Chinese Scalp Acupuncture

D1560539

JASON JISHUN HAO
& LINDA LINGZHI HAO

Blue Poppy Press

Published by:
BLUE POPPY PRESS
A Division of Blue Poppy Enterprises, Inc.
4804 SE 69th Avenue
Portland, OR 97206

First Edition, October, 2011
Second Printing, April, 2012
Third Printing, January, 2013
Fourth Printing, February, 2014
Fifth Printing, June, 2015
Sixth Printing, August, 2016
Seventh Printing, July, 2017
Eighth Printing, August, 2018
Ninth Printing, November, 2020
Tenth Printing, September, 2021
Eleventh Printing, September 2023

SBN 1-891845-60-8
ISBN 978-1-891845-60-4
LCCN #2011939115

DISCLAIMER: The information in this book is given in good faith. However, the author and the publishers cannot be held responsible for any error or omission. The publishers will not accept liabilities for any injuries or damages caused to the reader that may result from the reader's acting upon or using the content contained in this book. The publishers make this information available to English language readers for research and scholarly purposes only.

The publishers do not advocate nor endorse self-medication by laypersons. Chinese medicine is a professional medicine. Laypersons interested in availing themselves of the treatments described in this book should seek out a qualified professional practitioner of Chinese medicine.

COMP Designation: Compilation of functional translations using a standard translational terminology plus an original work.

16 15 14 13 12 11

Book design by Debra Topping
Color illustrations by Armando Espinosa Prieto
Caligraphy by Jason Jishun Hao

Printed at Frederic Printing, Aurora, CO

賀：

弘揚頭針

焦川友

2009. 4. 25

"Congratulations on your extensive development of scalp acupuncture."

—Jiao Shun-fa, the founder of
scalp acupuncture in China, April 25, 2009

Calligraphy Translations
Chinese Calligraphy by Jason Jishun Hao

Contents

Part Two: Common Clinical Applications of Scalp Acupuncture

Technical Illustrations

by Armando Espinosa Prieto

Acknowledgments

We acknowledge with sincere thanks our teachers, colleagues, friends, and families who helped us to write our first book in English.

We feel so grateful and blessed that we received our professional training directly from Jiao Shun-fa, the founder of Chinese scalp acupuncture, and Sun Shen-tian and Yu Zhi-shun, the famous professors of the research and development of scalp acupuncture.

We would like to express our gratitude to Maya Sutton for her knowledge, professionalism, concern, and support in creating a high-quality final edition of this text. Thank you to Betsy Amorous for helping us edit the first draft of the book, to Joseph Helms for organizing seminars for us, and Armando Espinosa Prieto for the wonderful technical illustrations.

We would like to thank all the acupuncture practitioners—our students, friends, and patients—who have encouraged us to persevere in our task with their positive attitudes and interest in this book.

Finally, this book would not have come into being without our parents, our son, David Hao and our daughter in-law Claire Parrish-Hao, and our brothers and sisters whose continuous encouragement, support, advice, and inspiration has meant so much.

Preface

In 2010, I had the rewarding experience of being a volunteer at a wonderful clinic in Kathmandu, Nepal, for a month. Among the many and varied patients that we treated there each day were several who had suffered brain injuries, strokes and related disorders such as aphasia, and serious trauma. Other patients had strange neurological disorders that Western medicine had been unable to help. These patients had been told there was nothing else that could be done for them, but they came to our clinic faithfully, almost every day, hoping for some small improvement in their terrible, disabling symptoms. One day in clinic, another volunteer who was working with us said, "It's too bad we don't know scalp acupuncture. I've heard that it can help with brain injuries and other difficult neurological disorders." She knew a few points on the head to try, but none of us, even with decades of experience as acupuncturists between us, knew enough about scalp acupuncture to be able to use it.

Shortly after returning from Nepal, the manuscript for this book arrived on my desk. Almost immediately after looking at its contents, we were certain we wanted to publish this text, and I knew I wanted not only to edit the book, but to learn this system before working as an acupuncturist in a third-world setting ever again.

What Jason and Linda Hao have created with this book is not just interesting reading, it is a reliable clinic manual for learning to use scalp acupuncture for many otherwise very difficult conditions. Readers will be unable to resist the obvious enthusiasm and faith these authors have in their work. Their joy in being able to help people who were thought to be beyond any help is palpable on every page, especially in the treatment section of the book. Add to that the precise illustrations and the detailed instructions for treatment, and they have created an accessible clinic manual for any acupuncturist to use.

Despite the Chinese origins of scalp acupuncture, authors with strong Chinese medical backgrounds, and the Chinese origins of acupuncture in general, readers will notice that there is proportionally more Western medicine than Chinese medicine in this text. This is not really surprising if you look at the history of this therapy. First, most of the research on scalp acupuncture, which in its current form is only 40 years old, has had to do with its impact on various brain and neurological functions and has been performed in relationship to those diseases. In other words, its use has been largely disease based, not pattern discrimination based. Furthermore, many of the practitioners in the West who have so far been interested in this system have been Western medical doctors, because it presents them with a new tool for helping patients whose other options are limited or nonexistent. Still, the authors have done their best to integrate Chinese medical concepts and diagnostic parameters where useful or relevant. You will note for most conditions in Part Two a pattern discrimination as well as related body and ear acupuncture to enhance the scalp acupuncture.

In Part One, the authors give you a history of modern scalp acupuncture, a crash course on neuroanatomy, some Chinese medical sources validating and supporting the use of scalp acupuncture, excellent illustrations to help you be certain of locating the treatment areas correctly, and finally a chapter on correct needle technique for making this system work the way it was designed.

Part Two is entirely a treatment formulary discussing some 40 conditions, supported and illustrated by case histories from the authors' considerable clinical experience. I believe that anyone practicing acupuncture will find this work impressive and inspirational.

In terms of acupuncture nomenclature, Lu = lung, LI = large intestine, St = stomach, Sp = spleen, Ht = heart, SI = small intestine, Bl = bladder, Ki = kidney, Per = pericardium, TB = triple burner, GB = gallbladder, Liv = liver, CV = conception vessel (*ren mai*), and GV = governing vessel (*du mai*). Extra channel points are identified by Bensky and O'Connor's numerical system as it appears in *Acupuncture: A Comprehensive Text* (Eastland Press, Seattle, 1981).

For Chinese medical terminology, wherever the authors have deviated from the term set in Wiseman and Feng's *A Practical Dictionary of Chinese Medicine*, we have put a footnote on the page where this first appears, along with the Chinese character(s) to which we refer.

As the editor and publisher of this book, I believe the information it contains is capable of changing lives for the better, even in cases where the patients and their families have all but given up any hope of improvement. All of us at Blue Poppy share this aspiration. Finally, I'd like to thank the authors for their years of dedication to this work, their perseverance, and their willingness to share this knowledge with anyone who is interested. All we need as recipients of their gift is the courage to try something new and the willingness to treat patients with these serious and painful conditions.

With good wishes for you and your patients,

Honora Lee Wolfe

Part One

Theory and Technique
of Scalp Acupuncture

Introduction

Chinese scalp acupuncture is a contemporary acupuncture technique integrating traditional Chinese needling methods with Western medical knowledge of representative areas of the cerebral cortex. It has been proven to be a most effective technique for treating acute and chronic central nervous system disorders. Scalp acupuncture often produces remarkable results with just a few needles and usually brings about immediate improvement, sometimes taking only several seconds to a minute.

History

Acupuncture, a therapeutic technique of oriental medicine, can be traced back more than 2500 years. Throughout its long history, acupuncture has evolved as its own unique traditional medicine. By embracing newly developed knowledge and technology, the profession continues to create additional methods of treatment. Techniques such as electrical and laser acupuncture and even new acupuncture points are currently being developed. We believe scalp acupuncture, which integrates Western medicine with traditional Chinese medicine, to be the most significant development that Chinese acupuncture has made in the past 60 years.

Scalp acupuncture is a well-researched natural science and incorporates extensive knowledge of both the past and present. Years of clinical experience have contributed to its recent discoveries and developments, but treatment of disorders by needling the scalp can also be traced back to early civilizations. In 100 BCE, the first Chinese acupuncture text, *Huang Di Nei Jing* (*The Yellow Emperor's Classic of Internal Medicine*) described the relationship between the brain and the body in physiology, pathology, and treatment as it was understood at that time, and citations of acupuncture treatments on the head can be found throughout classical Chinese literature.

The modern system of scalp acupuncture in China has been explored and developed since the 1950s. Various famous physicians introduced Western neurophysiology into the field of acupuncture and explored correlations between the brain and human body. In these early years of its development, there were several hypotheses for mapping stimulation areas. For example, Fan Yun-peng mapped the scalp area as a prone homunculus with the head toward the forehead and the legs toward the occipital area.[1] Taking a dividing line that connects the left ear to the vertex to the right ear, Tang Song-yan proposed two homunculi on the scalp, one in prone position and another in supine position.[2] Zhang Ming-jiu's and Yu Zhi-shun's scalp locations are formulated by penetrating regular head points, and Zhu Ming-qing created several special therapeutic bands on the scalp.[3, 4]

It took acupuncture practitioners in China roughly 20 years before they accepted a central theory that incorporated brain functions into Chinese medicine principles. Dr. Jiao Shun-fa, a neurosurgeon in Shan Xi province, is the recognized founder of Chinese scalp acupuncture. He systematically undertook the scientific exploration and charting of scalp correspondences starting in 1971. Dr. Jiao combined a modern understanding of neuroanatomy and neurophysiology with traditional techniques of Chinese acupuncture to develop a radical new tool for affecting the functions of the central nervous system. Dr. Jiao's discovery was investigated, acknowledged, and formally recognized by the acupuncture profession in a national acupuncture textbook, *Acupuncture and Moxibustion*, in 1977.[5] Ten years later, at the First International Acupuncture and Moxibustion Conference held in Beijing, China, scalp acupuncture began to gain international recognition. At the time, scalp acupuncture was primarily used to treat paralysis and aphasia due to stroke. Since then, the techniques and applications of this science have been expanded and standardized through further research and experience. Many studies on scalp acupuncture have shown positive results in treating various disorders of the central nervous system. The most outstanding results are with paralysis and pain management in very difficult neurological disorders.

Characteristics

Scalp acupuncture, sometimes also called head acupuncture, is a modern innovation and development. Just like any new technology and science, the discovery, development, and clinical application of scalp acupuncture has undergone a period of challenge because it falls outside some fundamental theories of Chinese medicine as well as being a new concept in the Western world. As a contemporary acupuncture technique, many of the specific treatments put forward in this book are also new, at least for a work that discusses Western medical concepts along with Chinese ones.

There are three new principles in this presentation of scalp acupuncture, however, which are of central importance and which depart considerably from traditional Chinese medicine. The first of these principles is the location of scalp acupuncture areas based on the reflex somatotopic system organized on the surface of the scalp in Western medicine. These do not relate to the theory of channels in Chinese medicine and are an essentially new type of conception. Second, because the technological innovation and invention of scalp acupuncture is fairly new, positive results can only reasonably be achieved by practitioners who have studied it; even an established doctor in China cannot perform it without at least seeing a demonstration of it. Third, scalp acupuncture consists of needling *areas* rather than *points* on the skull according to the brain's neuroanatomy and neurophysiology. Unlike traditional acupuncture, where one needle is inserted into a single point, in scalp acupuncture needles are subcutaneously inserted into whole sections of various zones. These zones are the specific areas through which the functions of the central nervous system, endocrine system, and channels are transported to and from the surface of the scalp. From a Western perspective, these zones correspond to the cortical areas of the cerebrum and cerebellum responsible for central nervous system functions such as motor activity, sensory input, vision, speech, hearing, and balance.

In clinical practice, acupuncture treatments are typically based not just on a systematic or rigidly applied system, but also on highly individualized philosophical constructs and intuitive impressions. The practitioner has a wide amount of discretion on the use of points and techniques. Therefore, even when treating the same complaint, the method of treatment chosen by one practitioner can vary significantly from another. Scalp acupuncture, on the other hand, applies more of a Western medicine approach, where patients with the same diagnosis usually receive the same or very similar treatment.

The scalp somatotopic system seems to operate as a miniature transmitter-receiver in direct contact with the central nervous system and endocrine system. By stimulating those reflex areas, acupuncture can have direct effects on the cerebral cortex, cerebellum, thalamo-cortical circuits, thalamus, hypothalamus, and pineal body. The scalp's unique neurological and endocrinal composition makes it an ideal external stimulating field for internal activities of the brain. Scalp acupuncture treats and prevents disease through the proper insertion of needles into scalp areas. It is accompanied by special manipulations to regulate and harmonize the functional activities of the brain and body, as well as to restore and strengthen the functions of the body, organs, and tissues.

Scalp acupuncture successfully integrates the essence of ancient Chinese needling techniques with the essence of neurology in Western medicine. Studying its results in clinical practice can also add clarity to ambiguities found in the practice of neurophysiology and pathology. In terms of Western medicine, it contributes significantly to the treatment of central nervous system disorders. In complementary and alternative medicine, it contributes new understanding to both theory and practice. Scalp acupuncture can successfully treat many problems of the central nervous system such as paralysis and aphasia, for which Western medicine has little to offer.

Applications

Scalp acupuncture areas are frequently used in the rehabilitation of paralysis due to stroke, multiple sclerosis, automobile accident, and Parkinson's disease. These areas may also be effectively employed for pain management, especially that caused by the central nervous system such as phantom pain, complex regional pain, and residual limb pain. It has been proven to have very effective results in treating aphasia, loss of balance, loss of hearing, dizziness and vertigo. The disorders covered in this book are commonly found in Western clinics. This book will show the scope of scalp acupuncture in treating many kinds of disorders and diseases, based on years of clinical experience. Scalp acupuncture not only treats disorders, but also can prevent illness and help to build the immune system. It can help increase energy, preserve youth, and promote longevity. The technique of scalp acupuncture is systematic, logical, easy to understand, and easy to practice. The techniques introduced in this book can be easily mastered and performed even by people with minimal acupuncture experience. Scalp acupuncture is more easily accessible, less expensive, entails less risk, can yield quicker responses, and causes fewer side effects than many Western treatments. Practitioners should consider scalp acupuncture as either the primary approach or a complementary approach when treating disorders of the central nervous system and endocrine system.

Although acupuncture and moxibustion have been used to prevent and treat disease in China for thousands of years, scalp acupuncture is a modern technique with a short history. In the West, many healthcare practitioners are familiar with acupuncture for pain management, while scalp acupuncture as a main tool for rehabilitation is a relatively new concept. It is still not easy for medical practitioners and the public to accept the reality that acupuncture can help in the recovery of paralysis, aphasia, and ataxia, while Western medical technology does not so far have effective treatments for those conditions. It is not surprising for a Western physician to claim that it is a coincidence if a patient recovers from paralysis after acupuncture. Therefore, there is an urgent need for Chinese scalp acupuncture to be studied and perfected, and extensive research done to fully explore its potential and utility. Chinese scalp acupuncture has been taught and used sparingly in the West and there are few books published on the subject. With such little information available, it has been almost impossible to apply this technique widely and with confidence. This book supplies all the needed information to practice scalp acupuncture.

In addition to more than 29 years of clinical practice of scalp acupuncture, we have taught scores of seminars for both practitioners of Chinese medicine and Western physicians practicing acupuncture in the USA and Europe, including eight years of seminars sponsored by UCLA and Stanford University. This book contains many amazing case reports from our years of clinical practice and teaching as examples of what is possible using these techniques. While it is not our intention to assert that scalp acupuncture is always effective with every patient, these clinical reports make a compelling case for its wider use. For example, in a report about the scalp acupuncture treatment of seven veterans with phantom limb pain at Walter Reed Army Medical Center in 2006, the results were as follows. After only one treatment per patient, three of the seven veterans instantly felt no further phantom pain, three others reported having very little pain, and only one patient showed no improvement. Such results warrant continued research into other possible uses for scalp acupuncture to alleviate human suffering.

During our lectures around the world, we are often asked why, if it is so effective in treating disorders of the central nervous system, has scalp acupuncture not spread to the whole world and been applied widely in practice? First, up to now there has been no authoritative and practical text for scalp acupuncture in English. Second, there is a very limited number of highly experienced teachers. Third, manual manipulation is very difficult to learn and master without detailed description and demonstration. And fourth, the names of stimulation areas are different from the standardized names given by the Standard International Acupuncture Nomenclature of the World Health Organization, Section 3.6 on Scalp Acupuncture, in Geneva in 1989 (see detail in the Appendix).

Furthermore, there have been few reports or articles published on treatment by scalp acupuncture. Most existing textbooks either lack detailed information or only introduce some new research on the topic. From their teachers and textbooks, students can learn only general information about scalp acupuncture and its locations and clinical applications. Therefore, many practitioners in both the West and the East are only mildly aware of this new technique, and few apply it in their practices. There is a high demand for a book that can provide teachers and students with useful knowledge and offer proper references to experienced practitioners. We feel confident that this book will meet these requirements.

Part One of this book is designed to give practitioners fundamental knowledge of neuroanatomy, neurophysiology, and pathology in Western medicine. Chapter One provides a review for practitioners with a Western medical background and an adequate introduction for practitioners new to this material. The next chapter is a review of essential theories of Chinese medicine related to scalp acupuncture including the Four Seas theory and the Four Qi Street theory that provide readers with a systematic explanation of function and indication based on Chinese medicine. Chapter Three describes in detail locations and techniques of scalp acupuncture in order to offer a wide range of useful information for teachers, experienced or new practitioners, and students. Readers may notice that the indications for treatment for each scalp area are many in order to demonstrate the variety of disorders that can benefit from scalp acupuncture therapy. Finally, Chapter Four presents a large number of treatment strategies and techniques with color figures clearly illustrating the location of stimulation areas.

In Part Two of our book, we discuss in detail many common central nervous disorders. All of these have proven to respond well to scalp acupuncture treatment. Forty-five successful case histories are given from our clinical experience. In these case descriptions, we explain in practical detail how to apply the needling techniques in order to obtain optimal results. These cases demonstrate practical application of the principles of scalp acupuncture. Each one reflects our experience, thought processes, strategies, and special techniques for treating patients suffering from disorders of the central nervous system. Wherever possible or useful, other modalities or techniques to enhance the scalp acupuncture treatments are included with the case histories, which demonstrates the integration of Chinese medical theory and application into the clinical practice of scalp acupuncture. A few "miracle" cases are presented in this book, such as the woman who was completely cured of quadriplegia after only two scalp acupuncture treatments and a man who was cured of aphasia after just five. While more the exception than the rule, such cases demonstrate not only how remarkable these new techniques are, but also provide the readers with examples of real clinical practice using them.

The information presented in the book is primarily a synthesis of two components of knowledge of scalp acupuncture. First, we were among an early group of people who studied these techniques and were very fortunate to have opportunities to learn it directly from famous scalp acupuncture specialists including Jiao Shun-fa, the brilliant founder of Chinese scalp acupuncture, Yu Zhi-shun, a well-known professor in scalp acupuncture development, and Sun Shen-tian, an outstanding professor in scalp acupuncture research. Second, we have been teaching, practicing, and researching it for 29 years, both in China and in the US and Europe, and have accumulated extensive and valuable experience, which has given us insight into the needs and questions of acupuncture practitioners in Western clinical settings. Through this book, we hope to contribute this knowledge and experience to current and future students, practitioners, and teachers, and that it will serve as a stepping stone for further teaching, practice, research, and development of Chinese scalp acupuncture.

CHAPTER ONE

Review of Anatomy, Physiology, and Neurology of Skull, Scalp, and Brain

The nervous system is the most complex system in the body, and learning it often overwhelms students and practitioners whose specialty is not neurology. It is difficult for acupuncture practitioners to remember neurological functions of the brain, understand how discrete lesions disrupt normal functions and cause symptoms, and apply knowledge of the brain in order to perform neurological examinations–especially if they must learn this information in a short period of time. For these reasons this chapter fulfills a real need by briefly reviewing the anatomy of the skull, scalp, and brain and discussing the neurophysiology and pathology that have close relationships to the practice of scalp acupuncture. This chapter integrates clear text with simple diagrams and figures in order to highlight and clarify the functionally important components

11

of the central nervous system. This information on neuroanatomy and neuro-physiology helps students and practitioners understand the origins of neuro-logical disorders and to use scalp acupuncture intelligently to resolve them.

Anatomy of the Skull

The skull is the bony framework of the head. It is comprised of the eight cranial and 14 facial bones. All of the bones of the skull are joined together by sutures except for the mandible. The eight cranial bones include one frontal, two tem-porals, two parietals, one sphenoid, one occipital, and one ethmoid, forming the neurocranium to protect the vault surrounding the brain. Fourteen facial bones form the splanchno-cranium to support the face. (See Figure 1.)

Anatomical Names of the Scalp Surface

Anatomical landmarks are standard reference points in the face and head used for the area locations of scalp acupuncture. These references are relatively fixed measurements, not affected by changes in appearance such as with aging, or with muscular actions. Figure 1 identifies the major anatomical divisions and landmarks on the scalp surface related to the locations and functions of scalp acupuncture. These areas are correctly located by using osseous marks on the skull. The most commonly used osseous marks are as follows:

- Glabella. This is the space between the eyebrows and just above the nose. It joins the two superciliary ridges and is slightly elevated. It is one of the main points used to measure many scalp acupuncture areas.
- Parietal Tubercle. This is the highest part of convexity, a little caudal area in the middle of the parietal bone. It marks the Speech II area and Praxia area.
- External Occipital Protuberance. This is a prominence on the outer surface of the occipital bone. It is near the middle of the occipital squama. It is a landmark for locating the Balance Area and Vision Area.

Anatomy of the Scalp

The scalp is the soft tissue envelope of the cranial vault. It extends from the supe-rior nuchal line on the posterior area of the skull to the supraorbital margins.

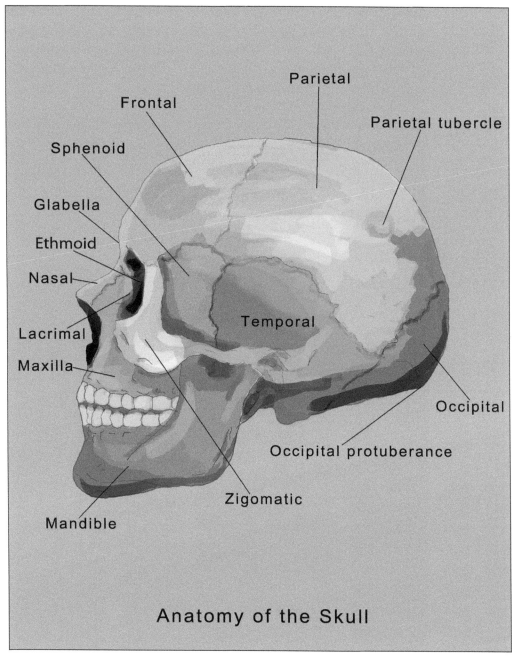

Anatomy of the Skull

Figure 1

Laterally, it extends into the temporal fossa to the level of the zygomatic arches. The scalp has five layers: they are the skin, the connective tissue, the epicranial aponeurosis, the loose areolar tissue, and the pericranium. The first three layers are bound together and work as a single unit. This unit can move along the loose areolar tissue over the pericranium. (See Figure 2.)

The skin of the scalp is thick and contains numerous sweat and sebaceous glands, a large blood supply, and hair follicles. Connective tissue (superficial

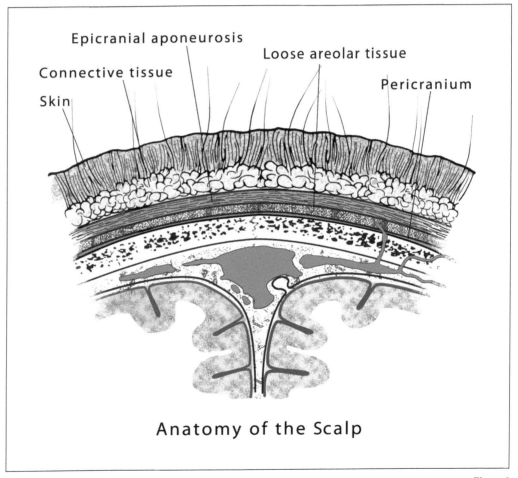

Anatomy of the Scalp

Figure 2

fascia) is a fibro-fatty layer that connects the skin to the underlying aponeurosis of the occipito-frontalis muscle, and provides a passageway for the nerves and blood vessels. The epicranial aponeurosis (*Galea aponeurotica*) is a tough layer of thick, fibrous tissue that runs from the frontalis muscle anteriorly to the occipital muscle posteriorly. Laterally, it continues as the temporal fascia. The loose areolar tissue connects the epicranial aponeurosis to the pericranium, and allows the three layers of the scalp to move superficially over the pericranium. This layer acts somewhat like a sponge because it contains innumerable potential spaces to provide an easy plane of separation between the upper three layers and the pericranium.[6] The loose areolar tissue, which lies approximately 5.7 mm (or .22 inches) from the surface on most adults, is the correct layer into which the needle should be inserted for scalp acupuncture. The pericranium is the periosteum of the skull bones and provides nutrition to the bone and capacity for repair.

Neuroanatomy and Neurophysiology Overview

The structures of the nervous system can be described on multiple levels. In this chapter, we will mainly review macroscopic brain divisions. This will help practitioners understand the functions and indications of scalp acupuncture later in the book, when a detailed study of the individual areas for scalp acupuncture begins. We will sketch the major features of the brain, paying particular attention to some of the most important functions related to scalp acupuncture. This will provide a framework for understanding how the central nervous system works as a whole. By the time the student or practitioner begins to read the clinical cases in this book, he or she should be able to picture the localized lesions in the central nervous system and understand the neurophysiologic changes in the body. Do not become discouraged if you have trouble remembering all of the details. As you read the clinical case reports in Part Two of this book and refer back to the information in Part One, the material will gradually become reinforced and solidified.

The human nervous system contains two parts: the central nervous system and the peripheral nervous system. The central nervous system includes brain and spinal cord, and the peripheral nervous system consists of sensory neurons, clusters of neurons called ganglia, and nerves connecting them to each other and to the central nervous system. The developing brain consists of three main divisions: the forebrain, the midbrain, and the hindbrain. The forebrain is the largest part of the nervous system in humans and is further subdivided into two other areas, the telencephalon and the diencephalon. The telencephalon is made up of the cerebral hemispheres, including the cerebral cortex, white matter, and basal ganglia. The diencephalon is composed of the thalamus, hypothalamus, and associated structures. The midbrain is a relatively short and narrow region connecting the forebrain and hindbrain. The hindbrain consists of the pons and cerebellum together with the medulla. The midbrain, pons, and medulla together form a connection between the forebrain and the spinal cord, and are referred to as the brainstem.

Major parts of the central nervous system made up of myelinated axons are called white matter. Areas made up mainly of cell bodies are known as gray matter. Most of the local synaptic communication between neurons in the central nervous system occurs in the gray matter, while axons in the white matter transmit signals over greater distances. A unique mantle of gray matter called the cerebral cortex covers the surface of the cerebral hemisphere. Beneath this lies the white matter, which sends signals to and from the cortex. Gray matter is also found in large clusters of cells called nuclei, located deep within the cerebral hemisphere and brainstem, such as the basal ganglia and thalamus.

The cerebral cortex has numerous crevices called sulci. The ridges of cortex that rise up between the sulci are called gyri. The cerebral hemispheres have four major lobes: the frontal, temporal, parietal, and occipital. The frontal lobes are in the front of the brain and extend backward to the central sulcus. The frontal lobes are separated inferiorly and laterally from the temporal lobes. The parietal lobes are bounded anteriorly by the central sulcus, but have no pointed demarcation from the temporal lobes or the occipital lobes when studied from the side of the brain. The parietal lobes and occipital lobes are divided by the parieto-occipital sulcus (Figure 3).

In addition to these four major lobes, another area of the cerebral cortex is located within the depths of the sylvian fissure, called the insular cortex. The two cerebral hemispheres are divided at the midline by the interhemispheric fissure. The corpus callosum, a large, C-shaped band of white matter, connects homologous areas in the two hemispheres.

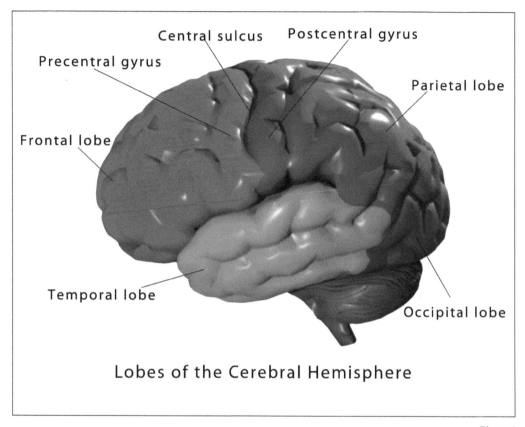

Lobes of the Cerebral Hemisphere

Figure 3

The nervous system receives, integrates, and transmits sensory stimuli. It generates motor activity, coordinates movements, and also regulates emotions and consciousness. In general, it controls all the activities that preserve the individual and the species.

Although there is some changeability, the sulci and gyri of the cerebral hemisphere form certain fairly consistent structures. An assortment of classification schemes exists for different regions of the cerebral cortex derived from their microscopic appearance and function. The most widely known of these was published by Korbinian Brodmann in 1909.[7] On the basis of microscopic studies, Brodmann cut the cortex into 52 cytoarchitectonic areas; each was assigned a number corresponding to how he prepared the slides (Figure 4). It turns out

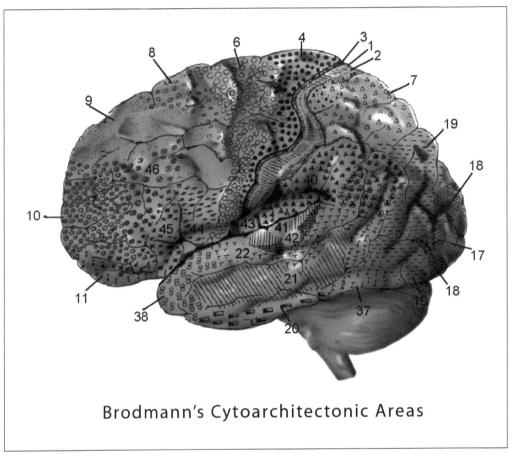

Brodmann's Cytoarchitectonic Areas

Figure 4

that many of the areas identified by Brodmann correlate well with the different functional areas of the cortex and, therefore, his classification is still often used today. Following is a brief review of the names of the major sulci and gyri along with their functions.

Primary Motor Cortex

The primary motor cortex lies in the precentral gyrus of the frontal lobe (Figure 5). This area controls movement of the opposite side of the body. Lesions occurring primarily in the motor cortex produce contralateral paralysis

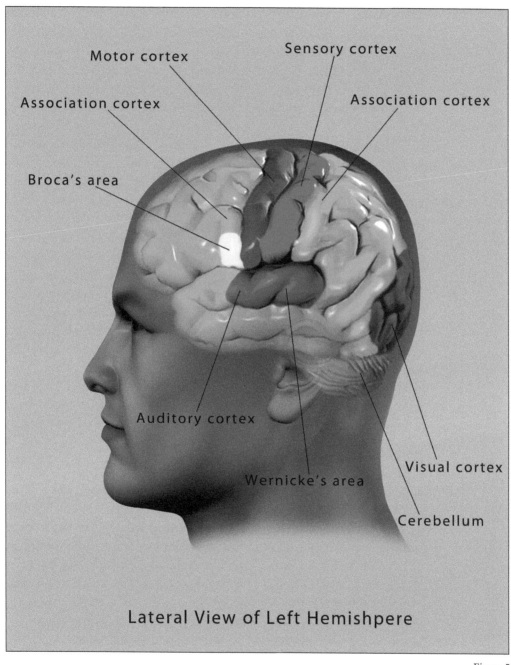

Lateral View of Left Hemishpere

Figure 5

and/or weakness with respect to the lesion. Motor control involves a delicate balance between multiple parallel pathways and recurrent feedback loops, such as the cerebellum and basal ganglia. The cerebellum and basal ganglia act by modulating the output of the corticospinal and other descending motor systems. Both the cerebellum and basal ganglia receive major input from the motor cortex; they, in turn, project back to the motor cortex via the thalamus.

Motor and sensory pathways are usually organized topographically. This means that adjoining areas on the motor surfaces are mapped to adjacent fibers in white matter pathways and adjacent regions of the cortex. For example, the primary motor and somatosensory cortex regions representing the foot are adjacent to regions representing the leg. These somatotopic maps on the cortex are at times called the motor or sensory homunculus (Figure 6). A homunculus is a physical representation of the anatomical division of the primary motor cortex and the primary somatosensory cortex. It is a projection of the parts of the body on the motor and sensory cortical areas and an upside-down representation of the human body, with the foot at the most superior position of the cortex and the face at the more inferior position. The proportion of the homunculus in the human brain is directly related to the movement and sensation of the rest of the body.[8] For example, the lips, hands, and feet have more motor neurons than other parts of the body, so the homunculus has correspondingly large lips, hands, and feet. A part of the body with fewer motor or sensory connections to the brain is represented as appearing smaller.

The Primary Somatosensory Cortex

The primary somatosensory cortex is located in the post-central gyrus of the parietal lobe (Figure 5, 6) and is involved with the sensations of the opposite side of the body. Somatic sensations refer to the perceptions of touch, pain, temperature, pulsation, and proprioception (sense of limb or joint position). The key input to this area arises from the ventral posterior nuclei of the thalamus (Figure 7), a somatotopically arranged protrusion in the form of a sensory homunculus (Figure 6). Like the motor homunculus, the body's distorted and uneven representation in the sensory homunculus is also based upon the relative densities of innervation. The lips, tongue, sex organs, and thumb have a larger representative area in the main somatosensory cortex.

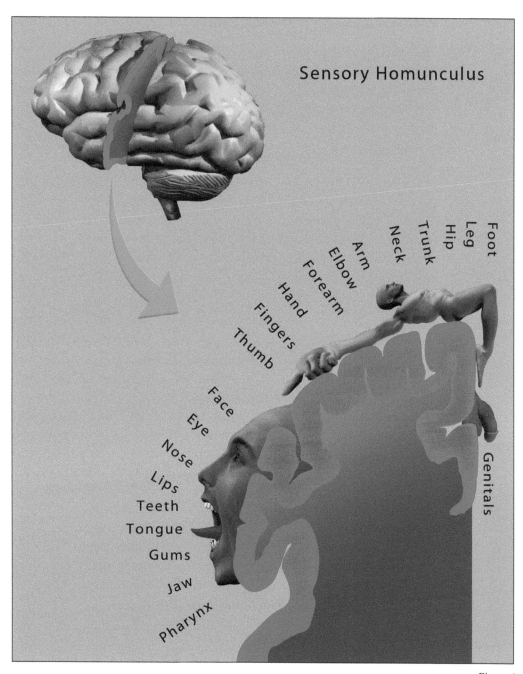

Sensory Homunculus

Foot
Leg
Hip
Trunk
Neck
Arm
Elbow
Forearm
Hand
Fingers
Thumb
Genitals
Face
Eye
Nose
Lips
Teeth
Tongue
Gums
Jaw
Pharynx

Figure 6

Primary Visual and Auditory Cortices

The primary visual cortex is located in the occipital lobes along the bands of a deep sulcus called the calcarine fissure (Figure 5). It is highly specialized for processing information about static and moving objects, and pattern recognition. The primary visual cortex receives visual inputs from the opposite visual field. Thus, the left half of the visual field of each eye is mapped to the right primary visual cortex.

The primary auditory cortex lies in the posterior half of the superior temporal gyrus and also enters into the lateral sulcus as the transverse temporal gyri (Figure 5). Sound reaching the primary auditory cortex is less lateralized and represents more of a mixture of input from both ears. The primary auditory cortex is responsible for processing auditory information and performs the basic functions of hearing, pitch, and volume.

Language Cortices

Language abilities are located in the association areas of the parietal-temporal-occipital complex, typically in the left hemisphere. Broca's area associates to language production, and Wernicke's area relates to understanding language. Broca's area is located in the frontal lobe, adjacent to the areas of the primary motor cortex responsible for moving the lips, tongue, face, and larynx (Figure 5). Linguistic rules and grammar (syntax) and the template for phonation are created, and speech, melody, and rhythm are regulated within Broca's area. Damage in Broca's area usually causes deficits in the construction of language. Wernicke's area is located in the posterior section of the superior temporal gyrus (Figure 5). It is involved in understanding both written and spoken language. Language is usually perceived first by the primary auditory cortex in the superior temporal lobe when we are listening or by the primary visual cortex in the occipital lobe when we are reading. From either the primary auditory cortex or the primary visual cortex, association fibers convey information to Wernicke's area. Damage in Wernicke's area often causes deficits in language comprehension.

Thalamus

The thalamus is located between the cerebral cortex and midbrain, above the brainstem and behind the basal ganglia (Figure 7). The thalamus is a major relay

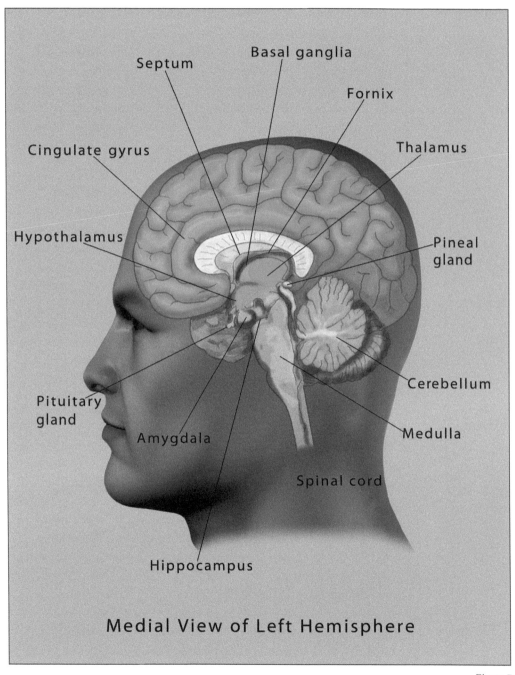

Septum

Basal ganglia

Fornix

Cingulate gyrus

Thalamus

Hypothalamus

Pineal gland

Pituitary gland

Cerebellum

Amygdala

Medulla

Spinal cord

Hippocampus

Medial View of Left Hemisphere

Figure 7

center: nearly all pathways that project to the cerebral cortex do so after synapsing in the thalamus. Its function includes integrating and modifying the sensory and motor inputs, and selectively tuning up the output signals to the cerebral cortex. Conscious awareness of pain, basic touch, temperature, and pressure sensations may all occur at the thalamic level. The thalamus also processes information that influences the electro-cortical activity of sleep and alertness. It is involved in consciousness and the adjustment of the affective component of behavior.

Hypothalamus

The hypothalamus is situated beneath the thalamus, just above the brain stem (Figure 7). The hypothalamus is an important region in the human brain and is involved in many different functions, such as control of the autonomic, neuroendocrine, limbic, and other bodily circuits. The hypothalamus synthesizes and secretes neurohormones, and these in turn regulate the secretion of pituitary hormones. The hypothalamus is responsible for both the sympathetic and the parasympathetic divisions of the autonomic nervous system. The hypothalamus is concerned with the reception and integration of sensory impulses from the internal organs and is the principal intermediary between the nervous and endocrine systems. Additionally, the hypothalamus controls appetite, thirst, fatigue, thermoregulation, the sleep-wake cycle, and sexual desire.

Pituitary Gland

The pituitary gland lies within the pituitary fossa and is linked to the bottom of the hypothalamus through the pituitary stalk (Figure 7). The pituitary gland is composed of an anterior and a posterior lobe. The anterior lobe synthesizes and secretes the following six hormones: adrenocorticotropic hormone (ACTH), growth hormone (GH), thyroid-stimulating hormone (TSH), luteinizing hormone (LH), and follicle-stimulating hormone (FSH). ACTH stimulates the adrenal cortex to produce corticosteroid hormones that are important for maintaining correct blood pressure, controlling electrolyte balance, and promoting glucose mobilization in the bloodstream. TSH stimulates the thyroid gland to produce thyroxin (T_4) and triiodothyronine (T_3), which promote cellular metabolism. Growth hormone stimulates growth in childhood and maintains a healthy body composition and well-being in adults. Prolactin stimulates the mammary glands to produce milk after childbirth to enable nursing and affects sex hormone levels of the ovaries in women and the testes in men. LH regulates estrogen in women and testosterone in men. FSH promotes sperm production in men and stimulates the ovaries to enable ovulation in women.[9] The posterior lobe stores and releases two hormones: oxytocin and vasopressin. Oxytocin controls the smooth muscles to contract in the breast for milk letdown to take place, and it controls contractions of the uterus during labor. Vasopressin regulates osmolarity and water in the body.

Pineal Gland

The pineal gland is an endocrine gland located near the center of the brain, between the two hemispheres, tucked in a groove where the two thalamic bodies join (Figure 7). The pineal gland secretes a melanocyte-stimulating hormone, which plays a pain-relieving role due to its endorphin content. It also secretes melatonin and other enzymes that show sensitivity to variations in diurnal light and circadian rhythms. In addition, it influences the secretion of the gonadotropic hormones that maintain a regulatory role in reproductive development. Through these hormones, the pineal gland may exert a regulatory role by modifying the actions of the pituitary, adrenal, and parathyroid glands, as well as the gonads.

Limbic System

Several structures in the brain are referred to collectively as the limbic system because they are located near the inner border of the cortex. It comprises the medial and anterior temporal lobes, anterior insula, prefrontal lobes, cingulate gyri, hippocampal formation, amygdala, hypothalamus, certain thalamic nuclei, epithalamus, pineal gland, septal area, basal ganglia, and brainstem (Figure 7). The limbic system has a direct influence on autonomic, neuroendocrine, and behavior mechanisms. It maintains homeostasis, integrates the olfactory impulses, and plays a role in sexual arousal. The limbic system is associated with emotion and motivation.[10]

Association Cortices

The cerebral cortex contains a large quantity of association cortices that carry out higher-order information processing. Any one association cortex is mostly located adjoining its primary area. The parietal, temporal, and occipital association cortexes are all located in the posterior part of the primary cortices, which organize functions from multiple sensory and motor modalities. The frontal and prefrontal association cortices are involved in planning actions, movements, and abstract thought. Since there are many association cortices in human beings, it is almost impossible to introduce all of them. We will briefly review the functions of several clinically important areas of association cortices that are closely related to scalp acupuncture.

The frontal lobes are the largest hemispheres and contain immense areas of association cortices involving the cognitive functions and personality (Figure 8). They are associated with reward, attention, planning, long-term memory, and drive. The prefrontal cortex is located in front of the premotor cortex, a well-developed area in the human brain. The prefrontal cortex plays an important role in the establishment of emotional responses, programming, and intellectual functions. Lesions in the frontal lobes cause a range of disorders in personality and cognitive functioning. Patients with frontal lobe lesions may have particular difficulty when asked to execute a sequence of repeated actions or to change from one activity to another. Personality changes caused by frontal lobe lesions can consist of impaired judgment, a cheerful lack of concern about one's illness, inappropriate joking, and other uninhibited behaviors.

The parietal lobe consists of the post-central gyrus, and is divided into a superior and inferior parietal lobule. This lobe is concerned with knowledge of numbers and their relations, manipulation of objects, imitation of speech or action, imitation of gestures without words, and copying. Damage in the inferior parietal lobule in the left hemisphere often causes difficulty with calculations, confusion with right-left orientation, an inability to identify fingers by name, and problems with written language. Damage in the front of the left parietal lobe may cause difficulty with motor conceptualization, planning, and execution. The parietal lobes also have an important role in spatial awareness. Damage in the parietal lobe often produces distortion of perceived space and neglect of the contralateral side.

The supplementary motor area is located in the medial frontal gyri, which form the medial extension of the superior frontal gyrus above the cingulate

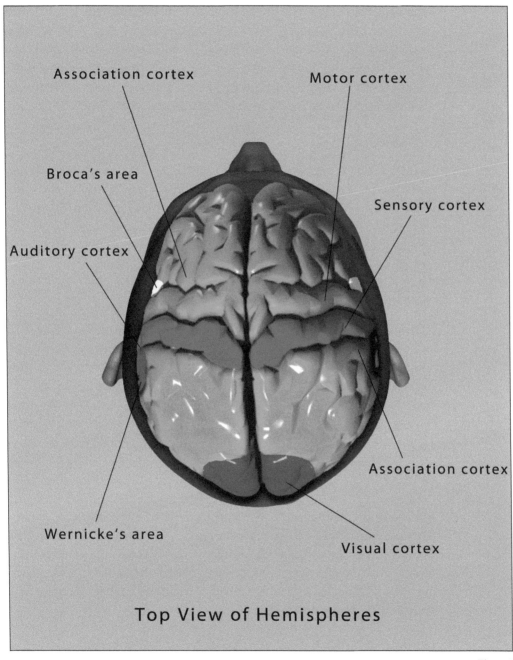

Association cortex

Motor cortex

Broca's area

Sensory cortex

Auditory cortex

Association cortex

Wernicke's area

Visual cortex

Top View of Hemispheres

Figure 8

one. This area exhibits a small motor homunculus that operates autonomously from the primary motor cortex. The supplementary motor cortex regulates the rhythm and strength of contraction of the muscles. It mediates contraction of postural muscles on both sides. It is also associated with the planning and initiation of movements. Damage in the supplementary motor cortex causes an increase in flexor muscle tone, leading to spasmodic contraction.

Cerebellum

The cerebellum is located at the bottom of the brain in the occipital lobe, underneath the cerebral cortex and underneath the pons (Figure 5). The cerebellum is divided into two large hemispheres. The cerebellum coordinates motor activities and eye movements, controls equilibrium, and regulates phonation. It also plays an important role in motor planning. Lesions in the cerebellum often cause complications in coordination and balance, referred to as ataxia.

Brainstem

The brainstem is composed of the midbrain, pons, and medulla (Figure 7). It is the lower part of the brain, adjoining and continuous with the spinal cord. Cranial nerves 3–12 arise from the brainstem, and all information passing between the cerebral hemispheres and the spinal cord must go through the brainstem. The brainstem plays an important role in the regulation of cardiac function, respiratory function, and the sleep cycle. It also is important in maintaining consciousness and regulating the central nervous system.

Blood Supply to the Brain

Reviewing the anatomy of the cerebral blood vessels is crucial because vascular diseases or accidents in the central nervous system cause most neurological disorders. Knowing about the blood supply to the brain is essential in performing and interpreting angiographic imaging, understanding the damage associated with vascular accidents, developing a treatment strategy and plan, and evaluating scalp acupuncture treatment.

There are two pairs of arteries that carry the blood supply to the brain and one pair of draining veins. The inner carotid arteries maintain the blood supply to

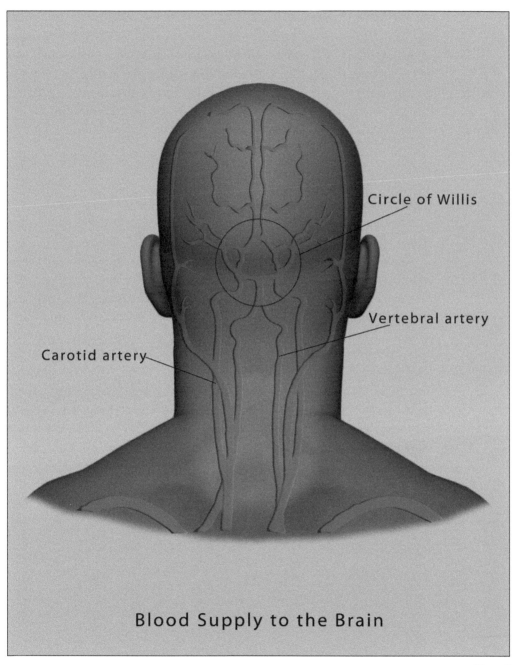

Blood Supply to the Brain

Figure 9

the anterior and middle cerebral cortices, while the vertebro-basilar arteries maintain the blood supply to the posterior cerebral cortex (Figure 9). Because of the importance of brain functions, the vascular supply to the brain is rich with collateral vessels. The anterior and posterior blood supplies from the carotid and vertebro-basilar systems join together in an anatomic ring at the base of the brain called the Circle of Willis. The main arteries supplying the cerebral hemispheres arise from the Circle of Willis (Figure 9).

The arteries supplying the brainstem and the cerebellum with blood also come from the vertebral and basilar arteries. These refer to the superior, anterior inferior, and posterior inferior cerebella arteries. Venous drainage for the brain is maintained by superficial and deep cerebral veins. The superficial veins include the superior and inferior cerebral, superficial middle cerebral, and anastomotic veins. The superficial veins drain blood from the cerebral cortex and medulla and open into the nearby sinuses. The deep cerebral veins are composed of the internal cerebral veins, great cerebral vein of Galen, basal, and occipital veins. The deep cerebral veins drain blood from inside the hemispheres and join nearby sinuses. The functions of the brain rely completely upon the nutrition and oxygen continually supplied by blood because the brain has no storage capacity for energy material. The human brain is approximately 2% of total body weight, yet it receives 15–20% of cardiac output, equivalent to 750 ml per minute. When the cerebral blood supply is deficient or blocked, the brain tissue may develop hypoxia and ischemia, which in turn cause general or localized symptoms and signs in the central nervous system.

CHAPTER TWO

Fundamental Theories of Scalp Acupuncture in Chinese Medicine

As a contemporary acupuncture method, the discovery, development, and clinical application of scalp acupuncture is not only based on modern knowledge of Western biomedicine, but also has a close connection with fundamental theories of traditional Chinese medicine. Specifically, the scalp acupuncture areas exist in close association with the channel system and acupuncture points on the head. While there was no systematic description of scalp acupuncture in the well-known ancient classics of Chinese medicine, in more recent Chinese medicine studies of brain function the use of points on the scalp to prevent and treat illness have been recorded in the fields of anatomy, physiology, pathology, diagnosis, and treatment as explained in this chapter.

Anatomy and Physiology

There are many books in earlier acupuncture literature that include a description of the anatomy and physiology of the brain. The *Huang Di Nei Jing Su Wen* (*Yellow Emperor's Classic of Internal Medicine–Simple Questions*) (100 BCE) said, "The head is the house of emotion and mind."[11] The descriptions of its location and size in the *Nan Jing* (*Classic of Difficulties*) (100 CE) are similar to anatomy in Western medicine. In the Ming dynasty (1368-1644 CE), Li Shizhen stated in the *Ben Cao Gang Mu* (*Grand Materia Medica*), "The head is the house of intelligence."[12] In the Qing dynasty (1644-1911 CE), in *Yi Fang Ji Jie* (*Essentials of Materia Medica*), Wang Ang stated, "The memory belongs to the brain function."[13] In the *Yi Lin Gai Cuo* (*Correcting the Errors in the Forest of Medicine*), Wang Qing-ren stated, "Ears, eye, nose, mouth and tongue connect with the brain; thus hearing, vision, smell, taste, and speech functions are all controlled by the brain."[14] Since the compilation of *The Yellow Emperor's Classic of Internal Medicine* in the second century BCE, many theories have been formulated to account for complexity in the function of the brain. It is important to review related fundamental theories of Chinese medicine for studying, mastering, applying, researching, and developing scalp acupuncture.

The Theory of Channels and Network Vessels

Channels and network vessels (*jing luo*, 经络) are the pathways in which the qi and blood of the human body circulate. The system of channels and network vessels on/in the head reflects symptoms and signs in the brain, transmits needling sensations, and regulates the conditions of deficiency (*xu*, 虚) or excess (*shi*, 实)* in the central nervous system.

Therapeutic areas in scalp acupuncture are related to distribution of the channels and network vessels in the head. The channels and network vessels in the head closely communicate with the entire body anatomical system. This occurs

---

Note: While many Chinese medical technical terms in this book are translated following *A Practical Dictionary of Chinese Medicine* by Wiseman and Feng, we prefer to use the more common terms in the profession for *xu* (虚) and *shi* (实). Wiseman and Feng translate these respectively as vacuity and repletion, while we are using deficiency and excess.

through the connections among the entire channel system, including the 12 channel divergences, the 12 muscle regions, 12 cutaneous regions, and network vessels. These connections and confluents make the head and brain a very important and extraordinary region and organ.

The theory of channels and network vessels constitutes one of the fundamental theories of scalp acupuncture for treatment of disorders in the central nervous system. The therapeutic action of Chinese scalp acupuncture is realized mainly through the channels and network vessels in regulating the function of the brain. Symptoms and signs will be relieved when brain functions become harmonized and return to normal following scalp acupuncture. There are eight channels that directly flow into the head among 12 main channels and eight extraordinary channels.[15] They are the du, foot tai yang urinary bladder, hand shao yang triple warmer, foot shao yang gallbladder, foot jue yin liver, foot yang ming stomach, yang wei, and yang qiao channels (Figure 10).

The foot yang ming stomach channel is distributed on the face and forehead and connects to the frontal lobe. The hand shao yang triple warmer channel, foot shao yang gallbladder channel, yang wei channel, and yang qiao channel are distributed on the side of the head and connect to the temporal and parietal lobes. The foot tai yang urinary bladder channel is distributed on the forehead, vertex, and occipital area and connects to the frontal, temporal, parietal, and occipital lobes. The du channel runs along the face, forehead, vertex, and occipital area and connects with the frontal lobe, temporal, parietal, and occipital lobes, as well as the cerebellum and brainstem. The foot jue yin liver channel connects to the eye system in the occipital lobe and runs up to the vertex. The three parallel channels of du or governing vessel (GV), foot tai yang urinary bladder (Bl), and foot shao yang gallbladder (GB) enter the brain through the vertex. Most location areas for scalp acupuncture overlap with the distribution of those channels labeled GV, Bl, and GB. These three channels perform important roles in regulating the functions of the central nervous system and the endocrine system.

The earliest acupuncture text in China is called *Huang Di Nei Jing Ling Shu* (*Yellow Emperor's Classic of Internal Medicine–Spiritual Axis*). It presents the following description:

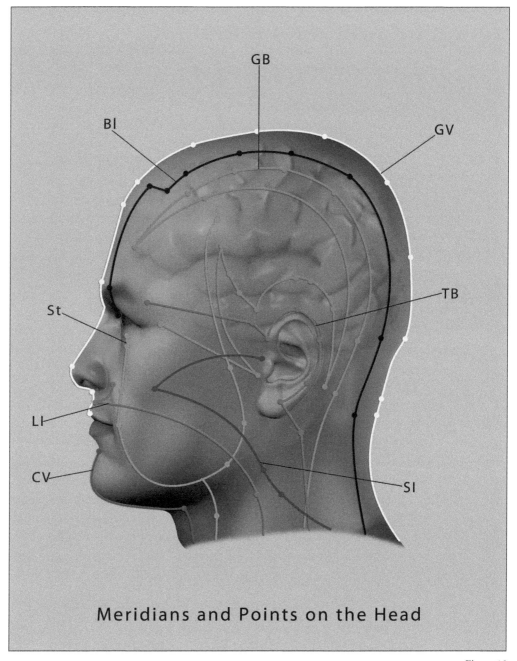

GB

BI

GV

St

TB

LI

CV

SI

Meridians and Points on the Head

Figure 10

The bladder channel of foot Tai Yang starts from the inner canthus. Moving up to the forehead, it joins the Governor Vessel at the vertex, where a branch arises, running to the temple. The straight portion of the channel enters and connects with brain from the vertex.

The liver channel of foot Jue Yin starts on the dorsum of the big toe. The channel ascends across the diaphragm and costal region, traverses the neck posterior to the pharynx, and enters the nasopharynx, connecting with the tissue surrounding the eye. Finally, the channel moves upward across the forehead and meets the Governing channel at the vertex.

The Governor Vessel arises from the lower abdomen and emerges from the perineum. Then it runs along the interior of the spinal column to Feng Fu (GV 16) at the nape, where is enters the brain. It further moves upward to the vertex and winds along the forehead to the columnella of the nose.

and finally

Yang Heel channel "starts below the lateral malleolus and moves upward to the posterior aspect of the hypochondrium. It then continues along the lateral side of the shoulder, transverses the neck and reaches the inner canthus. It ascends across the forehead and winds behind the ear to point Feng Chi (GB 20). It enters the brain at point Feng Fu (GV 16).

In addition, Chinese scalp acupuncture stimulates scalp areas to prevent and treat disorders according to the theory of the 12 cutaneous regions. These refer to the sites through which the qi and blood from the channels are transferred to the body surface. In fact, all channels and network vessels connect with the head and brain directly and indirectly just as described in the *Spiritual Axis*, which states, "The qi and blood of the 12 channels and 365 network vessels all go up the face and nourish the sense organs."

Zang-Fu (Viscera and Bowel) Theory

Zang-fu is the general concept of the internal organs of the human being in Chinese medicine and includes the five organs or viscera (*zang*, 脏), the six bowels (*fu*, 腑), and six extraordinary bowels. The brain is known as one of the six extraordinary bowels. They are called extraordinary because they function like an organ/viscus, storing a pure substance, while having the hollow form of a bowel.

In the *zang-fu* theory, physiological functions and pathological changes of each viscus and bowel is described along with their related tissues, connected sense organs, and complex interrelationships. Dysfunction or disorders of the internal *zang-fu* manifest as external symptoms and signs. A Chinese medical practitioner diagnoses these disorders through four diagnostic methods: inspection, auscultation and olfaction, questioning, and palpation.

Although the ancient Chinese scholars had some knowledge of the anatomy, neurophysiology, and pathology of the brain, they usually discussed the function and diagnosis of the brain through various *zang-fu* systems, especially in the heart, kidney, and liver. Consequently, disorders or patterns of the brain are often described in terms of the *zang-fu* system or the channel system. In addition, the normal functions of the brain rely on the supply of qi and blood. The production and circulation of qi and blood depend upon the functions of the *zang-fu*. According to *zang-fu* theory, for example, the heart system houses the mind, dominates mental activity, and controls the circulation of blood. The heart opens into the tongue and associates with speech and joy. Most of the functions of the brain in Western medicine are attributed to the heart system in Chinese medicine. The heart system controls consciousness, intelligence, memory, thinking, sleep, and emotion.

The kidney system stores congenital essence, manufactures marrow to fill up the brain and spinal cord, opens into ears, and associates with hearing and the emotion of fear. The kidney system includes the functions of the adrenal glands, sex hormones, and thyroid in Western medicine. Many of the functions of the central nervous system and endocrine system in Western medicine are often attributed to the kidney system in Chinese medicine, since the kidney system is said to produce marrow to fill the brain and spinal cord.

The liver system controls circulation of qi and dominates the function of tendons and ligaments. The liver opens into the eyes and associates with vision and with the emotions of depression and anger. The complicated functions of vision and emotion in Western medicine are attributed to the liver system in

Chinese medicine. The liver system stores blood and opens into the eye; it is the only one of the five *zang* that connects directly to the brain.

The spleen system is the source of engenderment of qi and blood and stores acquired (postnatal) essence. The spleen system opens into the mouth and associates with taste and with the emotion of worry. This system includes the functions of the stomach, pancreas, and spleen in Western medicine.

The lung system controls breathing, opens into the nose and associates with smell and the emotion of grief.

The gallbladder is the only bowel in traditional Chinese medicine that belongs to both the *fu* bowels and extraordinary bowels. It is associated with decision-making and courage in standard Chinese medicine. Most location areas of scalp acupuncture overlap with distribution of the channel associated with this bowel. This makes the gallbladder and its associated foot shao yang channel important to the regulation of the central nervous system and the endocrine system.

The Theory of Qi, Blood, Body Fluid, and Essence

Qi, blood, body fluid, and essence are essential materials to maintain the normal functions of the brain and *zang-fu* systems of the body. The vital activities of the brain rely on a normal supply and distribution of qi, blood, body fluid, and essence. As described in the *Yellow Emperor's Classic of Internal Medicine*, "The qi of five *zang* and six *fu* all flow up to enter into the eyes to generate vision." When the supply of qi or blood is interrupted, the qi and blood in the brain are deficient or stagnant. At that point, some sense organs, internal organs, and extremities may show symptoms and signs. This is similar to Western medicine's knowledge of damage to the brain due to a deficiency of oxygen and blood supply. Scalp acupuncture is used to regulate the functions of qi and blood. It promotes the free flow of qi and blood in the brain in order to restore brain function to homeostasis.

The Theory of the Three Treasures

Chinese medicine considers the health of the brain and body to result from the interaction of certain vital substances, namely essence, qi, and mind (*jing*, 精, *qi*, 气, and *shen*, 神). These are the three fundamental substances that maintain physical and psychic activity in human beings, and they are called the three treasures. The essence and qi are seen to be the material foundation of the mind. A healthy mind relies on the normal functions of essence and qi. The essence discussed here refers to the kidney essence, which derives from both congenital (prenatal) essence and acquired (postnatal) essence. The kidney essence manufactures marrow, which in turn fills the brain and spinal cord. Kidney essence governs growth, development, sexual maturation, reproduction, and aging. The qi referred to here is produced by the spleen and stomach and is an essential substance to preserve the normal functions of the brain. When kidney essence and spleen and stomach qi are abundant there is a healthy condition of the mind. If essence and qi are insufficient the mind is disturbed, causing emotional and mental disorders.

The Theory of Four Seas

The theory of four seas is a fundamental theory for Chinese scalp acupuncture. The 12 main channels are described as water all flowing into seas. The seas act as reservoirs and are distinguished by the substance they store. The *Huang Ti Nei Jing Ling Shu* (*Yellow Emperor's Classic of Internal Medicine–Spiritual Axis*) states,

> There are four seas and twelve channels of qi and blood in human beings. Twelve channels of qi and blood all flow into seas. They are seas of marrow, blood, qi, water and food. The brain is the sea of marrow. Its pathway rises to the top of the skull and descends to Feng Fu (GV 16). The points that influence the sea of marrow are Bai Hui (GV 20) in the upper part of head and Feng Fu (GV 16) in the lower part of the head.

The sea of marrow is represented by the brain and spinal cord, and includes neurological functions in the central nervous system. According to the *Yellow Emperor's Classic of Internal Medicine–Spiritual Axis*, the brain, as a sea of spinal marrow, is a vital organ to maintain normal activities of mental, physical, and emotional functions. It is said in the *Spiritual Axis*,

Sufficient sea of marrow increases strength and energy, physical activity and life span; whereas when the sea of marrow is deficient, there will be vertigo, tinnitus, soreness in legs, dizziness, fainting, blindness, lassitude, and sleepiness.

Thus, stimulating the correct areas of the scalp treats not only diseases of the brain, but also disorders of internal organs, sense organs, and the four extremities that the brain controls and regulates.

The Theory of Four Qi Streets

The theory of four qi streets is another fundamental theory of Chinese scalp acupuncture, described originally in the earliest acupuncture book. The *Yellow Emperor's Classic of Internal Medicine–Spiritual Axis* says,

> The four streets are the pathways of qi. The chest qi has a pathway; abdominal qi has a pathway, head qi has a pathway, and lower leg qi has a pathway. The qi pathway in the head terminates in the brain.[16]

This description correlates with Western medicine's knowledge of the brain and its neurological pathways. In the theory of the Four Qi Streets, the brain connects with internal organs, sense organs, and extremities through the qi pathways, and thus regulates those functions. Scalp acupuncture areas provide places to achieve homeostasis of the mind, emotions, and body because the brain is the place where the qi of the head accumulates.

The Theory of Root and Branch

There are several meanings to root and branch in theories of Chinese medicine. When discussing the onset of disease, an acute condition is the branch and a chronic condition is the root. When discussing the consequence of disease, the pathogenic factor is the root, while symptoms and signs are the branch.

As discussed here, root and branch refer to those terms in channel and network vessel systems. The root is the place where channel qi accumulates, while the branch is where channel qi distributes. Points on the head, face, and trunk are located in the upper part of the body and thus belong to the branch. Points on the four extremities below the elbow or knee are located on the lower part of body, and thus pertain to the root. Acupuncture points on the head can treat disorders in the extremities according to four seas theory. Based on root and branch theory, points on the extremities can treat disorders in the head.

Knowledge of root and branch theory is required to understand the relationship between the brain and extremities and to analyze the mutual influence between the functions of the *zang-fu* system and indications of points. There are eight locations of branches in the head according to ancient Chinese medical texts. They are described as follows: The branch of the foot tai yang urinary bladder channel reaches to the eye; the branch of the foot shao yang gallbladder channel is in front of the ear; the branch of the foot yang ming stomach channel is around the throat; the branch of the hand tai yang small intestine channel is above the inner canthus of the eye; the branch of the hand shao yang triple burner channel is above the outer canthus of the eye; the branch of the hand yang ming large intestine channel is located at the forehead; the branch of the foot tai yin spleen channel is at the root of the tongue; and the branch of the foot shao yin kidney channel is at the sides of the tongue.[17]

Pathology

According to the theory of channels and network vessels, each channel pertains to a specific *zang-fu* organ or bowel. When a *zang-fu* is out of balance, its pathological changes are often reflected to some particular points or areas on the body surface through its related channel. Thus, those particular points can be used to assist diagnosis and treat disorders.

When brain function is abnormal or there is a lesion or imbalance in the brain, certain regions of the scalp will reveal pathological changes or symptoms through connections of channels and network vessels. Those regions are used to diagnose the brain's dysfunction and restore it to normal. As the *Yellow Emperor's Classic of Internal Medicine–Spiritual Axis* states,

> When qi in the upper part of the body is deficient, there may be lightheadedness, tinnitus, loss of balance, dizziness, and blurred vision.

According to Wang Qing-ren in the *Yi Lin Gai Cuo* (*Correcting the Errors in the Forest of Medicine*), mental activities including memory, language, vision, hearing, and smell are all controlled by the brain. As a result, scalp acupuncture can treat disorders of memory, speech, vision, smell, and taste.

In another example, the *Spiritual Axis* states,

> All the essence and qi of the five organs and six bowels ascend to the eyes and form the vision. It communicates with many channels, constituting an eye system that ascends to the vertex and enters the brain, then descends and reaches the nape. Thus, when pathogenic factors invade the nape and encounter a deficiency of the body, they penetrate by this pathway to the eye system into the brain. This causes hyperactivity of the brain and tightness of the eye system.

Diagnosis

Areas to stimulate in scalp acupuncture are projections of areas of the brain onto scalp locations. Each area corresponds approximately to a specific neurophysiological function in the brain. Like the functions of back *shu* and front *mu* points of viscera and bowels, scalp areas have the property of transporting energy to and from the brain. Through the central nervous and endocrine systems, the structural, metabolic, hormonal, and energetic functions of the brain are accessible at specific areas of the scalp surface. The areas are located directly on the scalp surface bearing the same name as those in the brain, so those areas can directly influence the different functions of the brain. They derive their function from their neurophysiologic functions rather than their channel affiliations.

If the flow of qi and blood to the brain is blocked, the qi and blood stagnate at the scalp area and create tenderness when palpated. The pathways that flow from the stimulated areas in the scalp to the brain also return information to the surface areas. This allows the stimulated areas in scalp acupuncture to be employed for both diagnosis and therapy purposes. For this reason, palpating scalp areas for unusual sensitivity can detect a disturbance occurring within the associated brain cortex.

In general, excruciating or intense pain suggests an acute condition, whereas a dull ache suggests a chronic problem. Tender areas located on the scalp may relate strictly to structural damage, but might also be related to functional or organic lesions of the associated brain cortex. Scalp areas respond to the presence of brain disorders in a predictable fashion. Certain areas may become spontaneously tender or sensitive to the touch when brain function is abnormal. These areas are very useful not only in diagnosis, but also in the discovery of new areas for scalp acupuncture therapy.

Treatment

Scalp acupuncture treatment is based on fundamental theories of Chinese medicine. Stimulation areas in scalp acupuncture are places where both the qi and blood flow into, and connect with, channels and network vessels interiorly and exteriorly. They have the ability to move channel qi and blood, reinforce qi and eliminate pathogenic factors, and regulate deficiency and excess.

Through stimulation by scalp acupuncture, they can regulate the function of *zang-fu* and channels, benefit the immune system, balance yin and yang, and also harmonize hyperactive and hypoactive functions of the brain. Stimulation of projected areas of the brain can also restore the proper circulation of qi and blood so as to prevent and treat diseases. As the *Yellow Emperor's Classic of Internal Medicine–Spiritual Axis* describes, "Upper illness can be treated in the lower part of the body; lower illness can be treated in the upper part of the body."

Ancient Chinese practitioners found that needling the head could treat disorders in the lower part of the body, including extremities and urinary or bowel incontinence. There are hundreds of successful cases of needling head points to treat disorders of the limbs and internal organs in ancient acupuncture literature. These have served as a great source of inspiration for the development of scalp acupuncture treatment today.

Selecting scalp areas that have a close relationship with *zang-fu* functions or follow along the course of channels is presently an essential principle in scalp acupuncture treatment. Because many areas on the scalp interconnect with the brain through their channels and network vessels, their primary therapeutic properties are indicated for treating many disorders of the brain, including many psychiatric and neurological diseases.

Traditional functions of points on the scalp have been a great influence on the discovery and development of indications for scalp areas. Among the 37 points on the scalp commonly used in traditional acupuncture, 26 have a close relationship with the location, function, and indication of scalp acupuncture areas. For example Tian Zhu (Bl 10) is indicated for headache, vertigo, convulsive disease, depression, manic psychosis, vexation, and epilepsy. It is stated in *Spiritual Axis*, "Tian Zhu (Bl 10) treats sudden contraction of the extremities, seizures, vertigo, and difficulty in standing." It is interesting to note that indications of Shuai Gu (GB 8) in the *Zhen Jiu Da Cheng* (*Great Compendium of Acupuncture and Moxibustion*) in 1601 are exactly the same as indications of the Vertigo and Hearing Area in scalp acupuncture, which treat dizziness, vertigo, hearing loss, tinnitus, and auditory hallucination.

Ancient Chinese practitioners not only found therapeutic effects of points on the scalp, but also noticed the risk of needling scalp points that were contraindicated. For example, the *Yellow Emperor's Classic of Internal Medicine–Spiritual Axis* states, "When needling the head, if Feng Fu (GV 16) is punctured deeply and reaches the brain, the patient dies immediately." Therefore, when needling on scalp areas, practitioners should review their knowledge of anatomy of the skull and scalp to prevent acupuncture accidents.

CHAPTER THREE

Locations and Indications of Areas in Chinese Scalp Acupuncture

Precise location of Chinese scalp acupuncture areas requires identification of two imaginary lines on the head. The anterior-posterior line runs along the centerline of the head. The midpoint of this line on the skull is located halfway between the occipital protuberance and the glabella, which is midway between the eyebrows. The second line, the horizontal line, runs along the sides of the head from the highest point of the eyebrow to the occipital protuberance. Where this line intersects the anterior hairline at the temple defines the lower point of the Motor Area (Figure 11). In patients without a definite hairline, an alternative method for locating this point is to draw a vertical line up from acupuncture point Xia Guan (St 7) until it intersects the horizontal line.

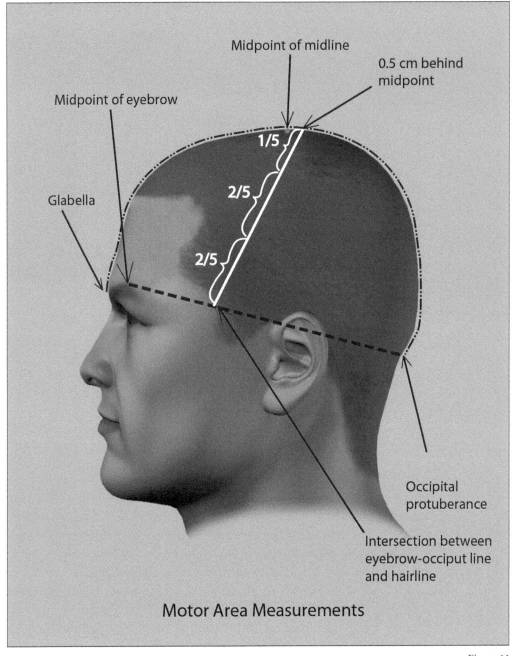

Motor Area Measurements

Figure 11

Motor Area Location

The Motor Area is located on the area of the scalp corresponding to the pre-central gyrus of the frontal lobe. The Motor Area is located in a strip beginning at the midline at a point 0.5 cm posterior to the previously located midpoint of the head, along the anterior-posterior line. The Motor Area runs from this point obliquely down to the point where the eyebrow-occipital line intersects the anterior hairline (Figure 11). The line of the Motor Area determines the angle and location of several other areas, such as the Sensory Area and Chorea and Tremor Area.

The Motor Area of the cerebral cortex controls and adjusts intersectional body movements. One side of the cerebral cortex controls the contralateral muscles of the body below the neck. In contrast, most head and face muscles are controlled bilaterally. The size of the motor gyrus of the cerebral cortex is associated with complexity and accuracy of body movement. A larger representative area equates to greater complexity and accuracy. The motor gyrus is depicted as a reversed homunculus. For example, the upper part of the gyrus controls the lower limbs, while the middle part of the gyrus controls upper limbs, and the lower parts control head and face movement.

The Motor Area is divided into three regions according to the homunculus projection. In order to correctly locate these three regions, the whole Motor Area is divided equally into fifths. Then three regions are measured as follows: upper one-fifth (1/5) region, middle two-fifths (2/5) region, and lower two-fifths (2/5) region (Figure 11). The upper 1/5 region is used to treat contralateral dysfunctional movement of the lower extremity, trunk, spinal cord, and neck. The middle 2/5 region is used to treat contralateral dysfunctional movement of the upper extremity. The lower 2/5 region is used to treat bilateral dysfunctional movement of the face and head.[18] It is also an effective area for treating dysphasia due to stroke and other brain damage. These areas are used to affect the contralateral side of the body. The direction of needling is usually from the upper part of the area downward, penetrating the entire area.

Motor Area Indications

Indications for the application of needles in the Motor Area are: paralysis or weakness in the face, trunk, or limbs caused by stroke, multiple sclerosis, traumatic paraplegia, acute myelitis, progressive myotrophy, neuritis, poliomyelitis, post-polio syndrome, periodic paralysis, hysterical paralysis, Bell's palsy, spinal cord injury, traumatic brain injury, Charcot-Marie-Tooth disease, and brain damage from brain surgery.

Among the disorders mentioned above, the most common problems are generally paralysis due to stroke, multiple sclerosis, and traumatic injury. When treating stroke from thrombosis and embolism, scalp acupuncture treatment should begin as soon as possible. When treating a hemorrhagic stroke, scalp acupuncture treatment should not be performed until the patient's condition is stable, typically at least one month after the stroke. Though stroke can be treated at any stage, the greatest response to treatment will be for strokes occurring less than a year prior to scalp acupuncture. The longer the duration of the impairment, the more gradual the improvement will be. With long-term cases of impairment, expectations need to be realistic, although some patients will occasionally surprise practitioners. Improvement is rare for patients with a long history of paralysis that has led to muscular atrophy, rigid joints, and inflexibility.

When treating chronic progressive diseases like multiple sclerosis and Parkinson's disease, the results from treatment are often temporary. Results may last for hours, days, weeks, or months, but ongoing follow-up treatments will be necessary. However, when treating paralysis from either stroke or trauma, improvements of movement are often permanent.

Each part of the cerebral cortex has its own functions, according to our current understanding of the brain. When one area is impaired, the impaired area can recover to a limited extent. In addition, by employing proper stimulation, other areas can compensate for the impaired area. This may be the answer to explaining the mechanism of scalp acupuncture in treating impairment in the cerebral cortex. Generally speaking, paralyzed extremities are targeted by treating the opposite site of the motor area in the scalp. For instance, if a patient has paralysis of the right leg and foot, needles should be inserted into the patient's left Motor Area of the scalp. However, for patients undergoing brain surgery or with an injury where part of the brain or the scalp has been removed, needling should be on the same side of the scalp as the side of the paralyzed limb.

Sensory Area Location

The Sensory Area is located on the projective area of the scalp corresponding to the post-central gyrus of the parietal lobe. The Sensory Area is one of the most commonly used in Chinese scalp acupuncture. It is located parallel to and 1.5 cm posterior to the Motor Area (Figure 12).

The sensory area of the cerebral cortex controls and adjusts sensations on the opposite side of the body. One side of the cerebral cortex controls contralateral sensations of the body in the level below the neck. In contrast, most of the sensations of the head and face are bilateral. The sensory gyrus, like the motor gyrus, is also distributed as an upside-down homunculus. That means the upper part of the gyrus controls the lower limbs, the middle part dominates the upper limbs, and the lower part controls head and facial sensations.

The Sensory Area is also divided into three regions according to the inverted homunculus projection and with the same proportions as discussed for the Motor Area: the upper 1/5, the middle 2/5, and the lower 2/5. These areas are used to affect the contralateral side of the body. The direction of needling is usually from the upper part of the area downward, penetrating the entire area.

Sensory Area Indications

Indications for the application of scalp acupuncture to the Sensory Area include abnormal sensations of face, trunk, and limbs that are either hyposensitive or hypersensitive, including pain, tingling, numbness, and loss of sensation in the contralateral side of the body. Disorders that have shown positive results when treated by scalp acupuncture include loss of sensation or pain from stroke and traumatic injury, numbness and tingling from multiple sclerosis, phantom pain, complex regional pain, residual limb pain, trigeminal neuralgia, temporomandibular joint (TMJ) pain, migraine headache, cluster headache, shingles, pain in the neck, shoulder, back and lower back, sciatica, gout, plantar fasciitis,

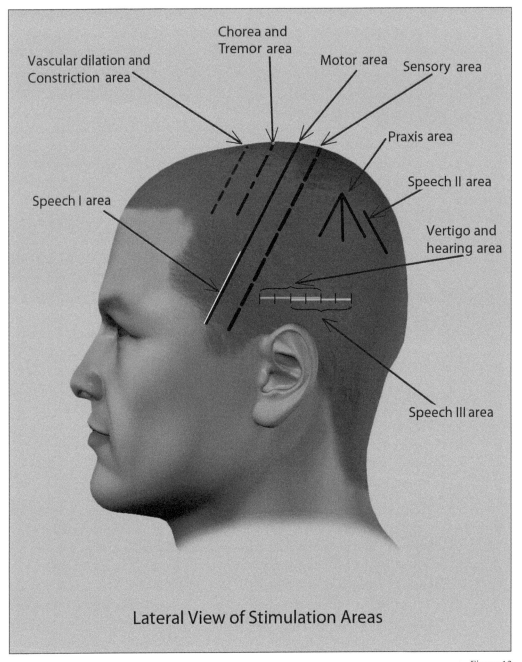

Lateral View of Stimulation Areas

Figure 12

fibromyalgia, neuropathy, and paresthesia. In general, abnormal sensations of an extremity are treated by choosing the opposite site of the sensory area in the scalp. For instance, if a patient has pain in the right leg and foot, the left side of the Sensory Area in the scalp should be needled. However, for patients having had brain surgery or an injury where part of brain or scalp was removed, needles should be placed on the same side of the scalp as the affected limb. For example, a patient with numbness in the left leg and foot would be treated with needles on the left side of the scalp's sensory area. Scalp acupuncture produces excellent results for pain, numbness and tingling. Many patients show significant improvement during the initial treatment. Scalp acupuncture results in much quicker effects compared to other types of acupuncture such as in the ear, hand, or body. Some patients feel improvement just a few seconds or a few minutes after the needles are inserted.

As with the Motor Area, the upper 1/5 of the Sensory Area is used to treat abnormal sensation and pain in the lower extremities, trunk, back, chest, and neck. The middle 2/5 is used for the upper extremities. The lower 2/5 is used for problems with the face and head, including migraines, headaches, trigeminal neuralgia, toothache, and temporo-mandibular joint (TMJ) pain.

Chorea and Tremor Area

The Chorea and Tremor Area is located on the projective area of the scalp corresponding to the premotor cortex. This gyrus has important functions in adjusting the stability of voluntary movement and the control of muscular tension.

The Chorea and Tremor Area is located parallel to and 1.5 cm anterior to the Motor Area (Figure 12) running 4 cm down in the same direction. It starts 1 cm anterior to the midpoint at its upper point. This area is always needled bilaterally and is used for any involuntary motor activity. This is the primary area for the treatment of Parkinson's disease, any type of tremor, shaking of the head, body, or extremities, chorea, tic, restless leg syndrome, and dystonia. This area is also very effective for treating patients with muscular tension and tightness in any part of the body. The direction of needling is usually from the upper part of the area downward, penetrating the entire area.

Vascular Dilation and Constriction Area

This area is parallel to and 1.5 cm anterior to the Chorea and Tremor Area, or 3 cm anterior to the Motor Area (Figure 12). This area is always needled bilaterally and can be used for essential hypertension, cortical edema, and other autonomic vascular dysfunctions. The direction of needling is usually from the upper part of the area downward, penetrating the entire area.

Vertigo and Hearing Area

This area is located over the temporal lobe on the lateral side of the head. It is on a horizontal line 4 cm long. It starts 1.5 cm superior to the apex of the auricle of the ear at its middle point, and extends 2 cm anterior and 2 cm posterior to the middle point (Figure 12). This area is also needled bilaterally and can be needled in either direction. This is a very useful area for treating vertigo, dizziness, Ménière's disease, tinnitus, hearing loss, and auditory hallucinations.

Speech I Area

There are three speech areas. Speech I Area is located on the posterior third of the gyrus frontalis inferior over the frontal lobe and controls groups of muscles for speech and phonation. This Area corresponds to Broca's area of the frontal lobe, which controls the muscles of the tongue and mouth that form speech. Speech I Area overlaps the lower 2/5 of the Motor Area (Figure 12). The indications for Speech I Area are dysarthria, dysphonia, or motor aphasia after a stroke or brain injury due to which the muscles of speech and vocalization have been paralyzed.[19] This area is needled bilaterally for motor aphasia. The direction of needling is usually from the upper part of the area downward, penetrating the entire area.

Speech II Area

This area lies over the reading and comprehension part of the parietal lobe, and is located by finding the parietal tubercle. From the parietal tubercle, run a line parallel to the anterior-posterior line 2 cm posteriorly. Using this as the starting point, the Speech 2 Area runs 3 cm in length, parallel to the anterior-posterior line (Figure 12, 13). This area is needled bilaterally for nominal apha-sia—the inability to name objects. In this disorder, the patient can describe an object, but cannot produce the noun. The direction of needling is usually from the upper part of the area downward, penetrating the entire length.

Speech III Area

This overlies Wernicke's area of the temporal lobe, and overlaps the posterior half of the Vertigo and Hearing Area. It lies on the same horizontal line 1.5 cm superior to the apex of the auricle but begins at the midpoint of the Vertigo and Hearing Area directly above the auricle and runs 4 cm posteriorly (Figure 12). It is used bilaterally for treatment of receptive aphasia, where the patient can articulate words but the words don't make sense. The direction of needling can go either from posterior to anterior or from anterior to posterior, penetrating the entire area.

Praxis Area

This is an uncommonly used area. Starting from the parietal tubercle, the Praxis Area joins 3 lines, one running straight downward and the other two at a 40-degree angle anterior and posterior to the vertical line (Figure 12). This area is for apraxia—the inability to execute certain fine motor activities such as buttoning a shirt.

Vision Area

The Vision Area is located over the occipital lobe on the posterior aspect of the head. It starts on a horizontal line at the level of the occipital protuberance. The Vision Area starts at a point 1 cm lateral to the occipital protuberance and runs upward for 4 cm, parallel to the anterior-posterior line (Figure 13). The Vision Area is often needled bilaterally. Unlike other scalp areas in Chinese acupuncture, into which needling could be any direction, the Vision Area must be needled from the top down. Needling from below pointing upward risks injury to the medulla if the needling angle or depth is wrong. Indications for needling are vision loss due to stroke or brain injury, visual field loss, double vision, visual hallucination, and nystagmus.

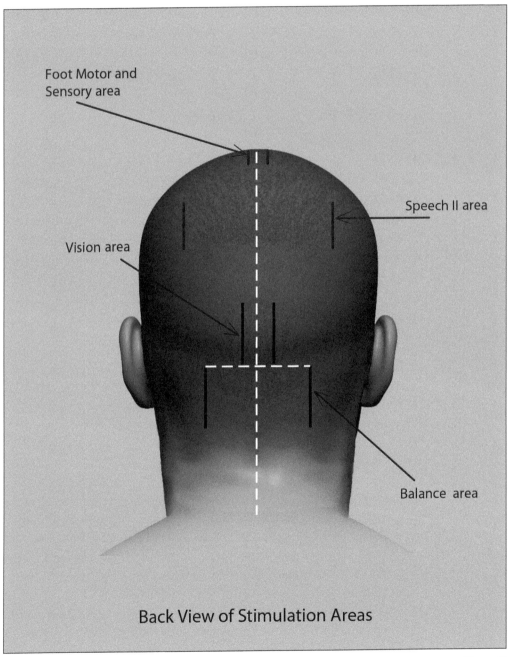

Foot Motor and
Sensory area

Speech II area

Vision area

Balance area

Back View of Stimulation Areas

Figure 13

Balance Area

The Balance Area is located over the cerebellum. It starts on a horizontal line at the level of the occipital protuberance. The Balance Area starts from a point 3.5 cm lateral to the occipital protuberance and runs 4 cm inferiorly (Figure 13). The Balance Area is needled bilaterally. Like the Vision Area, it must be needled from the top down. Needling from below pointing upward risks injury to the medulla. Indications for needling the Balance Area are disequilibrium, cerebellar atrophy, cerebellar strokes, multiple sclerosis, Parkinson's disease, ataxia, and loss of balance due to traumatic brain injury.

Foot Motor and Sensory Area

The Foot Motor and Sensory Area (FMSA) is the most commonly used one in Chinese scalp acupuncture. It has broad-ranging effects on both motor and sensory functions. The FMSA is located parallel to the anterior-posterior line, 1 cm lateral to the midline beginning at the level of the midpoint of the anterior-posterior line and running 4 cm posteriorly (Figure 13, 14). The Foot Motor and Sensory Area gets its name from including both the Motor Area and the Sensory Area in the region of the foot on the homunculus.

While it is useful for motor and sensory problems of the feet, the Foot Motor and Sensory Area has a much broader effect and is used for a wide range of symptoms. Since the area overlies many endocrine glands, such as the pituitary gland and adrenal glands, it not only affects the central nervous system but also regulates the endocrine system. That is why this area can treat many different kinds of disorders. The Foot Motor and Sensory Area is usually needled bilaterally, either from the front part of the area toward the back part or vice versa. However, it is relatively easier if the direction is from front to back.

Indications for needling the Foot Motor and Sensory Area include paralysis of the leg or foot, restless leg syndrome, pain in the legs and feet including gout, peripheral neuropathy, plantar fasciitis, reflex sympathetic dystrophy or complex regional pain, fibromyalgia, phantom pain, residual limb pain, numbness and tingling in legs and feet, pain in the neck and shoulders, incontinence of urine, bedwetting, incontinence of stool, irritable bowel syndrome, impotence,

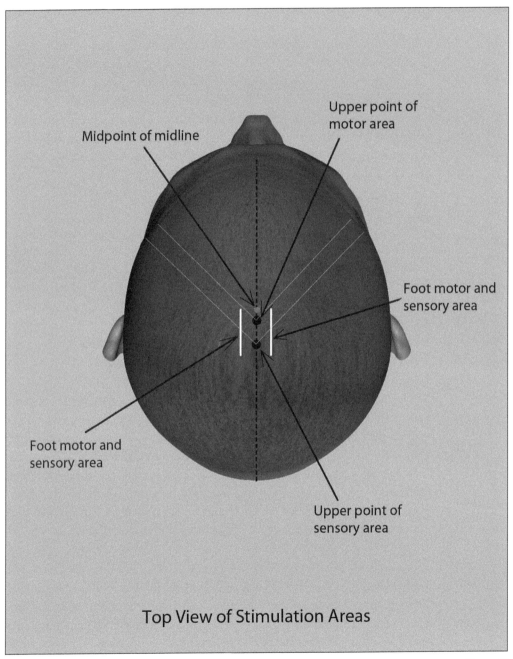

Top View of Stimulation Areas

Figure 14

premature ejaculation, decreased libido, infertility, prolapse of the uterus, prolapse of the bladder, amenorrhea, dysmenorrhea, abnormal uterine bleeding, psoriasis, neurodermatitis, shingles, ADHD, post-traumatic stress disorder, post-concussion syndrome, poor memory, poor concentration, emotional disturbances, and mental retardation. Avoid needling the Foot Motor and Sensory Area in pregnancy as there is a theoretical risk of inducing uterine contractions.

Internal Organ Areas

The internal organ areas are located on the front of the head. The location of these areas is based on clinical experience rather than anatomy and physiology as known in Western medicine. These scalp areas are not used very often since traditional body acupuncture produces excellent results.

Head Area

The Head Area is located on the midline at the forehead, running from the hairline 2 cm superiorly and inferiorly (Figure 15). This is the only area that we have added according to our experience. The area is used for treating mental and emotional disorders such as insomnia, poor memory, poor concentration, anxiety, and depression.

Stomach Area

This is located on the mid-pupillary line from the hairline 2 cm superiorly (Figure 15). This area is used for treating stomach pain and discomfort in the upper epigastric region.

Thoracic Cavity Area

This is located half the distance between the Stomach Area and the midline, running from the hairline 2 cm superiorly and inferiorly (Figure 15). This area is used for treating asthma and tachycardia.

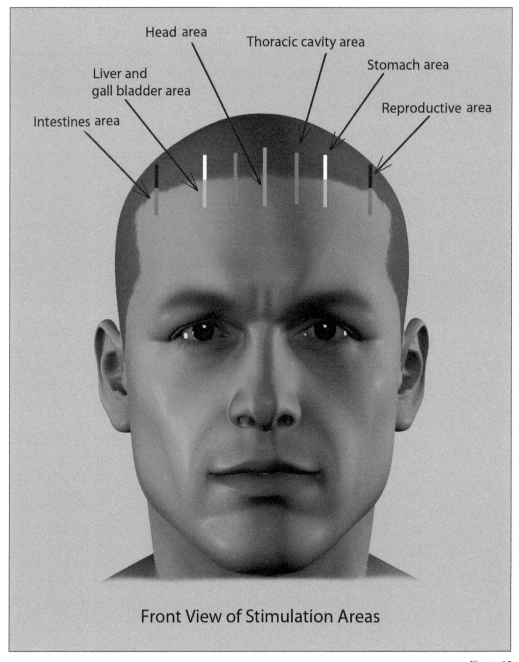

Front View of Stimulation Areas

Figure 15

Liver and Gallbladder Area

The Liver and Gallbladder Area or line descends onto the forehead for 2 cm along the mid-pupillary line (Figure 15). This area is used for treating costal pain and rib pain due to hepatitis, gallstones, and shingles.

Reproductive Area

This area starts at the frontal corner of the hairline, running 2 cm superiorly (Figure 15). It is useful for treating menstrual cramps, bleeding, and urinary tract infection.

Large Intestine Area

This descends onto the forehead for 2 cm along the Reproductive Area (Figure 15). The area can be used in cases of diarrhea or constipation.

CHAPTER FOUR

Scalp Acupuncture Techniques

Selection of Needles

Most modern acupuncture practitioners use disposable stainless steel needles of 0.18–to–0.30 mm diameter, sterilized with ethylene oxide or by autoclave. The upper third of these needles are wound with a thicker wire, a metal pipe, or covered in plastic in order to stiffen the needle and provide a handle for the practitioner to grasp and manipulate while inserting and stimulating. The size and type of needle used, and the depth of insertion, depend on the acupuncture modalities being practiced.

For scalp acupuncture, the size of Chinese needles is #30 to #36. The size of Japanese needles is #6 to #9. Needles 1 or 1.5 inches in length are commonly used for scalp acupuncture, depending on the area to be stimulated and the patient's condition. For the novice practitioner, relatively thicker needles are recommended because the scalp is tougher than the skin and thinner needles are too easily bent upon insertion.

Posture of the Patient

The positions of both patient and practitioner are important. Patients should be made as comfortable as possible in the treatment position because it is difficult to adjust this position once the needles have been placed. The ideal position for scalp acupuncture treatment is sitting. This allows the practitioner to easily inspect, identify anatomical landmarks, and insert and stimulate needles on different sides of the head based on the treatment design. Patients should be positioned so that they do not need to move their head while the needles are in place. Although most patients can be treated in this manner, some with motor or balance disorders must be treated with extra care, their bodies well supported in the prone, supine, or lateral recumbent position. This is especially useful for first-time treatment with scalp acupuncture as it allays feelings of nervousness or anxiety. The practitioner should be in a comfortable, upright, balanced position that allows freedom of movement in order to find the most suitable position to insert and stimulate the needles. While performing treatment, the practitioner should assume the *Tai Ji* posture. This means standing with the feet shoulder-width distance apart, relaxing the shoulders and elbows, and extending or opening the chest while contracting the abdomen. This posture allows the practitioner's qi to flow freely from the body to the hands, thus enhancing the results of the acupuncture treatment.

Insertion of Needles

Before needle insertion the needling area should be cleaned with a 75% alcohol swab or cotton ball. Hair or any other obstruction should be moved away to expose the stimulation area. The needle should be inserted by using the free-hand technique instead of a guide tube, which is a popular insertion technique in the West. This is due to the special anatomy of the scalp, which has five layers as described above: skin, connective tissue, epicranial aponeurosis, loose areolar tissue, and pericranium (Figure 2 on page 14).

Insertion with Two Hands

In Chinese scalp acupuncture, a 30–36 gauge stainless steel acupuncture needle with a length of 1.5 inches is placed into the loose areolar tissue layer beneath the epicranial aponeurosis and above the pericranium. To place the needle correctly, hold the needle with the non-dominant hand. Place the tip at a 15–25 degree angle to the skin. Use the dominant hand to quickly pierce the skin and thread the needle through the loose areolar tissue layer for the entire 1–1.5 inches length of the needle shaft (Figure 16).

It is much easier for the practitioner to insert the needle toward him/herself than toward the patient because the practitioner's wrist can then insert with much greater force and control. If resistance is encountered, the needle is most

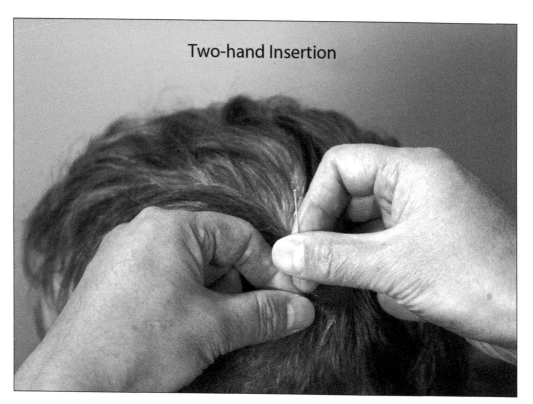

Figure 16

likely in the aponeurosis or the pericranium. Withdrawing the needle slightly and repositioning the angle will usually result in successful insertion.

In the Vertigo and Hearing Area, the Balance Area, and the lower 2/5 of the Motor and Sensory Areas, there is an additional muscle layer under the epicranial aponeurosis and above the pericranium. In these areas, the needle will be in the muscle layer. Insert the needles carefully to avoid a muscle spasm; having the patient relax the jaw will help. If muscle contraction prevents full insertion of the needle, you may use a second needle to cover the entire area.

Insertion with One Hand

Hold the needle 2–3 mm away from its tip with the thumb and index finger of the dominant hand. From a distance of 4–6 cm above the scalp, push the needle quickly into the areolar layer (Figure 17). This insertion method is relatively difficult to master and could cause patients additional pain if done by a novice.

It is highly recommended to insert a needle in ear point Shen Men at the very beginning of the treatment to help relax the patient, reduce any sensitivity to pain, and in general to ease him or her through the initial experience. The ear needles can be left in place for the duration of the scalp acupuncture treatment. If the patient experiences sharp pain during the needling, it is often caused by insertion of needles either too shallowly or too deep. Pushing the needle in a little more to a deeper desired depth or withdrawing the needle and relocating it at a smaller angle or a more shallow level can relieve this unpleasant feeling. It is advisable to adjust any needle that is painful as soon as the patient reports it. The practitioner should recheck with the patient often during and after the treatment to verify if there is any increase or change in the pain because some patients may experience discomfort later, such as when they talk, drink, or eat.

Angle, Depth, and Speed of Insertion

The proper angle, depth, and speed of inserting needles reduce sensations of pain and discomfort significantly. To review, the needle should be inserted at a 15–25 degree angle (close to parallel to the skin) and 1–2 inches in depth. While the needle penetrates the skin, the practitioner's fingers will have a slight sense of tightness at first. When the needle reaches the loose areolar layer, the

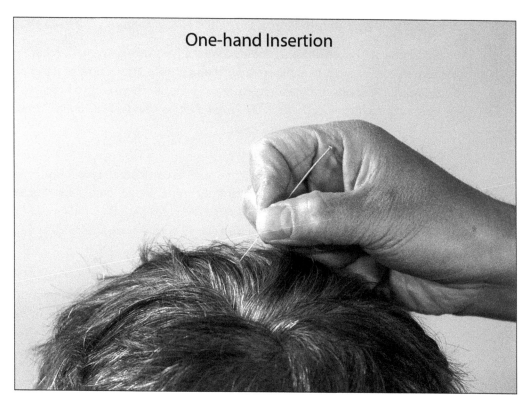

One-hand Insertion

Figure 17

practitioner's fingers will feel the tightness disappear or reduce. Once the layer becomes looser, the needle will smoothly push deeper with little or no resis tance. At this time, push the needle to the designated depth as quickly as possible. The speed of insertion is important for scalp acupuncture, the faster the needle is inserted, the less pain the patient feels.

It only takes 1–2 seconds for an experienced practitioner to insert a needle. After insertion, if the practitioner feels tightness in the skin or the patient feels much pain, it usually means the needle has been inserted either too shallowly or too deeply. If this happens, the needle should be pulled out a little, redirected, and pushed in again. Or more simply, take the needle out and insert a new one, heeding the above directions.

Special Needling Methods

In the past 38 years, many different needling methods have been applied in scalp acupuncture in order to enhance stimulation on scalp areas. Some of these are described in ancient acupuncture classics and some have been created by modern scalp acupuncture practitioners.[20] The most useful methods are described below.

Triple method (Qi Ci)

In this method three needles are inserted at different spots and are toward one point, with one needle in the center and the other two on both sides (Figure 18). This technique is very useful on Praxis Area for patients with apraxia or on the lower 2/5 of the Motor Area for patients with a paralyzed hand.

Adjacent method (Pang Ci)

In this method one needle is inserted in the appropriate scalp acupuncture area first and another adjacent needle is placed near the first needle with its tip toward the first needle (Figure 18). This technique is often used on Speech I Area for patients with motor aphasia or Speech III Area for patients with sensory aphasia.

Opposing method (Dui Ci)

In this method one needle is inserted at the beginning of a stimulating area along the area line. A second needle is placed at the opposite end of this stimulating area. The two needles are pointing toward each other but the needles' tips do not reach or touch each other (Figure 18). This technique is very useful for Foot Motor and Sensory Area or Liver Area and Stomach Area for the patient with disharmony between the liver and stomach.

Parallel method (Pingxin Ci)

In this method two or three needles are inserted at different spots or in different stimulation areas and are parallel to each other, with one needle in the center and another on one side or one on either side (Figure 18). The technique of two parallel needles is very useful for patients who present both movement and sensation disorders and is commonly used in the Vision Area, Balance Area,

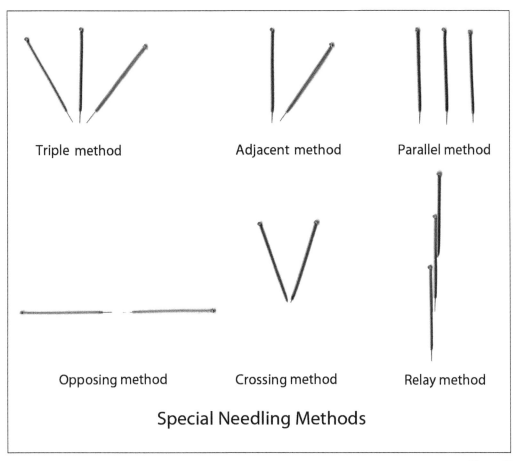

Triple method   Adjacent method   Parallel method

Opposing method   Crossing method   Relay method

Special Needling Methods

Figure 18

and Foot Motor and Sensory Area. The technique of three parallel needles is often used on the Head Area, Thoracic Cavity Area, and Stomach Area for the patient with insomnia or poor memory because heart and spleen are both deficient and weak.

Crossing method (Jiao Ca Ci)

This is another new method created by scalp acupuncture practitioners. Two or three needles are inserted at different spots and cross under the skin (Figure

18). This technique is often applied on Chorea and Tremor Area for a patient with Parkinson's disease or on Vascular Contraction and Dilation Area for patients with essential hypertension.

Relay method (Jie Li Ci)

In this new method created by modern scalp acupuncture practitioners, the second and third needles are inserted immediately after insertion of the initial needle, as if they were in a relay race (Figure 18). It is a common technique to treat patients with paralysis of both upper and lower limbs so the entire Motor Area can be stimulated quickly.

Penetrating method (Tou Ci)

In this method one needle is inserted so it is transversely penetrating more than one "point." This method is the most commonly used technique in scalp acupuncture treatment because the place needled on the scalp is in fact not a "point" but an "area." Using the penetrating method, one needle can cover and stimulate an entire area.

Contralateral method (Niu Ci)

This is one of nine needling methods described in the *Huang Di Nei Jing* (*Yellow Emperor's Classic of Internal Medicine*). Needle the points on the right side of the body when the disorder is located on the left side or vice versa. This method is very useful to treat hemiplesia, pain, and abnormal sensation in one side of the body due to stroke and other upper neuron damage, because the right side of the cerebral cortex controls movement and sensation on the left side of the body and vice versa. For example, when a stroke patient presents paralysis on the left arm and leg, his right Motor Area on the scalp should be needled.

Manipulation

Rotating or Twirling

Once the needle is in the correct position, it is stimulated with manual manipulation. Grasp the handle of the needle between the thumb and the distal interphalangeal joint of the index finger (Figure 19). By moving the index finger and keeping the thumb stationary, you can twirl the needle at a rate of 200

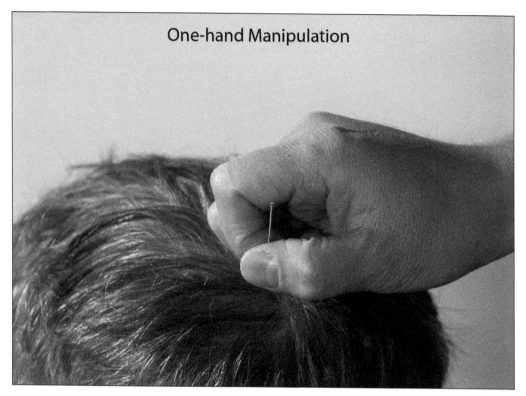

One-hand Manipulation

Figure 19

times per minute.[21] Rotate clockwise and counter-clockwise with amplitude ranging from 360 to 720 degrees. In other words, make one-to-two turns in each direction. Rotate needles every 10 minutes for 2–3 minutes. Take care not to push or pull the needle while twirling, as this can be quite painful. Two-hands stimulation is very useful for some of the special needling methods such as crossing method (Figure 20) During stimulation of the needles, encourage the paralyzed patient to move the affected area actively and passively.

Lifting and Thrusting

After the needle has reached its desired depth, lift and thrust it perpendicularly using a small range of 2–3 mm at 10-minute intervals. Manipulate the needle for 2–3 minutes at a time. It is not recommended to lift and thrust with too much range because the scalp is very sensitive and it may cause severe pain.

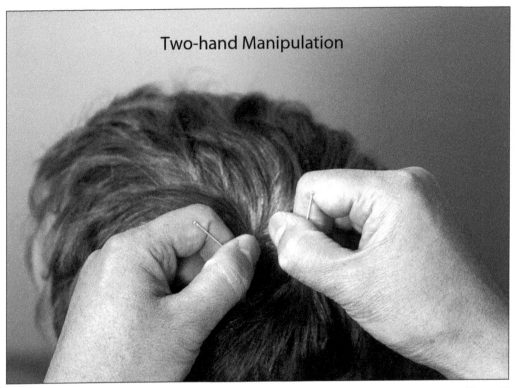

Two-hand Manipulation

Figure 20

Electrical Stimulation

Electrical stimulation may be used to replace hand stimulation. It can strengthen the stimulation and improve the therapeutic effect for practitioners who cannot rotate needles at the minimum of 200 times per minute. If this method is chosen, a pair of needles is connected to the electric stimulator. It is generally recommended to stimulate a pair at one time, usually choosing pairs on the same scalp area. The negative lead from the stimulating device is connected to the secondary area and the positive lead is connected to the primary stimulating area on the scalp. The recommended frequency for the Sensory Area is in the 100–150 hertz range and for other areas in the 4–30 hertz range.[22] This is equal to approximately 200-400 rotations per minute. The ideal intensity should be at the level that the patient can feel some tingling or vibrating sensation without causing any pain. The duration of electrical stimulation is 10–20 minutes. During the stimulation period, the patient may feel that the sensation of tingling or vibration gradually diminishes or disappears due to adaptation. It often happens after the first few minutes. If this occurs, the electrical output should be adjusted in intensity to re-establish the sensation.

It is necessary to inform patients who receive electrical acupuncture that it may produce sensations of tingling, numbness, sleepiness, heaviness, or distention. Their prior knowledge of this will help to allay any feelings of anxiety or fear they may have about the treatment. The device should not be turned on until after the acupuncture needles are in place and the electrodes connected. Frequency should be set first when the device is turned on with intensity starting from zero hertz and increasing gradually to avoid a shock. The wave form chosen can provide slightly different stimulation and responses. It is generally believed that intermittent waves produce more stimulation than continuous waves, and mixed waves have an effect between the two. For patients with severe heart disease or who faint easily, electrical stimulation should be avoided.

Observation of Needle Sensation Response

Arrival of qi is an especially important phenomenon for predicting the effect of acupuncture treatment. In the *Huang Di Nei Jing Ling Shu* (*The Yellow Emperor's Classic of Internal Medicine–Spiritual Axis*), it says that, "acupuncture therapy does not take effect until the arrival of qi." Quick arrival of qi suggests good effects in treatment; slow arrival of qi shows a retarded effect. The term "arrival of qi" means that the acupuncture practitioner manipulates the inserted needle so as to induce in the patient a sensation of soreness, numbness, heaviness, and distention around the point, or the transmission of these sensations upward and downward along the channels. In regular body acupuncture, needle manipulation may induce signs of the "arrival of qi" around or radiating from the insertion point. In contrast, needle manipulation in scalp acupuncture may induce the "arrival of qi" in areas distal to the needling site such as the face, neck, back, abdomen, or limbs. Quite interestingly, the distal sensations often occur in the affected limb rather than the normal limb. While inserting and stimulating scalp needles, pay close attention to the patient's reactions. Patients may experience some sensations in the body such as tingling, numbness, heat, cold, movement, or twitching of certain muscles. Alteration in the color or moisture of the skin along a channel can also be observed during scalp acupuncture treatment. Although such reactions vary from patient to patient depending upon both the patient's constitution and the quality of the scalp acupuncture treatment, they provide a useful tool to predict the patient's response and prognosis. Some patients respond more quickly than others. It is a good prognostic sign if the patient does feel something during the needle stimulation. This is not, however, necessary for recovery.

During or after scalp acupuncture, the patient may occasionally experience some sensations in the affected body part. This is considered a normal reaction. Besides the sensations listed above, patients may also feel heaviness, electrical sensation, muscle spasm, a sensation of water or energy moving, visible muscle twitching, and even involuntary movement. In addition, a few patients may experience temporary exacerbation of some symptoms in the affected area during or after the process of stimulation. This is considered a positive sign, as those patients usually show faster improvement. However, this is not essential, and many patients will still experience immediate, satisfactory results. Approximately 80% of our patients show minor to major improvement after their first scalp acupuncture treatment. In many cases, patients' abnormal sensations of pain, numbness, tingling, burning, or increased sensitivity to touch may also be partially or completely relieved during or after the process of scalp acupuncture treatment.

Retention of Needles and Course of Treatments

The needles are stimulated for approximately 2–3 minutes and re-stimulated at 10-minute intervals over the course of treatment. Most treatments of scalp acupuncture last 30–45 minutes. Some practitioners have left needles in place for as many as one to three days. Do not leave them in for more than 72 hours due to the risk of infection.

Most disorders that respond quickly to acupuncture require treatment two to three times per week initially. Exceptions to this are acute disorders that may need daily treatment. The interval between treatments may be extended to a week once improvements are stable for the full period between visits. Once the improvements have lasted from several days to a full week, treatments may be spaced every 10 days to two weeks. After recovery from the initial complaints, patients can return on an as-needed basis or schedule monthly maintenance visits. A therapeutic course in the West consists of 10 treatments at intervals between visits of from five to seven days. In China and other Asian countries, patients are usually treated daily if they are in a hospital. This is because the cost of acupuncture treatment in Asia is inexpensive compared to Western countries. According to our experience, two or three treatments per week are efficient and effective for patients who are not hospitalized; these patients can recover as quickly as if they were treated every day.

Withdrawal of Needles

Needle removal is accomplished with one swift motion. Begin by pressing down the hair around the needle with one hand. Meanwhile, hold the needle between the thumb and index finger of the other hand. Rotate the needle gently to make sure it is loose and then withdraw it quickly. After that, press the needled area with a dry cotton ball for a short while to prevent bleeding. Because of the scalp's rich blood supply, the needled sites bleed more frequently on removal of the needle than at other body sites. It is therefore important to press the needled site a little longer and recheck it after removing the cotton ball. For some patients there is bleeding not at the moment the needles are removed, but later, after removal. To be safe, it is always best to recheck the scalp for bleeding as well as for needles, as sometimes they become hidden in the hair.

After Scalp Acupuncture Treatment

Most patients do not experience abnormal feelings at the conclusion of their treatment. However, it is recommended that patients rest in the clinic for about 10–30 minutes if they feel at all lightheaded or disoriented. But by far, most patients feel relaxed after a treatment. The rare patient who experiences exhaustion after treatment should be advised to take it easy for the rest of the day. Whatever the immediate subjective or objective responses reported by the patient, be they symptoms and signs of improvement or exacerbation of complaints, these should be considered as positive responses. Any exacerbations usually diminish after a few hours or at least by 48 hours.

Contraindications and Precautions

It is inadvisable to apply scalp acupuncture on any scalp area where there is infection, ulcer, tumor, or a postoperative skull defect. Also it is inadvisable to treat an infant whose fontanel has not yet closed. Do not use scalp acupuncture on patients with a tendency to hemorrhage or on those with severe hypertension, high fever, or in an acute stage of cerebral hemorrhage.

Management of Scalp Acupuncture Accidents

Scalp acupuncture is a relatively safe treatment and has no risk of injury to the brain because of the skull beneath the scalp. Some common incidents and their management are listed below.

Fainting

Needling in scalp acupuncture into the correct layer is a relative challenge, at least initially. This is especially true for practitioners who usually use a guide tube for needle insertion and who have little experience with freehand needle insertion. It could be relatively painful for the patient and could easily cause fainting if s/he is in a sitting position, too nervous, hungry, or very weak. In mild cases, the patient may experience lightheadedness, dizziness, nausea, shortness of breath, palpitation, cold sweats, or become pale. In severe cases, there may be loss of consciousness, a drop in blood pressure, or incontinence of urine or stool.

When fainting occurs, stop needling and stimulating immediately and withdraw all the needles already in place. The practitioner needs to assist the patient to lie down and then offer the patient some warm water or candy. The patient usually feels better after resting for a short period of time. In severe cases, if the patient has shown loss of consciousness, do acupressure or needle Shui Gou (GV 26), Nei Guan (Per 6), Zhong Chong (Per 9), and He Gu (LI 4), or use moxibustion on Qi Hai (CV 6), Guan Yuan (CV 4), and Yong Quan (Ki 1).

Stuck Needles

Stuck needles are more commonly seen in scalp acupuncture treatment than other types of acupuncture because of the five layers in the scalp. After a needle is inserted it could become stuck in the scalp, making it difficult to manipulate or impossible to withdraw. Quite often this results from inserting the needle in a wrong layer of the scalp, rotating the needle in one direction only, or uneven manipulation. Occasionally it is caused by muscular tension or cramping in a very nervous patient.

A stuck needle should be managed in different ways according to its cause. If the stuck needle is caused by insertion of the needle in the wrong layer of the scalp, the condition will release after the needle is withdrawn. If the stuck needle is due to rotating it in only one direction, the condition usually releases when the needle is twirled in the opposite direction. For the patient with a stuck needle due to muscular tension or spasm, the needle often loosens up after the patient has relaxed for a few minutes. Massaging the scalp near the stuck area or inserting another needle nearby can be very effective in loosening up the tense muscle and releasing the stuck needle as well.

Hematoma

Hematoma is much less seen in scalp acupuncture treatment due to the anatomy of the scalp. It may be caused by injury to blood vessels and not pressing the area after withdrawing the needle. Usually there is no special management needed. Mild hematoma will disappear by itself in a few days if it occurs. A cold compress and light massage are recommended if there is severe hematoma.

Subsequent Modifications to Treatment

Most patients are responsive to the initial scalp acupuncture treatment and show some improvement with the first session or at least within three treatments. In our practice, about 80% of our patients have a good response and even major improvement early on. The likelihood of experiencing a positive response following the initial treatment is dependent on the nature and duration of the disease, the patient's constitutional condition, and his/her motivation to improve. Generally speaking, patients fall into several categories of improvement. Some show a gradual and progressive improvement; some have an amelioration of symptoms followed by a return to the presenting conditions (such as in multiple sclerosis and Parkinson's disease); and some appear to have an exacerbation of their symptoms followed by major improvement. In a few cases there will be no change in their symptoms at all.

It may take two or more treatments for patients to notice a difference in their disorder. Therefore, it is inappropriate to change the treatment plan prematurely if the practitioner has confidence in the diagnosis and choice of treatment. As a general rule, the practitioner should repeat the same initial program at the second and third sessions of treatment with a modification in intensity of manual stimulation or electrical stimulation to accommodate for deficiencies or excesses in the first treatment.

If a patient is not responsive by the third treatment, the practitioner should reconsider the accuracy of the diagnosis, treatment principle, and location of the area stimulated. If these parameters appear to be correct, the practitioner's next step should be to reassess both the patient's vitality and motivation, and the practitioner's choice of treatment location.[23] A patient with low vitality and motivation usually responds more slowly than one with normal vitality and greater motivation. With such a patient, it is appropriate to add body acupuncture at source points, back *shu* points, or front *mu* points, combined with supplementing methods such as moxibustion to enhance the treatment program. Increasing the duration or frequency of the treatment will not change the results at all.

For the patient with multiple symptoms, the goal of the initial treatment should be focused on the major complaint. The secondary clinical manifestations can be addressed after the major complaint has shown marked improvement. In such cases, this will maintain the confidence and interest of the patient in the treatment so that s/he will look forward to continuing treatments. The practitioner should avoid addressing too many symptoms at once, especially for the patient with no prior acupuncture experience.

In supervising many scalp acupuncture clinics, it is often observed that the initial location and preliminary stimulation might have been incorrect. The revised choice of therapeutic location may start at the fourth visit or, in the case of a patient with low vitality, the fourth treatment may be focused more on general supplementing of the qi with little attention to the chief complaint.

Sometimes patients show no change from the presenting condition after a few treatments because they have reduced or stopped the medication that has been used to control the symptoms. It is necessary to explain to patients that they should continue to take any medication they were taking before acupuncture started until consulting their primary physician. If a patient is still not responding after the fourth visit, the practitioner should consider shifting to a different treatment strategy by reviewing the initial interview and all earlier notes. The practitioner should consider shifting to a different kind of treatment altogether if the patient's symptoms and signs have not changed after five to six visits.

It is common for patients to experience early positive results and then to reach a plateau of improvement after only a few treatments. It is also common that the patient's initial positive responses do not relieve the symptoms of their major complaints. In such conditions, an additional technique or needling area in combination with the original ones can be very helpful. For example, it might be necessary to stimulate the Speech II or Speech III areas after a patient with motor aphasia has shown some signs of improvement.

After a patient has shown major improvement, the treatment strategy would change to focus on continuation of treatments as infrequently as possible with the objective only to maintain and consolidate the improvements already achieved. As the reader can see, every case is different based on a myriad of conditions and practitioners must be ever vigilant and open to the changes and needs of their patients.

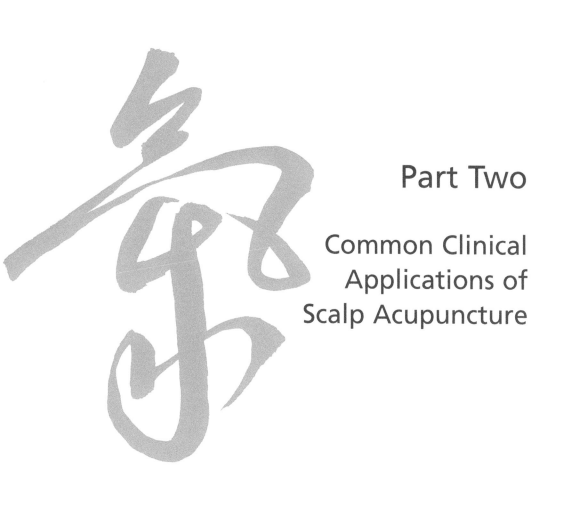

Part Two

Common Clinical Applications of Scalp Acupuncture

CHAPTER FIVE

Paralysis

Paralysis refers to complete or partial loss of muscle strength and voluntary movement for one or more muscles. Paralysis can be localized, generalized, or it may follow a certain pattern. Paralysis is most often caused by damage to the nervous system, especially the brain and spinal cord. Such damage may be due to stroke, trauma with nerve injury, poliomyelitis, amyotrophic lateral sclerosis, botulism, spinal bifida, and multiple sclerosis. Paralysis due to stroke, multiple sclerosis, and traumatic injury of the brain or spinal cord are the most commonly seen problems in our practice. Most paralyses caused by nervous system damage are constant in nature. There are forms of periodic paralysis, including sleep paralysis, which are caused by other factors. Paralysis can be accompanied by a loss of feeling in the affected area if there is sensory nerve damage as well.

The chain of nerve cells that runs from the brain through the spinal cord out to the muscles is called the motor pathway. Normal muscle function requires intact connections all along this motor pathway. Damage at any level often interrupts the brain's ability to control muscle movements resulting in paralysis. Paralysis almost always causes a change in muscle tone. Paralyzed muscles may be flaccid, flabby, and without appreciable tone, or may be spastic, tight, and with abnormally high tone that increases when the muscle is moved. Paralysis may affect an individual muscle but it usually affects an entire body region. The distribution of weakness is an important clue to locate the level of nerve damage that caused the paralysis.

The types of paralysis are classified by region. Monoplegia is impairment in the motor function of only one limb. Diplegia affects the same body region on both sides of the body (both arms, for example). Hemiplegia, affects one side of the body. Paraplegia is impairment in motor function of both legs and the trunk. Quadriplegia, also known as tetraplegia, is paralysis with partial or total loss of use of all limbs and the torso. Paralysis is also divided into four types in neurological practice, namely upper motor neuron paralysis, lower motor neuron paralysis, paralysis due to neuromuscular transmission diseases, and the paralysis caused by muscular diseases.

To test the strength of each muscle group and record it in a systematic fashion is important before and after scalp acupuncture treatment for paralyzed patients. It can help localize a lesion to a particular cortical region and spinal cord level, evaluate scalp acupuncture treatment, and give the patient encour-

TYPES OF PARALYSIS CLASSIFIED BY REGION

- monoplegia is impairment in the motor function of only one limb
- diplegia affects the same body region on both sides of the body (both arms, for example)
- hemiplegia affects one side of the body
- paraplegia is impairment in motor function of both legs and the trunk
- quadriplegia, also known as tetraplegia, is paralysis with partial or total loss of use of all limbs and the torso

agement when there is subtle improvement that the patient might not notice. When evaluating a patient with paralysis, the practitioner should follow a systematic approach that includes inspection of muscle, palpation and percussion of muscle, manual muscle strength testing, and assessment of motor function. It is useful to pair the testing of each muscle group immediately with the testing of its contralateral counterpart to enhance detection of any asymmetries and record detailed information of any changes.

Muscle strength is often rated at six levels on a scale of 0 out of 5 to 5 out of 5.[24] The level of 0 out of 5 shows no muscular contraction, which means complete paralysis; the level of 1 out of 5 shows some muscular contraction, but no limb or body movement; the level of 2 out of 5 shows limb movement is possible but not against gravity, which means the limb can only move in its horizontal plane; the level of 3 out of 5 shows limb movement is possible against gravity but not against resistance by the examiner; the level of 4 out of 5 shows limb movement is possible against some resistance by the examiner but it is still weak compared to a normal limb; and the level of 5 out of 5 shows normal muscular strength, which means complete recovery from paralysis.

Scalp acupuncture is frequently used in rehabilitation of paralysis due to stroke, multiple sclerosis, spinal cord injury, and traumatic brain injury. It has been proven effective in treating any type of paralysis, sometimes taking only one to two treatments for an amazing amount of recovery. We have treated hundreds of paralyzed patients with remarkable results in the US, China, and Europe, allowing many patients to leave their wheelchairs, walkers, crutches, and canes behind.[25, 26, 27, 28, 29, 30]

Since scalp acupuncture is a modern technique with just 39 years of history, much more research needs to be done so that its potential can be fully explored and utilized and more paralyzed patients helped to regain a normal life.

Stroke

Stroke is an acute neurological disease in which the blood supply to the brain is interrupted causing brain cells to die or be seriously damaged, thus impairing brain functions. Stroke is classified into two major categories, ischemic and hemorrhagic. In an ischemic stroke, a blood vessel becomes occluded and the blood supply to part of the brain is blocked. Ischemic stroke is divided into thrombosis stroke, embolic stroke, systemic hypoperfusion, and venous thrombosis. A hemorrhagic stroke occurs when a blood vessel in the brain ruptures and bleeds. The bleeding vessel can no longer carry the blood to its target tissue and interrupts the brain's blood supply. Hemorrhagic stroke is commonly divided into two types, intracerebral and subarachnoid.

The symptoms of stroke depend on the type of stroke and the area of the brain affected. These include weakness, paralysis or abnormal sensations in limbs or face, aphasia, apraxia, altered vision, problems with hearing, taste, or smell, vertigo, disequilibrium, altered coordination, difficulty swallowing, and mental and emotional changes. Some stroke patients may have loss of consciousness, headache, and vomiting at the onset. If the symptoms disappear within several minutes up to a maximum of 24 hours, the diagnosis is transient ischemic attack (TIA), which is a mini or brief stroke. Those symptoms are warning signs and a large proportion of patients with TIA may develop full strokes in the future.

Stroke is the third leading cause of death in the United States after heart attack and cancer and it is a leading cause of adult disability. It is necessary for stroke patients to receive emergency treatment with Western medicine and it is important to identify a stroke as early as possible because patients who are treated earlier are more likely to survive and become less disabled. Stroke survivors usually have some degree of sequelae of symptoms depending primarily on the location in the brain involved and the amount of brain tissue damaged. Disability affects about 75% of stroke survivors and it can affect patients physically, mentally, emotionally, or a combination of all three.

Because each side of the brain controls the opposite side of the body, a stroke affecting one side of the brain results in neurological symptoms on the other side of the body. For example, if stroke occurs in the motor area of the right side of the brain, the left side of the body may show weakness or paralysis. Although there is no cure for stroke, most stroke patients now have a good chance for survival and recovery. When stroke patients pass the acute stage they should start rehabilitation as soon as possible. Stroke rehabilitation therapy helps patients return to normal life as much as possible by regaining and relearning skills of everyday living such as speaking or walking. Treatment may include acupuncture, physical therapy, occupational therapy, speech and language therapy, and massage.

In Chinese medicine, the stroke itself is thought to involve several interpromoting disease mechanisms, possibly including qi stagnation, heat, phlegm, blood stasis and, of course, wind. Hence the common name for stroke in Chinese medicine is wind stroke. Many of these same patterns will be present in cases involving post-stroke symptomology discussed in this book such as paralysis, dysphagia, and aphasia. See reference #55 on page 258 for more details about the Chinese medical description of stroke.

CASE HISTORY #1

At a workshop conducted at Tri-State Acupuncture College in New York City in 1998, a patient named Tom volunteered for scalp acupuncture. The manager at the college told us that the patient had had a stroke from cerebral thrombosis only 11 months before and was a good candidate for the class demonstration. While interviewing Tom, we were shocked to find that his right arm and hand had actually been paralyzed for 11 years. Although we were not at all certain that we could help this patient, it had taken several hours for the family member to give him a ride here and we did not want to turn him away. His tongue was a little purple with a normal coating and his pulses were bilaterally fine and wiry.

As an additional source of concern, we had only a few hours earlier told the students that any patient with paralysis enduring for more than three years was unlikely to respond to scalp acupuncture therapy. Unsure how to proceed, we considered simply demonstrating the location and technique of scalp acupuncture on this patient and not immediately showing the results to the students. After demonstrating two needles in his scalp, we moved Tom to another room to rest, inserted more needles, and then continued with the lecture.

Chinese medical pattern discrimination: Qi stagnation and blood stasis in the channels and network vessels

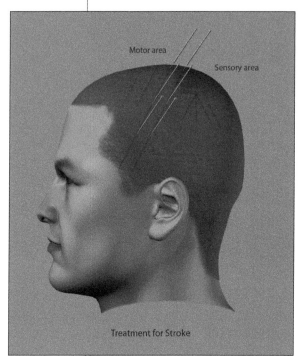

Motor area

Sensory area

Treatment for Stroke

Scalp acupuncture treatment

Area selection

Primary area: Upper 1/5 and middle 2/5 of the Motor Area
Secondary area: Upper 1/5 and middle 2/5 of the Sensory Area

Manipulation

For treating motor dysfunction, place the needles and rotate them at least 200 revolutions per minute for 1–3 minutes every 10 minutes for a total of 30–60 minutes. The worse the symptoms or longer the duration of disease, the longer the duration of each treatment should be. As stated above in Chapter Four, unless the paralysis is due to the removal of damaged tissue by brain surgery, a paralyzed extremity is generally treated by choosing the opposite side of the Motor Area on the scalp. The upper 1/5 region is used to treat contralateral dysfunctional movement of the lower extremity, trunk, spinal cord, and neck. The doctor should twirl the needle as vigorously as the patient can tolerate and have the patient move the affected limb actively and passively. It is helpful to have the patient exercise the affected limbs with or without assistance as indicated, between needle stimulations.[31] During treatment, some patients may have sensations of heat, cold, tingling, numbness, heaviness, distention, or the sensation of water or electricity moving along their affected limbs. Those patients usually respond and show improvement quickly. However, those who don't have such sensations could still have immediate effects. Initially, treatment should be two to three times a week until major improvements are achieved, then once weekly, then every two weeks, and then spaced out as indicated by the patient's condition. A therapeutic course consists of 10 treatments.

Results of Case #1

Tom was instructed to do some passive exercise while the needles were in place, having his wife move his hand and raise his arm. While we were continuing our lecture, we heard screaming from the other room. The patient's wife rushed back into the lecture room saying repeatedly, "He can move his arm and hand now" in a loud, excited voice. Tom was able to move his arm, hand, and even his fingers in any way or direction that he was asked by the audience. This patient's experience has caused us to change the information we give students about whether treatment could be successful after a specific number of years. It is now our opinion that a patient with paralysis should be treated no matter how long ago a stroke has occurred as long as the limb shows no muscular atrophy. One student at this class offered the conclusion, "It's never too late to treat a paralyzed patient with scalp acupuncture."

Discussion

Scalp acupuncture has been found to have very good effects on the sequelae of stroke including hemiplegia, aphasia, and abnormal sensations in the limbs. Thanks to advanced stroke research and brain imaging technology, doctors are continuing to gain new understanding of how the brain can adapt after stroke in order to regain its ability to function. New research suggests that normal brain cells are highly adaptable. They can undergo changes not only in function and shape but also can take over the functions of nearby damaged cells. Because of these abilities, scalp acupuncture is geared toward stimulating and restoring affected brain tissue or retraining unaffected brain tissue to compensate for the lost functions of damaged brain tissue.

In Tom's case, the hemiplegia was caused by cerebral thrombosis, which has the best prognosis for recovery from stroke compared to cerebral embolism and cerebral hemorrhage. It is necessary to point out, however, how unusual it is that a patient gets only one scalp acupuncture treatment and recovers completely. In our normal practice it often takes from several weeks to several months for stroke patients to improve and recover.

Also, the time frame for patients with stroke to be treated by scalp acupuncture is crucial; the earlier the treatment the better the prognosis. When treating stroke from thrombosis or embolism, scalp acupuncture treatment should begin as soon as feasible. When treating a hemorrhagic stroke, however, scalp acupuncture should not be performed until the patient's condition is stable, probably one month after a stroke.

As we discovered with Tom, a patient with any duration of stroke disabilities can be treated, but treatment within a year brings about the greatest response in our experience. The longer the duration of the impairment, the more gradual will be the improvement. With long-term conditions expectations need to be realistic, although occasionally a patient will surprise practitioners. It is hardest to achieve improvement for a patient with paralysis for a long time, especially if there is also muscular atrophy and rigid, inflexible joints.

There are several different acupuncture techniques to treat paralysis. Although scalp acupuncture has the best and fastest response, other techniques are necessary for a fuller recovery. According to the individual's condition, regular body acupuncture, electrical acupuncture, and moxibustion, as well as physical therapy and massage can combine with scalp acupuncture to speed up the time of recovery. Regular acupuncture treatment has been found to have positive therapeutic effects on the recovery of movement in the hands, fingers, feet, and toes. In treating unilateral paralysis of the limbs, traditionally more points from yang ming channels are selected because yang corresponds to movement and agility, and foot yang ming stomach channel controls muscle functions. Commonly used points are He Gu (LI 4), Wai Guan (TB 5), Qu Chi (LI 11), Bi Nao (LI 14), and Jian Yu (LI 15) for upper limb paralysis, and Kun Lun (Bl 60), Cheng Shan (Bl 57), Yang Ling Quan (GB 34), Zu San Li (St 36), and Huan Tiao (GB 30) for lower limb paralysis. Although more yang ming points are used for paralysis, points from yin channels, especially tai yin and jue yin channels should not be ignored. Yin corresponds to nourishing muscles and tendons and points from yin channels have positive results for pronounced stiffness and contraction of the limbs. Commonly used points are Chi Ze (Lu 5) and Nei Guan (Per 6) for upper limbs and San Yin Jiao (Sp 6), Yin Ling Quan (Sp 9), Xue Hai (Sp 10), and Qu Quan (Liv 8) for lower limbs. Hand or foot paralysis is relatively difficult to recover and often requires a longer process, especially for a contracted hand and foot. To relax contractures of the hand, thread a two-inch needle from He Gu (LI 4) under the palm toward Lao Gong (Per 8) and Hou Xi (SI 3). Stimulate this needle with vigorous thrusting, lifting, and twirling. Thread another needle deeply from Wai Guan (TB 5) toward Nei Guan (Per 6) and stimulate in a similar fashion. To relax the upper arm and shoulder, thread a needle from Jian Yu (LI 15) to Bi Nao (LI 14) and stimulate vigorously. To relax contractures of the foot and ankle, thread a two-inch needle from Jie Xi (St 41) toward Qiu Xu (GB 40) and Sheng Mai (Bl 62). Thread a second needle from Jie Xi (St 41) toward Zhong Feng (Liv 4) and Zhao Hai (Ki 6). Thread a third needle from Tai Chong (Liv 3) through the foot to Yong Quan (Ki 1) on the sole of the foot. Stimulate all needles with vigorous thrusting, lifting, and twirling. For additional effect, thread a long needle from Yang Ling Quan (GB 34) through to Yin Ling Quan (Sp 9) and from Kun Lun (Bl 60) through to Tai Xi (Ki 3).

Electrical stimulation is very helpful if the practitioner has difficulty performing needle rotation of more than 200 times per minute. It is suggested that only one to two pairs of the scalp needles be stimulated at any one session or the brain can become too confused to respond. For electrical stimulation in body acupuncture, fewer than four needles should be stimulated in each limb. Best results are achieved by applying low frequency (for example, 3 hertz) with high intensity (for instance, when visible muscle contraction is observed). Moxibustion can enhance the therapeutic results of scalp acupuncture, especially for older or weaker patients.

Research on the effect of scalp acupuncture for stroke

There are considerable clinical studies and experimental research showing the excellent results obtained from scalp acupuncture on paralysis due to stroke.

- Jiao Shun-fa, the founder of scalp acupuncture, collected and analyzed 20,923 cases of paralysis caused by stroke from 1970 to 1992. After treatment on the Motor Area of the scalp, 7,637 cases were cured (36.5%), 7,117 cases showed marked improvement (34%), and 5,196 cases showed some improvement (24.8%), yielding a total effective rate of 95.13%.[32]
- Jia Huai-yu reported on 1,800 cases of paralysis due to stroke treated on the Motor Area by scalp acupuncture in 1992. The result were as follows: 462 cases fully recovered (25.67%), 950 cases markedly improved

(52.78%), 292 cases somewhat improved (16.22%), 96 cases failure (5.33%), yielding a total effective rate of 94.67%. Findings in these two studies are very similar.[33]

- Liu Jian-hao and colleagues reported on the treatment of 60 cases of paralysis due to stroke using scalp acupuncture in 2010. The duration of the paralysis was from one day to 14 days. The patients were randomly divided into a body acupuncture group and a scalp acupuncture group, 30 in each group. The body acupuncture group was treated with needling from Bai Hui (GV 20) penetrating to Tai Yang (extra point) and the scalp acupuncture group was treated at the Motor Area. Treatments were given once a day and 14 treatments comprised a course. The neurological deficit scores (NDS) and the therapeutic effects were compared before and after treatment and the contents of plasma endothelins (ET) and calcitonin gene related peptide (CGRP) were tested on the second and fourteenth days respectively after initial treatment. The results showed that the effective rate was 86.7% (26/30) in the body acupuncture group and 80.0% (24/30) in the scalp acupuncture group. The NDS of both groups were statistically decreased ($P < 0.01$). The ET level was also decreased and the CGRP level was effectively increased in both groups ($P < 0.01$).[34]

Dysphagia

Dysphagia is the medical term for the symptom of difficulty in swallowing. The signs and symptoms of dysphagia include difficulty controlling food in the mouth, inability to control food or saliva in the mouth, difficulty initiating a swallow, coughing, choking, frequent pneumonia, unexplained weight loss, gurgly or wet voice after swallowing, nasal regurgitation, and swallowing difficulty. When asked where the food is getting stuck, patients will often point to the cervical region. The actual site of obstruction is always at or below the level at which patients perceive the obstruction. The most common symptom of esophageal dysphagia is the inability to swallow solid food, which the patient often describes as "becoming stuck" or "held up" before it either passes into the stomach or is regurgitated. Some people present with "silent aspiration" and do not cough or show outward signs of aspiration. When the airway is unprotected and foreign material is aspirated into the lungs, the person is at risk for development of pulmonary infection and aspiration pneumonia. A swallowing disorder can occur in people of all age groups but it is more likely in the elderly, patients who have had strokes, and in patients who are admitted to acute care hospitals or chronic care facilities.

Dysphagia is classified into two major types, oropharyngeal dysphagia and esophageal dysphagia. Oropharyngeal dysphagia is often caused by stroke, multiple sclerosis, myasthenia gravis, Parkinson's disease, amyotrophic lateral sclerosis, and Bell's palsy. Esophageal dysphagia can be subdivided into mechanical and functional causes. Functional causes include achalasia, myasthenia gravis, and bulbar or pseudobulbar palsy. Mechanical causes usually comprise peptic esophagitis, carcinoma of the esophagus or gastric cardia, candida esophagitis, and pharyngeal pouch. Medicines can help some people, while others may need surgery. Treatment with a speech-language pathologist can help. Patients may find it helpful to change their diet or hold their heads or necks in a certain way when they eat. In very serious cases, patients may need feeding tubes.

CASE HISTORY #2

Fred, a 62-year-old male in a wheelchair, was brought to our clinic in Santa Fe, NM. His wife gave a brief medical history because of his aphasia. One month before, Fred had severe headache, slurred speech, and the right side of his body became paralyzed. A local hospital diagnosed stroke caused by cerebral hemorrhage in his left hemisphere. He initially was totally paralyzed on the right side and had lost his speech. He had been receiving physical therapy and speech therapy since he was admitted to the hospital. Although his aphasia gradually improved, his speech was not clear. His voice was low and it was very difficult to understand him. He had severe dysphagia and could not swallow any food or water at all, which was his primary complaint at our clinic. He felt depressed, irritable, angry, and severely fatigued. A nasogastric tube was inserted to provide non-oral feeding. Examination showed he was unable to move his right leg and foot at all with muscular tone at 0 out of 5. He could move his right arm slightly with muscular tone at 2 out of 5. He could not elevate the hyoid bone, indicating a probable swallow reflex problem. Maximum phonation duration of seven seconds indicated reduced breath support, likely resulting from vocal cord paralysis. He had a weak cough and diminished throat-clearing ability. His aphasia, dysphasia, and paralysis on the right side had shown no further improvement for the past two weeks. A hospital physician recommended that Fred try acupuncture treatment. Upon examination he looked very tired and depressed, his tongue was red with a dry, thick, yellow coating, and his pulses were wiry and slippery.*

Chinese medical pattern discrimination: Liver depression qi stagnation, spleen qi deficiency, blood stasis in the channels, liver-gallbladder damp heat

Scalp acupuncture treatment

Area selection

Primary area: Upper 1/5, middle 2/5 and lower 2/5 Motor Area
Secondary area: Speech I Area (same as lower 2/5 Motor Area), Neck point, (a new extra point for dysphagia, located at 1 inch below Feng Chi (GB 20)

Manipulation

The entire Motor Area should be needled and stimulated on the opposite side of the paralyzed limbs. Always put one needle in the ear point Shen Men to help a depressed and angry patient relax and to reduce the sensitivity of needle insertion and stimulation of the scalp. Use the fewest number of needles possible in the scalp and rotate the needles at least 200 times per minute with the thumb and index finger for 2–3 minutes, twirling as gently as possible so that the depressed patient can tolerate the sensation and repeating the stimulation every 10 minutes. Select the Speech I Area or some local points in the neck accordingly if the patient has aphasia or difficulty swallowing. Retain the needles in place for 30–45 minutes. The treatment is given two to three times per week and a therapeutic course consists of 10 treatments. Communicate with the patient and any relatives often in order to gain their confidence, to encourage them, and reduce their fear and anxiety.

Note: We are choosing to use the authors' translation for the *xian mai* (弦脉). In *A Practical Dictionary of Chinese Medicine*, Wiseman and Feng translate this pulse image as the "string-like" pulse, but "wiry" is the more common usage.

During the treatment, some patients may experience sensations of heat, cold, tingling, numbness, heaviness, distention, or the sensation of water or electricity moving along their spine, legs, or arms. Telling the patient that those are normal and that people who experience some or all of these sensations usually respond and improve more quickly encourages them to come back for additional treatments. However, those who do not have such sensations could still have immediate positive results.

Results of Case #2

Fred was very negative and showed no interest in treatment by scalp acupuncture at the initial visit. He was reluctant to do any active exercise when being instructed. Even after showing some improvement of his aphasia and the paralyzed arm and leg, he demonstrated no excitement and simply said, "I do not notice any difference about my throat and swallowing."

At the second treatment, Fred presented with severe depression and no motivation. He did not like to perform speech, swallowing, and body exercises. His treatment strategy was modified to take care of depression. The ear points Heart, Liver, and Shen Men along with the Head Area and Chest Area on the scalp were needled.

At the beginning of the third visit, his wife reported that Fred's mood and attitude were much better after the last treatment. He talked a little more and was easier to understand. To her surprise he reminded her what time he had the acupuncture appointment that day. Since the patient's attitude was relatively more positive toward acupuncture therapy, we were able to perform stronger stimulation after inserting needles at the same locations as for the initial treatment. Fred was able to follow instructions to practice his speech and do oral and pharyngeal exercises. He started to smile after hearing himself count from one to 10 very clearly. He refused to try drinking a little bit of water to test his swallowing function and said he was afraid that it could induce severe coughing and choking and cause aspiration. With continued encouragement Fred finally agreed to try. To his astonishment he did not choke at all when he took a first sip of water. He drank more and more and finished a whole cup of water without a problem.

The patient thrived on this program. He began to tolerate a soft/semi-solid diet and the nasogastric feeding was gradually tapered down to overnight only as his oral intake improved. At this point his weight increased and his stamina was markedly improved. Fred started to eat more solid food and add more kinds of food gradually.

With every treatment, Fred showed dramatic improvements in speech, eating and drinking, and movement of his right arm, hand, leg, and foot. By the fifth treatment, Fred wanted to add more foods and soon could eat and drink anything like a normal person. The nasogastric tube was removed and he had no problem with talking or depression after his sixth treatment.

His subsequent treatments were focused on his paralyzed arm and leg. He was treated by combined scalp acupuncture and body acupuncture. For body acupuncture, Qu Chi (LI 11), Wai Guan (TB 5), and He Gu (LI 4) on the right upper limb and Zu San Li (St 36), Kun Lun (Bl 60), and Jie Xi (St 41) on the right lower limb were needled. Sometimes those points were stimulated with electrical acupuncture. Fred could move his right arm up and down more and he was able to start walking to our clinic on his own. After the sixteenth treatment he had gained more mobility and use of his right hand and gained more muscular strength in that hand. At the end of 20 treatments his walking appeared almost normal. At his last visit, Fred said, "Thank you very much for giving me back my normal life."

Discussion

Scalp acupuncture offers great rehabilitation tools for dysphagia. Most patients with dysphagia whom we have treated showed some improvement after three treatments and some of them appear better right way. However, to treat dysphagia patients who have depression is very challenging because patients are not always willing to participate in the treatment. It requires very good needle technique as well as good communication skills. Sometimes it is necessary to treat the depression first and then address the difficulty in swallowing. Compared to other patients, in general depressed patients should receive fewer needles, milder stimulation, and a shorter time of needle retention. Whether you are treating a child or adult with depression, it is important to observe the response and reaction while inserting, stimulating, or withdrawing needles, and adjust the techniques accordingly. Although each part of the cerebral cortex has its own functions, some variation is possible. When one area is impaired, this area can recover to a certain extent or can be compensated somewhat by other areas with proper scalp stimulation. This may be the mechanism by which scalp acupuncture is successful in treating dysphagia.

Correct food consistency, texture, and temperature are important for the dysphagia patient's success during acupuncture treatment. All three factors are important as they act to heighten lingual control, reduce oral muscle fatigue, minimize the patient's fear of choking, and provide a cohesive bolus to stimulate a swallow reflex. A dysphagia diet uses foods that stimulate swallowing and minimize mucus build-up around the larynx. Dysphagia may lead to malnutrition and dehydration and at the most severe stages can cause choking, aspiration, and airway obstruction. Therefore it is imperative to deal with the dangers of dysphagia through dietary management once acupuncture has been instituted. Overall, our patient Fred had a very successful recovery, progressing from dysphagia to total normal eating within just a few weeks. This case study followed the patient as his post-stroke swallowing status changed and various acupuncture decisions were made. In addition to scalp acupuncture, the ear and body acupuncture were very helpful in the patient's progress and recovery. This case illustrates that scalp acupuncture could be the primary approach to manage swallowing disorder.

Research on the effect of scalp acupuncture for dysphagia

- Li Min and colleagues reported the treatment of 60 cases of dysphagia due to stroke using scalp acupuncture in 2009. The duration of the condition was from 30–360 days. The 60 cases were randomly divided into a five–needle–in–nape (FNN) group and a routine acupuncture (RA) group, 30 cases in each group. The FNN group was treated with needling Ya Men (GV 15), Tian Zhu (Bl 10), and Zhi Qiang Xue (new extra point). The RA group was treated with needling at Lian Quan (CV 23), Tong Li (Ht 5) and Zhao Hai (Ki 6). Treatment was given six times a week and 16 treatments made a course. Results showed seven cases fully recovered, 13 cases markedly improved, eight cases some improvement and two cases failure in FNN group. Five cases fully recovered, eight cases markedly improved, 11 cases some improvement, and six cases failure in the RA group. The effective rate was 93.3% in the FNN group, better than that of 80.8% in RA group (P< 0.05).[35]

Multiple Sclerosis

Multiple sclerosis (MS) is a progressive disease of the central nervous system in which communication between the brain and other parts of the body is disrupted. Its effects can range from relatively benign in most cases, to somewhat disabling, to devastating for some people. During an MS attack, inflammation occurs in areas of the white matter of the central nervous system in random patches. These are called plaques. This is followed by the destruction of myelin. Myelin allows for the smooth, high-speed transmission of electrochemical messages between the brain, the spinal cord, and the rest of the body. When myelin is damaged, neurological transmission of messages may be slowed or blocked completely resulting in some body functions being diminished or lost. Approximately 300,000 people in the US and 2.5 million people worldwide suffer from MS. It primarily affects adults, with age of onset typically between 20 and 40 years, and is twice as common in women compared to men.

Symptoms and signs of multiple sclerosis vary widely depending on the location of affected myelin sheaths. Common symptoms include numbness, tingling or weakness in one or more limbs, partial or complete loss of vision, double or blurred vision, tremor, unsteady gait, fatigue, cognitive impairment, and dizziness. Some patients may also develop muscle stiffness or spasticity, paralysis, slurred speech, dysfunction of urine or bowels, and depression. In the worst cases, people with MS may be unable to write, speak, or walk. Multiple sclerosis is unpredictable and varies in severity. In some patients it is a mild disease but it can lead to permanent disability in others. Multiple sclerosis may occur either in discrete attacks or slowly over time. Although symptoms may resolve completely between the episodes, permanent neurological problems usually persist, especially as the disease progresses.[36] Many risk factors for multiple sclerosis have been identified, but no definitive cause has been found. It likely occurs as a result of some combination of environmental and genetic factors. Currently, multiple sclerosis does not have a cure in terms of conventional treatments. However, a number of therapies including acupuncture can be used to treat the disease symptomatically and convert MS into remission.

In Chinese medicine, there are at least six or more patterns of disharmony that can account for the signs and symptoms of multiple sclerosis. The common denominators in most cases are external invasion or internal engenderment of damp heat, which damages qi and consumes yin and blood, thus giving rise to internal stirring of wind. Former heaven or prenatal natural endowment insufficiency may also play a role.

CASE HISTORY #3

Denise, a 79-year-old female in a wheelchair, was brought to our clinic in Santa Fe, New Mexico in 1994. She had suffered from multiple sclerosis for more than 25 years. Her initial symptoms were an onset of numbness in the right arm followed by subsequent numbness descending down both her legs. Over the past 25 years, Denise had multiple relapses and remissions with episodes of lower extremity weakness, stiffness and muscle spasm, incontinence of urine, loss of balance, and fatigue. Those symptoms typically lasted a few weeks to several months. Five years ago she had a dramatic neurological decline during which she was unable to stand up and lost strength and sensation in her lower extremities. For the last three years and currently, she could not stand or walk by herself due to weakness in her legs and loss of balance. Denise also complained of numbness, tingling, and spasms in her legs accompanied by incontinence of urine and severe fatigue. The examination revealed she had paraparesis of the left lower extremity that was more affected than the right. Her tongue was purple with a thin white coating. Her pulses were wiry and fine overall, with especially weak pulses in the cubit (*chi*) positions bilaterally.

Chinese medical pattern discrimination: Liver blood deficiency with internal stirring of liver wind, kidney qi deficiency, liver depression qi stagnation, blood stasis

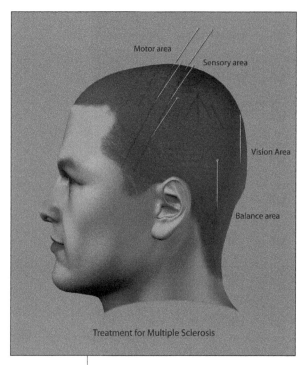

Motor area

Sensory area

Vision Area

Balance area

Treatment for Multiple Sclerosis

Scalp acupuncture treatment

Area selection

Primary area: Motor Area, Sensory Area, Foot Motor and Sensory Area
Secondary area: Balance Area, Chorea and Tremor Area, and Vertigo and Hearing Area

Manipulation

Insert needles in the Motor Area, Sensory Area, and Foot Motor and Sensory Area and stimulate unilaterally or bilaterally according to the patient's symptoms. Rotate the needles at least 200 times per minute with the thumb and index finger for 1–3 minutes, twirling them as vigorously as the patient can tolerate and repeating the stimulation every 10 minutes. During treatment, some patients may have all or some of the following sensations: increasing tingling or numbness, heat, cold, heaviness, distention, or the sensation of water or electricity moving along their spine, legs or arms. Patients with some or all of these sensations usually respond and improve more quickly. However, those who do not have such sensations could still have immediate positive results. If balance, dizziness, or vertigo is present, select the Balance Area or the Vertigo and Hearing Area. The Chorea and Tremor Area should be chosen if the patient has tremor or limb spasms. Keep the needles in for 25–30 minutes. Treatment is given two to three times per week and a therapeutic course consists of 10 treatments.

Results of Case #3

Denise had a very positive response to her initial scalp acupuncture treatment. She was amazed to feel the spasms and numbness in her legs improve just minutes after a few needles were inserted. Although she was nervous when the doctor asked her to stand up, her family was thrilled to see her not only stand up with improved stability, but also start to walk a few steps. At the second treatment, Denise reported that the incontinence of urine had improved remarkably after the first treatment and the numbness, spasms, and weakness of both legs showed some improvement as well. She continued to get better with each additional treatment and by the sixth treatment, Denise was able to enter our clinic with a walker instead of in a wheelchair. She also had more energy and started to do some housework again.

By the fifteenth treatment, Denise reported that she was able to walk around her home by herself and walk much longer distances. The numbness and tingling in her limbs did not bother her as much, she had more energy, and had not experienced incontinence of urine for several weeks. However, her right foot was still weak and was sometimes difficult to pick up and she had to drag it to walk. During each treatment, however, her right foot was getting stronger and she could pick it up more easily. This ability would last for several days after treatment, so Denise liked to get a tune-up treatment every other week. At each session, a few needles would be inserted in her scalp and she would go out for a walk and come back later for withdrawal of the needles.

Discussion

When compared to other acupuncture modalities including acupuncture on the ear, body, and hand, scalp acupuncture has proven to have the most success in treating MS and other central nervous system damage. Not only can it improve symptoms, the patient's quality of life, and slow the progression of physical disability, but it can also reduce the number of relapses. The patient should get treatment as soon as possible as the earlier the treatment, the better the prognosis. Scalp acupuncture treatment for MS has had much success in reducing numbness and pain, decreasing spasms, improving weakness and paralysis of limbs, and improving balance. Many patients also have reported that their bladder and bowel control, fatigue, and overall sense of well-being significantly improved after treatment.

Recent studies have shown that scalp acupuncture can be a very effective modality in controlling MS, often producing remarkable results after just a few needles are inserted. It usually relieves symptoms immediately and may take only a few minutes to achieve significant improvement. Although scalp acupuncture areas may be chosen according to the patient's particular symptoms, primary areas for patients with motor problems such as paralysis, weakness of limbs, or abnormal sensations in limbs including tingling, numbness, or pain, are the Motor Area and the Sensory and Foot Motor Areas. Those areas should be stimulated unilaterally or bilaterally, according to the patient's manifestations. Select the Balance Area or Vertigo and Hearing Area of the scalp, respectively, depending on the symptoms. The Chorea and Tremor Area should be chosen if patients have limb spasm. Many patients have a very quick and positive response in controlling urine and bowel functions when the Foot Motor and Sensory Area is stimulated.

There are many different acupuncture techniques for treating MS. Although scalp acupuncture has the fastest track record for improving symptoms, other techniques are also necessary for further improvement. Regular body acupuncture, electrical acupuncture, and moxibustion as well as physical therapy and massage can be combined with scalp acupuncture to speed up recovery. Regular acupuncture treatment has been found to have a positive therapeutic effect on the recovery of movement and reducing abnormal sensations of the hands, fingers, feet and toes. Commonly used points are Feng Chi (GB 20), Yu Zhen (Bl 9), Nao Kong (GB 19), Huan Tiao (GB 30), Yang Ling Quan (GB 34), Tai Chong (Liv 3), and Tai Xi (Ki 3) for lower limbs, and Qu Chi (LI 11), He Gu (LI 4), and Wai Guan (TB 5) for upper limbs.[37] Electrical stimulation is very helpful if the practitioner has difficulty performing needle rotation more than 200 times per minute. It is suggested that no more than two of the scalp needles be stimulated at any session so the brain does not become too confused to respond. Moxibustion can enhance the therapeutic results of scalp acupuncture, especially for older or weak patients. Recommended points are Zu San Li (St 36), San Yin Jiao (Sp 6), Guan Yuan (CV 4), Yong Quan (Ki 1) and Shen Shu (Bl 23).

When treating chronic progressive diseases like multiple sclerosis, Parkinsonism, and amyotrophic lateral sclerosis (ALS), the effects are sometimes temporary. Improvement may last for hours, days, weeks, or months, but follow-up treatments will be necessary on an ongoing basis. When treating paralysis, whether from stroke or trauma, improvements in movement are often permanent. The practitioner should consider scalp acupuncture as the primary approach rather than as a complementary approach for the patient with multiple sclerosis. Although other acupuncture techniques can be effective, scalp acupuncture seems to bring about quicker and often immediate improvement. In a recent investigation, scalp acupuncture was applied to 16 patients with multiple sclerosis at our National Healthcare Center in Albuquerque, NM. After only one treatment per patient, eight of the 16 patients instantly showed significant improvement, six patients showed some improvement, and only two patients showed no improvement, thus yielding a total effective rate of 87%.

CASE HISTORY #4

Michael, a 52-year-old patient referred by his primary care physician, walked with the aid of a cane. He sought treatment from us during a conference in Phoenix, Arizona in 2006. He had suffered from multiple sclerosis since 1982 and had received many kinds of treatments with no positive results. Five years before, his medical team had noted his condition "has been slowly going downhill." Because his legs were very stiff and weak, Michael had to drag both legs in a shuffling manner when he walked. Other symptoms included an inability to lift his feet or wiggle his toes. His fatigue was so great he could only walk 2–3 minutes at a time. Further examination showed that he could not stand with stability due to losing his balance when standing on both legs, and it was impossible for him to stand on one leg. He could neither utilize a normal gait from heel to toe nor walk backwards. His tongue was red and slightly purple with a thick, white coating and his pulses were wiry and slippery.

Chinese medical pattern discrimination: Spleen qi and kidney essence deficiency, liver depression with depressive heat leading to the internal stirring of liver wind

Results of Case #4

While needles were being inserted in Michael's scalp the audience was quiet, waiting to see how he would respond to his first treatment. Michael showed remarkable improvement right away. When told that it was time for him to "show off," he stood up straight with great stability and even stood on one leg for several seconds without losing his balance. The audience reported that he was taking much larger steps, was lifting up his legs rather than dragging them, and was turning around without hesitation. During the break, Michael went outside for a bit more exercise. He walked back into the conference room without using his cane and his face glowed with pleasure as he told the audience, "I walked for about 30 minutes without any rest and without my cane except for security. I am so overjoyed with these unexpected wonderful results. I can walk solidly from heel to toe and walk backwards with no difficulty."

Discussion

Although multiple sclerosis (MS) remains an incurable disease of the central ner-vous system, scalp acupuncture provides an important complementary/alternative treatment approach for improving many symptoms and the patient's quality of life by slowing or reversing the progression of physical disability and reducing the number of relapses. By directly stimulating affected areas of the central nervous system, scalp acupuncture has shown more effective results compared to other acupuncture techniques. Our studies showed that 87% of patients had instant improvement after only one treatment. Scalp acupuncture for MS is accessible, less expensive, safer, more effective, and causes fewer side effects than Western medical treatments. It not only benefits MS patients, but also significantly helps us to better understand the mechanisms that cause the condition. It may lead to the discovery of new effective treatments and hopefully to a cure for this disease in the future.

Spinal Cord Injury

Often caused by a car or sporting accident, spinal cord injury is extremely serious. When cervical discs are injured, compression fractures may cause permanent disability. Also hernias or bulges of intervertebral discs may cause spinal cord compression. Common symptoms of spinal injuries include arm and leg paralysis or weakness, difficulty breathing, tingling, numbness, or pain in affected limbs, and incontinence of both bowel and urine.

Modern medicine has not yet found a cure for spinal cord injury. The majority of treatments available in Western medicine involve drugs or surgery and are often ineffective. Acupuncture treats the patient as a whole entity and helps patients with spinal cord injury to recover function more effectively than Western medical treatment. If the spinal cord injury is not total, it is possible for some people to recover all bodily functions including touch and pain sensations, bladder and bowel functions, and motor control. Through acupuncture treatment, some patients can be cured and many others witness a variety of significant improvements.

CASE HISTORY #5

Julia, a 49-year-old female in a wheelchair was brought to our clinic in Santa Fe, NM in 1992. Four months prior to the first visit, this patient was injured in a car accident. Her neck was severely damaged at the level of C-5 and C-6. Upon examination, it was found that she had paralysis of all four extremities. Below the level of injury on the neck there was minimal contraction and movement of arm muscles, which indicated that the muscular tone of her arm was a 2 out of 5. Her hand, legs, and feet were completely paralyzed, which meant that muscular tones were 0 out of 5. Julia had incontinence of urine and was experiencing muscle spasms throughout her entire body. Her tongue was purplish with a thin, sticky, yellow coating. The pulse reading showed lack of force in the inch (*cun*) and bar (*guan*) positions, with faint pulses in the cubit (*chi*) position.

Chinese medical pattern discrimination: Qi stagnation and blood stasis in the channels, kidney qi deficiency

Scalp acupuncture treatment

Area selection

Primary area: Upper 1/5 Motor Area and middle 2/5 Motor Area
Secondary area: Foot Motor and Sensory Area, Chorea and Tremor Area

Manipulation

Needles should be inserted in both upper 1/5 Motor Area and middle 2/5 Motor Area and stimulated bilaterally. Rotate the needles at least 200 times per minute with the thumb and index finger for 1–3 minutes, twirling them as vigorously as the patient can tolerate and repeating the stimulation every 10 minutes. During the treatment, some patients may experience sensations of heat, cold, tingling, numbness, heaviness, distention, or the sensation of water or electricity moving along their spine, legs, or arms. Patients with some or all of these sensations usually respond and improve more quickly. However, those who do not have such sensations could still have immediate, positive results. Select the Chorea and Tremor Area or Foot Motor and Sensory Area according to whether the patient has muscular spasms or other abnormal sensations such as pain or burning. Retain the needles for 25–30 minutes. Treatment is given two to three times per week and a therapeutic course consists of 10 treatments.

Results of Case #5

During the first treatment, Julia experienced immediate relief from the muscle spasms. She also experienced a sensation like electricity shooting downward through her spine, radiating to her feet. With more stimulation of the needles on her head, she started to feel a hot sensation in her hands and feet. She felt so excited about these improvements that she began to cry. While Julia was starting to wiggle her paralyzed toes, we told her that her responses were a good prognosis for significant improvement in the near future. During the third treatment she was able to stand on her feet with someone holding her knees and could lift her arms much higher. The incontinence of urine also showed some improvement. After each treatment from the third to the fifth visit there were gradual improvements in all her limbs.

During the sixth treatment, Julia was able to kick her legs with some strength and she could bend her legs at the knee and hold this position for a few minutes. This was a signal that she could possibly stand and walk. With strong encouragement, she struggled up and stood by herself for one minute, two minutes, and then three minutes. After resting for a while, she stood up again and started to walk, managing 20 halting steps before needing to sit down, exhausted. Julia was also in much better control of urination, now holding her urine for six hours at night. After the eighth treatment she was able to walk with the assistance of a walker, experienced much more mobility in her hand movements, and her body spasms were almost entirely gone. With the increase in hand functions she was able to hold a knife with both hands and cut vegetables. To be able to cook again brought her such tremendous joy and gratitude that she laughed and cried at the same time.

Though she continued to improve with each treatment, the most dramatic changes occurred in the twentieth treatment. At that time her leg and arm muscles were so much stronger that she was able to write and make phone calls. She called the Western medicine physician who had told her she would be paralyzed for the rest of her life and gave him the wonderful news. Not believing that she was once again able to walk, he went to her house in person to see this miraculous change. Though shocked and stunned watching her walk up to greet him, her doctor was thrilled with her progress and hoped for more excellent results. After 39 treatments, she had gained back all movement of her hands and arms, was able to walk with a cane, and began living without the aid of personal assistants. After 48 treatments, Julia felt well enough to end treatment and start a new life in San Francisco where her son was living.

Discussion

Scalp acupuncture is the best therapy for spinal cord injury. Having proven effective through clinical results recorded over the last 35 years, it can effectively stimulate the paralyzed area in order to restore the body's energy flow to a normal state so that the body can heal itself. In other words, scalp acupuncture is able to treat the cause and thus heal the injury. It is also the most useful technique for the patient to improve quickly in the initial visits. In our practice, the combination of scalp acupuncture and regular body acupuncture ensures the best results, especially for the further recovery of paralyzed fingers and toes. Common acupuncture points include Qu Chi (LI 11), He Gu (LI 4), Jian Yu (LI 15), and Wai Guan (TB 5) for upper limb paralysis and Yang Ling Quan (GB 34), Huan Tiao (GB 30), Feng Shi (GB 31), Zu San Li (St 36), and Kun Lun (Bl 60) for lower limb paralysis. Electrical acupuncture is very helpful for speeding up recovery and can be applied on the above points as well as at the Hua Tou Jia Ji points on the back. When choosing Hua Tou Jia Ji points, the pair of points for stimulation should be one above and one below the site of injury level. The electrical stimulation usually lasts 10–20 minutes. Exercise is very important for the recovery of affected limbs. Regular exercise helps the blood circulation and keeps muscles active, and this also accelerates the results from ongoing acupuncture treatments.

Traumatic Brain Injury

Traumatic brain injury is a serious condition that may lead to permanent or temporary impairment of the brain's functions. Brain damage is often related to quick acceleration and deceleration of the brain, which results in injury to the area of impact and its opposite area. The symptoms of brain injury depend on the area of the brain affected. When the speech and motor areas are damaged, body dysfunctions appear such as aphasia and paralysis.

According to Chinese medicine, trauma to the head (or anywhere else in the body) causes the blood to extravasate outside its normal vessels, obstructing the flow of fresh new blood to the area. Any tissue of the body requires nourishment by blood to perform its proper function. Blood stasis must be resolved for the tissue to once again receive the nourishment of healthy blood.

CASE HISTORY #6

Lisa, a 10-year-old girl in a wheelchair, was brought by her mother to our clinic in Santa Fe, New Mexico in 1993. Four months before, Lisa fell off her bicycle and hit her head on the left side, above and behind her ear. She had had a concussion on the left side of the brain in the internal capsule and initially was totally paralyzed on her right side and lost the ability to speak. She had been receiving rehabilitation treatment including physical therapy, osteopathic therapy, and speech therapy starting two weeks after her injury. Her aphasia gradually improved and she was able to drag her right leg while walking and move her right arm slightly but the paralysis had shown no further improvement for the past eight weeks. Her primary doctor recommended that she try acupuncture treatment. Upon examination, her tongue was red with a thin white coating and her pulse was slippery and wiry.

Chinese medical pattern discrimination: Qi stagnation and blood stasis in the channels

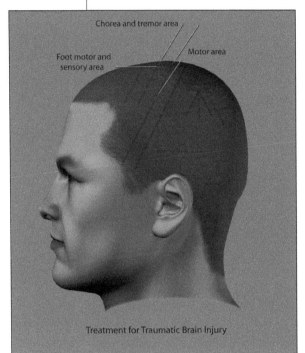

Chorea and tremor area

Motor area

Foot motor and sensory area

Treatment for Traumatic Brain Injury

Scalp acupuncture treatment

Area selection

Primary area: Upper 1/5 Motor Area and middle 2/5 Motor Area
Secondary area: Foot Motor and Sensory Area, Chorea and Tremor Area

Manipulation

Needles should be inserted in both upper 1/5 Motor Area and middle 2/5 Motor Area and stimulated on the opposite side of the paralyzed limbs. With children, select the thinnest needles that you can insert into the scalp. Always put one needle in the ear point Shen Men to help a young patient relax and to reduce the sensitivity of needle insertion and stimulation of the scalp. Use the fewest number of needles possible in the scalp and rotate them at least 200 times per minute with the thumb and index finger for one minute, twirling as gently as possible so that the child patient can tolerate the sensation and repeating the stimulation every 10 minutes. Communicate with children and their parents more often than with adult patients in order to reduce their fear and anxiety. During the treatment, some patients may experience sensations of heat, cold, tingling, numbness, heaviness, distention, or the sensation of water or electricity moving along their spine, legs, or arms. Tell the child that those are normal and are a good sign for improving more quickly.

Select the Chorea and Tremor Area or Foot Motor and Sensory Area according to whether the patient has muscular spasms or other abnormal sensations such as pain or burning. Retain the needles in place for 10–20 minutes.

Treatment is given two to three times per week and a therapeutic course consists of 10 treatments.

Results of Case #6

Lisa was afraid of needles and started to cry and refuse the treatment before the first needle was inserted. She agreed to allow the needle insertion only after her mother told her that she might ride a bike again if these treatments worked. The insertion of two needles on the left side of her scalp did not seem to bother her at all. Two minutes after the treatment began, Lisa announced that she felt "a lot of blood move to my head." After that, the child was able to lift her right arm with much more ease. Her walking also showed some improvement as she was able to lift her right leg more easily.

Lisa experienced dramatic improvements of her right arm, hand, leg, and foot with every visit. By the sixth treatment, Lisa could move her right arm up and down very quickly and was able to start writing with that hand again. After the fifteenth treatment, she had gained more mobility and use of her right hand as well as more muscle strength in that hand, which was now as strong as her left hand. Her walking appeared almost normal, and she was again able to run, at least slowly. At the end of the twenty-second treatment her right hand was completely back to normal and all paralysis was gone. She had participated in running a race and did very well.

Discussion

Scalp acupuncture can be an excellent rehabilitation tool for traumatic brain injury patients. However, while treating children with body acupuncture can be challenging, it can be even harder with scalp acupuncture. Children and their parents might not be willing to participate in needling as a therapeutic method. It requires the doctor to have very good techniques of insertion and manipulation of needles as well as good communication skills. Sometimes it is necessary to show a patient how tiny the needles are or demonstrate the insertion of a needle in the practitioner's own body. This helps to reduce fear and anxiety for both patient and parents.

It is very helpful to play or chat with young patients as if they are friends or family members before the treatment. It is also a good strategy to ask the parents to talk, play with, or feed young patients during the insertion and stimulation of needles, which acts as a diversion to turn the child's attention away from the needles and makes them less sensitive to the procedure. For a child who is extremely sensitive to needles, stimulation by twirling should be avoided during the first one or two visits. For children less than two years old, an effective technique is to hide each needle from their sight while inserting and stimulating. Compared to adult patients, generally speaking, young patients should receive fewer needles, milder stimulation, and shorter time of needle retention. Whether you are treating a child or adult, it is important to observe responses and reactions while inserting, stimulating, or withdrawing needles, and adjust the techniques accordingly.

Monoplegia

CASE HISTORY #7

David, a 52-year-old man, was vacationing with his wife in Santa Fe, NM in 1993. A waitress who noticed that he was paralyzed told him that he should come to our clinic, which specialized in treating that affliction. The man had developed paralysis in the right arm and hand after an operation on the left side of his brain to remove a tumor. Following the surgery, the left front side of his head no longer contained any scalp and there was a depression where the tumor and surrounding tissue had been removed. Because he was feeling very frustrated with his condition, David took the advice of the waitress and made an appointment at our clinic for a free consultation the same day. In addition to the paralysis on the right side, his tongue was purple with teeth marks and a thin, white coating. His pulses were wiry and fine.

Chinese medical pattern discrimination: Qi stagnation and blood stasis in the channels

Scalp acupuncture treatment

Area selection

Primary area: Upper 1/5 Motor Area and middle 2/5 Motor Area

Manipulation

Needles should be inserted in the upper 1/5 Motor Area and the middle 2/5 Motor Area on the unaffected side of the scalp for patients who develop paralysis from brain surgery. Always put one needle in the ear point Shen Men to help nervous patients relax and reduce the sensitivity of needle insertion and stimulation of the scalp. Rotate the needles at least 200 times per minute with the thumb and index finger for 1–3 minutes, twirling them as vigorously as the patient can tolerate and repeat the stimulation every 10 minutes. During treatment, some patients may experience sensations of heat, cold, tingling, numbness, heaviness, distention, or the sensation of water or electricity moving along their spine, legs, or arms. As mentioned previously, those patients with some or all of these sensations usually respond and improve more quickly. One may also choose the Chorea and Tremor Area or Foot Motor and Sensory Area accordingly if the patient has muscular spasms there. Retain the needles for 25–30 minutes. Treatment is given two to three times per week and a therapeutic course consists of 10 treatments.

Results of Case #7

During the initial consultation, David and his wife asked many questions because they were doubtful that scalp acupuncture could help him. They asked, "How quickly could he notice any improvement?" David decided to try the treatment but was still skeptical after being told that some patients had immediate improvement and others did not. Examination showed that the sensations in his right arm and hand were still normal. There was a little twitching in the muscles of his arm but no movement at all in his right arm or hand and the hand appeared puffy and swollen.

After two needles were inserted on the right side of his scalp, David immediately noticed tingling sensations in his right arm and hand. A few minutes later he was able to move his paralyzed arm and hand, amazed as he raised it over his head. The following day he returned to the clinic for another treatment. David appeared to be very tired because, he said, "Everyone at the hotel came to our room for hours to shake my recovering hand." By the end of his fifth treatment David had full use of his right hand and arm and the edema in his hand was completely gone.

Bell's Palsy

Bell's palsy is a paralysis and weakness of the muscles that control expression on one side of the face. The disorder results from damage or trauma to one of a pair of facial nerves (Cranial Nerve VII) that controls the muscles of the face. Symptoms of Bell's palsy usually appear suddenly and reach their peak within 48 hours. Symptoms range in severity from mild weakness to total paralysis of the face, and Bell's palsy can often cause significant facial distortion. Until recently, in most cases its cause was unknown. Most scientists believe that a viral infection causes the disorder and that the facial nerve swells and becomes inflamed in reaction to the infection.

Signs and symptoms of Bell's palsy may include sudden onset of weakness or paralysis on one side of the face making it difficult to smile or close the eye on the affected side, and deviation and droop of the corner of the mouth making facial expressions difficult. Other symptoms include pain behind or in front of the ear on the affected side, sounds that seem louder on the affected side, and changes in the amount of tears and saliva the body produces. Babies can be born with facial palsy and they exhibit many of the same symptoms as adults with Bell's palsy. This is often due to a traumatic birth that causes irreparable damage to the facial nerve resulting in acute facial nerve paralysis.

Patients with facial paralysis for which an underlying cause can be readily found are not generally considered to have Bell's palsy. These underlying problems include tumor, stroke, diabetes, meningitis, head trauma, and inflammatory diseases of the cranial nerves. However, the neurological findings are rarely restricted to the facial nerve in these conditions. There is no cure or specific treatment for Bell's palsy, although three in four patients' symptoms may subside on their own within two to three weeks. Others may be left with deficits of varying degrees, and some patients have permanent damage.

Major complications of the condition include chronic loss of taste (ageusia), chronic facial spasm, and corneal infections. To treat loss of taste, the lower 2/5 Sensory Area in the scalp should be stimulated. It is not advisable to use electrical stimulation on the needles in the face because it may cause facial muscle spasm. To treat facial muscle spasm the Chorea and Tremor Area and the lower 2/5 Motor Area should be stimulated. To prevent corneal infections, the eyes may be protected by covers or taped shut during sleep and for rest periods. Tear-like eyedrops or eye ointments may be recommended, especially in cases of complete paralysis.

Facial paralysis, according to Chinese medicine, involves both disregulation of qi and blood causing malnourishment of the channels in the facial region, as well as invasion by pathogenic wind-cold or phlegm.

CASE HISTORY #8

Jimmy, a 52-year-old male, came to our clinic in Santa Fe, NM in 2000. He had been diagnosed with Bell's palsy two weeks prior and was suffering from cold-like symptoms. He was experiencing moderate pain running along the line of his jaw and behind his left ear. As well, he could not close his left eye, raise his left eyebrow, show his upper teeth, frown, or puff out his left cheek. If this was not enough, the corner of his mouth on the affected side drooped and his mouth deviated to the right side, which was aggravated when he smiled. Because of all these symptoms, he was extremely agitated, angry, and fearful that his face would never look normal again. He had a red tongue with a thin, yellow coating. His pulses were wiry and slippery.

Chinese medical pattern discrimination: Damp heat obstructing the channels and network vessels

Scalp acupuncture treatment

Area selection

Primary area: Lower 2/5 Motor Area
Secondary area: Lower 2/5 Sensory Area

Manipulation

Needles should be inserted on both lower 2/5 Motor Area and lower 2/5 Sensory Area on the contralateral side. Select the finest gauge needles that you can insert into the scalp for the initial treatments. Always put one needle in the ear point Shen Men to help the patient relax and reduce sensitivity to needle insertion and stimulation of the scalp. For two minutes, rotate the needles at least 200 times per minute with the thumb and index finger, twirling them as gently as possible at the beginning of treatment and repeating stimulation every 10 minutes so that the patient can tolerate the sensations better. During treatment, some patients may have all or some of the following sensations: heat, cold, tingling, numbness, heaviness, distention, or the sensation of water or electricity moving in the affected side of the face. Retain the needles in place for 20–30 minutes and request the patient to exercise the affected side of his facial muscles during scalp acupuncture treatments, especially if there are no needles in his face. The treatment is first given two times per week and then gradually reduced to fewer sessions after patients have experienced major improvement. A therapeutic course consists of 10 treatments.

Results of Case #8

Jimmy had a very good response to his first scalp acupuncture treatment. He was immediately able to close his left eye better and the pain around his ear and jaw significantly reduced just a few minutes after two needles were inserted. After the third treatment, the deviation and drooped corner of his mouth showed remarkable improvement, especially after more needles were inserted into his face, hands, and feet. He was able to raise his left eyebrow, reveal his upper teeth, and puff out his left cheek after only six visits. However, he still could not squeeze his left eye completely closed and his smile was a little crooked. After nine scalp acupuncture treatments, he regained all functions of expression in his face and was very pleased with the outcome.

Discussion

Scalp acupuncture is an effective treatment for Bell's palsy. It can repair damaged nerves and restore full use and strength to injured areas. Most patients can recover completely after five to 15 treatments. The sooner patients get treatment, the quicker their recovery. However, facial paralysis may continue to develop and get worse for seven to 10 days after initial symptoms occur.

If treating a patient with Bell's palsy within seven days of its onset, it is wise to inform patients that their condition is not yet stable and more or worse symptoms can continue to develop. Otherwise, patients may conclude that acupuncture made their symptoms worse. Although scalp acupuncture has been successful in the treatment of Bell's palsy, body acupuncture with threaded techniques is very effective for this disorder as well. Common points are Si Bai (St 2) threaded toward Di Cang (St 4), Di Cang (St 4) threaded toward Jia Che (St 6), Yu Yao (extra point) threaded toward Tai Yang (extra point), Yang Bai (GB 14) threaded toward Yu Yao (extra point), and Xia Guan (St 7), He Gu (LI 4), and Tai Chong (Liv 3).

Research on the effects of scalp acupuncture for Bell's palsy

There are several clinical studies showing the excellent results obtained from scalp acupuncture and regular body acupuncture on facial paralysis.

- Wu Jian-min reported on treating 80 cases of facial paralysis using scalp acupuncture in 1989. The duration of the ailment was from four days to two years. Scalp acupuncture treatments were given once a day and 10 treatments made a course. The results showed Bell's palsy fully resolved in 72 cases (90%) and markedly improved in 8 cases (10%) with zero failure, yielding an effective rate of 100%.[38]
- Based on Liu Fang-shi's report of research done in 1994, 48 cases of facial paralysis were treated by scalp acupuncture on the Motor Area. The results were 25 cases fully recovered (52%), 18 cases markedly improved (38%), and 5 cases failed to improve at all (10%), yielding a total effective rate of 90%.[39]

Motor Neuron Diseases

The motor neuron diseases (MNDs) refer to a group of progressive neurological disorders that affect motor neurons associated with controlling voluntary muscle activity including speaking, walking, breathing, swallowing, and general movement of the body. They commonly have distinctive differences in their origin and causation but a similar result in their outcome for the patient, which is severe muscle weakness. Common MNDs include amyotrophic lateral sclerosis (ALS), primary lateral sclerosis, progressive muscular atrophy, and poliomyelitis. Amyotrophic lateral sclerosis (ALS), also known as Lou Gehrig's disease, is a disorder that generally involves either the lower or upper motor systems of the body. In advanced stages, both regions of the body are affected. It is caused by sclerosis in the corticospinal tracts.

Primary lateral sclerosis is a rare motor neuron disease that resembles ALS but there is no evidence of the degeneration of spinal motor neurons or muscle wasting that occurs in ALS.

Progressive muscular atrophies are a wide group of genetic disorders characterized by primary degeneration of the anterior horn cells of the spinal cord, resulting in progressive muscle weakness.

Poliomyelitis, also called polio or infantile paralysis, is a highly infectious viral disease that may attack the central nervous system and is characterized by symptoms that range from a mild nonparalytic infection to total paralysis. Common symptoms and signs include progressive weakness, muscle wasting, muscle fasciculations, spasticity or stiffness in the arms and legs, and overactive tendon reflexes. Patients may present dragging foot, unilateral muscle wasting in one or the other hand, or slurred speech.

Causes of many motor neuron diseases are unknown and others have varying causes according to the specific motor neuron disease. There is no cure or standard treatment for motor neuron diseases and treatment focuses on reducing the symptoms of muscle spasm and pain while maintaining the highest practical level of overall health.

Diseases such as progressive muscular atrophy, poliomyelitis, and ALS are categorized as *wei zheng* (痿证) or wilting conditions in Chinese medicine. The patterns presenting in these diseases usually include a complex combination of liver blood, kidney yin, and spleen qi deficiencies along with damp heat further consuming the blood and damaging the qi, and thus depriving the limbs of strength and the flesh and muscles of nourishment. The damp heat may become congested in the network vessels causing the sinews and muscles to further lose their nourishment. Other patterns based on the patient's constitutional tendencies may also present or arise as the disease progresses.

Sherry, a 38-year-old female, came to our clinic in 2007. It was difficult for her to walk even with her mother's support and because of Sherry's aphasia, her mother gave the medical history. Sherry fell frequently, lost her balance easily, and had had difficulty walking since the age of 19. Her slurred speech sometimes even her mother could not understand. She could not control her urine, choked when eating, and always felt fatigued. Her left ovary hurt and the pain was worse during menses. She often had a migraine headache and premenstrual syndrome (PMS), and she had considerable mucous in her nose and throat much of the time. Sherry had been to several famous hospitals but there was no clear diagnosis. Several doctors thought she suffered from a motor neuron disorder or ALS. Her mental activity presented as normal and she was then in graduate school for a master's degree.

Examination showed she was unable to stand and walk straight by herself. Her gait was wide-based and unsteady and she had to hold on to someone to walk in order to maintain her balance. Her ataxia was even more apparent when she tried to turn and her whole body was stiff and rigid, but worse on the left side. She had lost her fine motor skills. Her legs had severe tremors when she put her toes on the ground and she could not stand on one leg. She counted the numbers from one to 20 with a slow, slurred, weak voice. She could hardly be understood when she said her home phone number. Her tongue had a red tip, a peeled coating on the right side, was purple in the center, had major teeth marks along the sides, a severe tremor, and a thick, white coating. Her pulses were fine and wiry, and were faint in both cubit (*chi*) positions.

Chinese medical pattern discrimination: Liver wind stirring internally, kidney qi deficiency

Scalp acupuncture treatment

Area selection

Primary area: Upper 1/5 Motor Area and Speech I Area
Secondary area: Foot Motor and Sensory Area, Chorea and Tremor Area, and Praxis Area

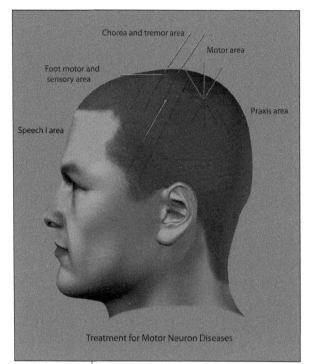

Chorea and tremor area

Motor area

Foot motor and sensory area

Praxis area

Speech I area

Treatment for Motor Neuron Diseases

Manipulation

Insert needles in the upper 1/5 Motor Area, Speech I Area, Foot Motor and Sensory Area, Chorea and Tremor Area, and Praxis Area and stimulate bilaterally. Rotate the needles at least 200 times per minute with the thumb and index finger for 1–3 minutes, twirling them as vigorously as the patient can tolerate and having the patient move her affected limbs actively and passively. Repeat the stimulation every 10 minutes. During treatment, some patients experience sensations of heat, cold, tingling, numbness, heaviness, distention, or the sensation of water or electricity moving in the affected limbs. Those patients usually respond and improve more quickly. However, those who don't have such sensations could still experience immediate and positive effects. Retain the needles for 30–45 minutes and treat two or three times a week. A therapeutic course consists of 10 treatments.

Results of Case #9

A few minutes after being needled on her head, Sherry felt a whole-body hot sensation, which then moved from her hips to her feet, stronger on the left side. Afterwards, her speech was so much clearer, faster, and stronger that even she was surprised. Her walking was much more stable and she was able to lift both legs much higher. She could stand on either leg alone and had to look down to check if it was true.

She returned for the second treatment a day later, having had traveled across the country for these treatments. Sherry reported without her mother's help that her body was less stiff and that she could walk and move better. Her speech was clearer, she didn't feel that her tongue was thick when talking, and very little choking had occurred. Her fatigue and bladder control were improved but she still had a lot of mucous and leg tremor. Her bowel movements were a little loose and she had experienced some nausea and gas after taking the prescribed Chinese herbs. Examination showed that the tremor as well as teeth marks in her tongue were less, the thick, white coating was less, and it was peeled more on the front part of her tongue. Her pulses remained unchanged.

During the second treatment, Sherry experienced a hot sensation again, more so on the left side of the body. She was able to count from one to 20 without breathing. She felt that her legs were not as heavy when walking. For scalp acupuncture, the Chorea and Tremor Area replaced the Foot Motor and Sensory Area in this second treatment. Body acupuncture was added 15 minutes after scalp acupuncture began. The points were Tai Chong (Liv 3), Tai Xi (Ki 3), Yang Ling Quan (GB 34), Feng Long (St 40), Wai Guan (TB 5), and Lian Quan (CV 23).

During the third treatment the next day, the patient reported that she walked better with more control of her left leg and that it felt less heavy. Her speech continued improving with less of a heavy sensation in her tongue. She was able to eat better because of less choking. She had less mucous in her nose and throat and no nausea since the last visit. Although the tremor in both legs was better, she still had some fine movement problems such as difficulty with buttons and writing and still had some stiffness in her legs. Examination showed that her tongue was less red with fewer teeth marks and tremor only on the left side. The thick, white coating was less. Her pulses remained unchanged and were still fine and wiry.

The treatment strategy was modified. While the same scalp areas of upper 1/5 Motor Area and Speech I Area were still used, the Praxis Area and Chorea and Tremor Area were added to address her secondary complaints. The manipulation and retaining of needles remained the same. She could pick up pennies on a table with either hand during the treatment.

Two days later, Sherry arrived for her fourth session and reported very positive reactions to the last treatment. Eating was easier because she could swallow without choking and had less mucous in the throat. Her breathing was less labored when she was active, and friends noticed major improvement in her speech during phone conversations. Sherry's fine motor movement showed some improvement such as turning on a light switch. Unfortunately, that morning she had lost her balance and fallen backward, but with no severe injury. Her tongue showed a red tip, only a thin, white coating, and a peeling coating at the front. There were almost no teeth marks remaining. Her fine pulses had become a little larger and stronger, were still slightly wiry, and showed more strength in the cubit (*chi*) positions.

She received more aggressive treatment that day because it was her last treatment for this trip. The upper 1/5 Motor Area and Speech I Area were still considered primary according to her condition. The Speech III Area, Balance Area, and Foot Motor and Sensory Area were added to assist and consolidate her improved clinical signs. She responded immediately after the needles were inserted, her voice sounding much clearer and stronger. She reported that her balance was improving and her legs felt lighter during the walking exercises. She watched and listened to herself on the video screen while she walked and talked like a normal person. At the end of her final treatment she was both laughing and crying.

Discussion

Scalp acupuncture has been found to have very a significant positive impact on hemiplegic aphasia due to various central nerve disorders, even during the initial few treatments. In Sherry's case, the hemiplegia was caused by a motor neuron disorder. For patients such as Sherry who present with multiple symptoms and signs, it is, in our experience, more effective to treat major complaints first with a few needles. Secondary symptoms can be addressed after patients have significant improvements in their major complaints. As the above case study demonstrated, doctors should modify the treatment strategy and stimulate areas according to changes in a patient's condition.

In our practice, the combination of scalp acupuncture and regular body acupuncture ensures the best results, especially for the further recovery of paralyzed fingers or toes. Common acupuncture points include He Gu (LI 4), Qu Chi (LI 11), Jian Yu (LI 15), and Wai Guan (TB 5) for upper limb paralysis and Yang Ling Quan (GB 34), Feng Shi (GB 31), Huan Tiao (GB 30) Zu San Li (St 36), and Kun Lun (Bl 60) for lower limb paralysis. Electrical acupuncture is very helpful for speeding up recovery. The electrical stimulation usually lasts 10-to-20 minutes. Exercise is also important for the recovery of affected limbs. Active and passive exercise during scalp acupuncture treatment is very important for improvement. It helps the blood circulation and keeps muscles active, accelerating the results from ongoing acupuncture treatments.

Quadriplegia

Quadriplegia means paralysis of all four limbs or of the entire body below the neck. When the arms, legs, and torso are paralyzed, this is commonly caused by damage to the brain, injury of the cervical spinal cord, polyneuritis, myasthenia gravis, progressive myodystrophy, multiple myositis, or acute infective multiple radiculoneuritis.

The severity of quadriplegia depends on both the level at which the spinal cord is injured and the extent of the injury. Although the most obvious symptom is impairment to the limbs, function is also impaired in the torso. That results in loss or impairment of bowel and bladder control, sexual function, digestion, breathing, and other autonomic functions. Because sensation is usually impaired in affected areas, this can manifest as numbness, reduced sensation, or burning sensation and pain. Quadriplegics are often vulnerable to pressure sores, osteoporosis and fractures, frozen joints, spasticity, respiratory complications and infections, poor autonomic reflexes , deep vein thrombosis, and cardiovascular disease because of depressed functioning and immobility.

CASE HISTORY #10

Barbara was in a wheelchair when she was brought to our 2006 scalp acupuncture seminar in Phoenix, Arizona. She had little hope that our treatment would help her condition. Infected by West Nile virus, she had immediately developed quadriplegia. She lost control of her body below the neck and had paralysis of all four limbs. As a result, she had incontinence of bowel and urine. After trying many kinds of therapies that brought no improvement, she became depressed. Examination showed that all four extremities were very tight and had occasional spasms. The muscular tone of her right arm ranked 2 out of 5 degrees, and her left arm and both legs were 0 out of 5 degrees, or completely paralyzed. Her tongue was red with a thin, white coating; her pulses were fine and wiry.

Chinese medical pattern discrimination: Qi stagnation and blood stasis in the channels, kidney qi deficiency, liver blood deficiency and liver depression qi stagnation

Scalp acupuncture treatment

Area selection

Primary area: Upper 1/5 and middle 2/5 of Motor Area
Secondary area: Foot Motor and Sensory Area

Manipulation

Needles should be inserted in both upper 1/5 Motor Area and middle 2/5 Motor Area and stimulated bilaterally. Rotate the needles at least 200 times per minute with the thumb and index finger for 1–3 minutes, twirling them as vigorously as the patient can tolerate and repeating the stimulation every 10 minutes. During treatment, some patients feel heat, cold, tingling, numbness, heaviness, distention, and/or the sensation of water or electricity moving along their spine, legs, or arms. Patients who experience some or all of these sensations usually respond and improve more quickly. As stated previously, however, those who do not have such sensations could still have immediate, positive results. It is important to instruct patients to move their

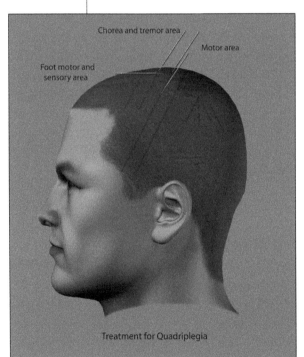

Chorea and tremor area
Motor area
Foot motor and sensory area
Treatment for Quadriplegia

affected limbs actively and passively, if possible. Select either the Chorea and Tremor Area or the Foot Motor and Sensory Area, depending whether the patient has muscular spasms or other abnormal sensations such as pain or burning. Retain the needles for 30–45 minutes. Treatment is given two to three times per week and a therapeutic course consists of 10 treatments.

Results of Case #10

Barbara had very positive responses to scalp acupuncture treatment. As soon as we inserted two needles in her scalp at the Chorea and Tremor Area, the tightness in all four limbs loosened up and the spasms were gone. Soon after that, both of her arms began to move and lift. When we told Barbara that some similar patients were able to walk again, her eyes filled with tears. After inserting four more needles in her scalp, we encouraged Barbara to stand up. She was very surprised to find that she had regained the ability to control her legs again. Although she felt nervous and was assisted by two people, she stood up. She couldn't believe it when we encouraged her to start walking. With much excitement and audience applause, she followed our instruction and started to move: one step, then two, three, and four steps. She walked as much as she could, turning about every 30 steps, walking with confidence and a smile on her face.

At another scalp acupuncture seminar in Phoenix, Arizona later the same year, the audience was waiting to see Barbara, whom we had treated several months before. We were astonished and barely able to recognize her when she walked into the conference room by herself. Barbara reported that she had not received further acupuncture treatment after the last two scalp acupuncture treatments because neither her insurance nor her own money could cover further sessions. Instead, she did intensive exercise as we had instructed seven months before and had recovered completely. Barbara felt it was like a miracle.

For the benefit of the seminar audience, Barbara demonstrated many different kinds of movement of her four extremities such as jumping, running, and easily raising her arms, which brought audience applause. She had gotten married and returned to work.

The only remaining problem was urgent, frequent urination and some incontinence of urine. That was one of the reasons that she returned to this second seminar half a year later. We put two needles in the Foot Motor and Sensory Area and two needles in the Reproductive Area. Barbara had constantly felt pressure and a "strange feeling" there, but she left the seminar very happy. She no longer had that urgent feeling in her bladder and was able to hold her urine for two hours.

Discussion

We need to emphasize that this patient received only three scalp acupuncture treatments and had recovered completely. That is highly unusual and by no means the norm. Treating quadriplegia by acupuncture is very challenging. Normally it takes several months or even as much as one to two years for this treatment to be effective. Even then, only 50% of patients have a chance of improving. Quadriplegia can be treated after any duration, but less than three months from the date of injury or illness shows the greatest improvement. The longer the duration of impairment, the more gradual the improvement occurs. With long-term conditions expectations need to be realistic, although some patients will occasionally surprise practitioners.

There are many different acupuncture techniques to treat paralysis. Although scalp acupuncture has the best and fastest response, other techniques are necessary for a more complete recovery. Regular body acupuncture treatment has been found to have a positive therapeutic effect on the recovery of movement of hands, fingers, feet, and toes. Electrical stimulation is very helpful if the practitioner has difficulty rotating the needle more than 200 times per minute. Only two of the scalp needles should be stimulated at any one session, or the brain can become too confused to respond. For electrical stimulation in body acupuncture, fewer than four needles should be stimulated in each limb. The best results are usually achieved by applying low frequency (for example, 3 hertz) with high intensity (for instance, when visible muscle contraction is observed). Electrical stimulation can be applied above and below the damaged level at Hua Tuo Jia Ji points on the back, which is another important technique for treating quadriplegia in addition to scalp acupuncture.

CHAPTER SIX

Pain

Pain refers to any unpleasant sensory and/or emotional experience associated with actual or potential tissue damage. Pain is the most common reason for patients to seek physician consultation in the US. It is a major symptom in many medical conditions and can significantly impact a person's quality of life and general functioning. The International Association for the Study of Pain uses five categories to classify pain: duration and severity, anatomical location, body system involved, cause, and temporal characteristics.

Regarding duration, pain that lasts a long time is called chronic; pain that arises suddenly but is of short duration is called acute. Traditionally, the distinction between acute and chronic pain has relied upon an arbitrary interval of time from onset, the two most commonly used markers being three months and six months.

Pain can be described based on its location in the body such as in the stomach, or based on the body system involved such as myofascial pain or neuropathic pain.

The crudest example of classification by cause simply distinguishes somatogenic pain from psychogenic pain. Somatogenic pain is subdivided into nociceptive, which is caused by activation of nociceptors, and neuropathic, which is caused by damage to or malfunction of the nervous system.

The temporal characteristics of pain refer to intermittent and constant.

The treatment of pain is guided by its history, intensity, duration, aggravating and relieving conditions, and structures involved in causing the pain. Treatment approaches to pain include interventional procedures, medication, psychological counseling and support, acupuncture, physical therapy, chiropractic, and other alternative therapies.

Acupuncture has been used to treat a wide variety of pain and to maintain an optimal state of health for more than 2,500 years. Most people in the West go to acupuncture practitioners for pain control. In the last two decades there has been increasing interest in the use of acupuncture in pain management. According to a recent National Institutes of Health study, acupuncture is most frequently used for musculoskeletal pain relief in both China and the US. There are several acupuncture modalities for pain management including acupuncture of the body, scalp, ear, hand, and foot.

Scalp acupuncture has been proven to be the most effective technique to remove a wide range of pain. It is especially successful in removing or reducing pain due to central nervous system disorders, which in Western medicine might be treated with pain-masking drugs or surgery. Effective results have been achieved in treating such difficult conditions as phantom limb pain, complex regional pain, and residual limb pain, often producing remarkable results with just a few needles. It usually brings about improvement immediately, sometimes taking only several seconds to a minute.

Beyond the statement of fact in Chinese medicine that says, "Where there is pain there is no free flow; where there is free flow there is no pain," it would be impossible to give any generalization about the Chinese medical pattern discrimination of pain. A wide range of complex and inter-promoting patterns can lead to lack of free flow. As is usually true in Chinese medicine, pattern discrimination can only be done on a case-by-case basis.

Phantom Limb Pain

Phantom limb pain is the term for abnormal sensations perceived from a previously amputated limb. Patients may feel a variety of sensations emanating from the absent limb, which may feel completely intact despite its absence. Patients often describe their pain as burning, squeezing, cramping, prickling, shooting, or stabbing. Several studies have shown that approximately 70-80% of patients develop pain within the first few days after amputation.

Several theories have been proposed regarding the cause of phantom limb pain. Some studies have indicated that phantom pain originates in the brain. When the area of the brain that controlled the limb before it was amputated no longer has a function, other areas of the brain fill in. There is a reorganization of the primary sensory cortex, subcortex, and thalamus after amputation. The reorganization of the sensory cortex is currently considered to be responsible for phantom limb pain. Conventional medicine provides only limited help in alleviating these types of pain. Acupuncture, on the other hand, is becoming a preferred method of treatment for phantom limb pain.

CASE HISTORY #11

We treated a 22-year-old male soldier with scalp acupuncture at Walter Reed Army Medical Center in Washington, DC in 2006. Although both legs had been amputated for several months, the patient still felt severe phantom pain. Various types of medication had been provided, but with little relief. The pain interrupted his sleep and caused him to lose emotional control. The patient described severe painful tingling sensations in both of his absent feet, with the feeling in his right foot worse than his left. The examination showed his tongue to be red with a thin, white coating, and his pulses were wiry and slippery, and somewhat fast.

Chinese medical pattern discrimination: Qi stagnation and blood stasis in the channels, liver qi stagnation transforming heat or fire

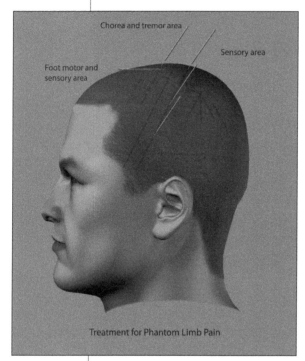

Chorea and tremor area

Sensory area

Foot motor and sensory area

Treatment for Phantom Limb Pain

Scalp acupuncture treatment

Area selection

Primary area: Upper 1/5 Sensory Area and Foot Motor and Sensory Area

Secondary area: Chorea and Tremor Area

Manipulation

The Foot Motor and Sensory Area is known as the primary center to treat phantom limb pain. The Sensory Area is another important treatment site. The upper 1/5 Sensory Area is unilaterally selected to treat opposing leg and foot pain. The middle 2/5 Sensory Area is unilaterally selected to treat opposing arm and hand pain. The Chorea and Tremor Area is classified as a secondary area to treat limb pain and is bilaterally selected to treat spasm pain on either or both sides.

Proper manipulation techniques are crucial in obtaining the desired results. Rotate the needles at least 200 times per minute with the thumb and index finger for 1–3 minutes, twirling them as vigorously as the patient can tolerate and repeating the stimulation every 10 minutes. As mentioned previously, during treatment some patients may feel heat, cold, tingling, numbness, heaviness, distention, or the sensation of water or electricity moving along their spine, legs or feet. Patients who experience some or all of these sensations usually respond and improve more quickly. However, those who do not have such sensations could still have immediate, positive results. Retain the needles for 30–45 minutes. Patients are often treated two to three times a week depending upon the degree of pain and a therapeutic course consists of 10 treatments.

Results of Case #11

As soon as the needles were inserted in his scalp, the patient began to feel heat sensations in both his phantom legs followed by a tingling and almost electric-like sensation in his toes. Five minutes later his phantom pain had diminished considerably and after 10 minutes it had completely disappeared. The patient was worried that the pain might come back after the needles in his scalp were removed, so he insisted on sitting in the treatment room for some time after the treatment was finished. He was relieved and happy to leave without any phantom pain two hours after his first treatment.

Discussion

In our experience, scalp acupuncture is a very effective form of pain relief for phantom limb pain. Other acupuncture techniques for alleviating phantom pain have been proven effective as well. The more commonly practiced techniques are acupuncture of the ear and body, as well as electrical acupuncture. Commonly used ear points are Shen Men, Brain, Subcortex, Sympathetic Nerve, and corresponding limb points. Commonly used body acupuncture points are He Gu (LI 4), Tai Chong (Liv 3), Xing Jian (Liv 2), Nei Guan (Per 6), Tong Li (Ht 5), Xue Hai (Sp 10) in existing limbs. The cleft (*xi*) point is also used in existing limbs that have the same channel names, such as hand shao yang for foot shao yang or left hand shao yang for right hand shao yang.[40] Some research has found that certain circumstances such as emotional stress, anger, fatigue, anxiety, and insomnia can trigger or aggravate the feeling of pain. Therefore, the selection of ear and body acupuncture points should be individualized, and the treatment should be varied among patients according to their symptoms and signs. Electrical acupuncture stimulation of ear points, Hua Tuo Jia Ji extraordinary points, and the sensory cortex of the brain all have very good results in alleviating phantom limb pain.

Although few scientific investigations have directly assessed the efficacy of scalp acupuncture for limb pain, in our clinic at least seven out of eight patients feel improvement after only one treatment. Scalp acupuncture for pain relief is accessible, less expensive, safe, and perceived as having fewer side effects than Western medical treatments. It not only benefits patients with limb pain, but also significantly contributes to our understanding of phantom pain. It can directly stimulate the central nervous system to release neurotransmitters, hormones, or the body's natural pain-relieving endorphins. It may also alter blood pressure, blood flow, and body temperature that are thought to regulate and respond to phantom limb pain.

Complex Regional Pain

Complex regional pain is a chronic pain syndrome that may occur after an injury to an arm or leg. It has been called reflex sympathetic dystrophy (RSD) when skin, bones, joints or tissues are injured. It has been named causalgia when major nerves are injured. Patients with complex regional pain may experience intense burning pain accompanied by changes in the color and temperature of the skin, sweating, swelling, or hypersensitivity on the affected limb. The cause and mechanism of complex regional pain is still unknown. However, it often involves a problem in the sympathetic nervous system. Conventional medicine has provided limited help in alleviating these types of pain. Acupuncture, on the other hand, is becoming a more popular method of treating acute and chronic pain. Other alternative treatments include transcutaneous electrical nerve stimulation, vibration therapy, biofeedback, hypnosis, massage, physical therapy, and electroconvulsive therapy.

CASE HISTORY #12

Jeff, a 45-year-old soldier, received scalp acupuncture from us at Walter Reed Army Medical Center. After being shot twice in each leg during a battle in Iraq, this patient suffered from severe complex regional pain in his right leg. His right leg and foot were so sensitive that even the lightest touch or contact with a thin blanket or sock would induce severe pain that the patient could barely tolerate. Jeff had severe insomnia and felt angry and irritable. He had lost the ability to stand or walk due to sensitivity in the right foot.

Chinese medical pattern discrimination: Qi stagnation and blood stasis in the channel, flare-ups of liver fire

Scalp acupuncture treatment

Area selection

Primary area: Upper 1/5 Sensory Area and Foot Motor and Sensory Area
Secondary area: Chorea and Tremor Area

Manipulation

The Foot Motor and Sensory Area is known as a primary treatment center to treat lower limb pain. The upper 1/5 Sensory Area is unilaterally selected to treat opposing leg and foot pain. The Chorea and Tremor Area is secondary for treating limb pain and is bilaterally selected to treat pain on either or both sides.

Proper manipulation techniques are crucial toward obtaining the desired results. Rotate the needles at least 200 times per minute with the thumb and index finger for 1–3 minutes, twirling them as vigorously as the patient can tolerate and repeating the stimulation every 10 minutes. As mentioned, some patients will have a variety of sensations, and they usually respond and improve more quickly. However, those who do not have such sensations could still have immediate, positive results. Retain the needles for 30–45 minutes. Patients are treated two to three times a week depending upon the degree of pain and a course of treatment consists of 10 sessions.

Results of Case #12

As soon as the needles were inserted in his scalp, Jeff experienced a "water bubble-like sensation" moving first from his right hip to his leg, then to his foot and toes. Five to eight minutes later, his leg and foot pain started to diminish and he was able to touch his leg and toes with little discomfort. He continued touching them to verify that they really were better. He was asked to put a sock on his right foot and did so without any pain or discomfort. The patient felt relaxed and took a short nap. The next day when we returned, Jeff was lying on his bed with both socks on. He had very little pain and was much less sensitive than previously. After a second scalp acupuncture treatment with four needles, he was able to walk with almost no pain. Each step he took brought applause from observers.

Discussion

When compared to other acupuncture modalities including acupuncture on the ear, body, and hand, scalp acupuncture has proven to have the most success in treating complex regional pain. It often produces remarkable results after just a few needles are inserted. It usually relieves symptoms immediately, sometimes taking only minutes to achieve remarkable results. Scalp acupuncture areas may be chosen according to the patient's particular symptoms. The primary areas for patients with abnormal sensations in limbs, including pain, burning, tingling, or numbness are the Sensory Area and Foot Motor and Sensory Area.

There are many different acupuncture techniques to treat complex regional pain. Although scalp acupuncture has the fastest track record for improving symptoms, for some patients other techniques are also necessary for further improvement. Regular body, ear, or electrical acupuncture can be combined with scalp acupuncture to speed up the time of recovery. Commonly used body acupuncture points are He Gu (LI 4), Nei Guan (Per 6), and Qu Chi (LI 11) for upper limb, Tai Chong (Liv 3), Xing Jian (Liv 2), Xue Hai (Sp 10) for lower limb. Commonly used ear points include Shen Men, Subcortex, Sympathetic Nerve, and corresponding limb points. Some research has found that certain circumstances such as emotional stress, anger, fatigue, anxiety, and insomnia can trigger or aggravate the feeling of pain. Therefore, the selection of ear and body acupuncture points should be individualized, and the treatment should be varied among patients according to their clinical manifestations. Electrical acupuncture stimulation of ear points, Hua Tuo Jia Ji (extra points), and the Sensory Area all have very good results in alleviating complex regional pain.

Residual Limb Pain

Residual limb pain is another common problem for patients following partial amputation. It is often caused by surgical trauma, bone abnormality, local scarring, neuroma, or central neuropathic phenomenon. It also may result from an underlying disease process such as infection, ischemia, tumor recurrence, joint dysfunction, or stress fracture that injures nerves at the amputation site. Residual limb pain is a complex condition involving psychological, neuroanatomical, neurochemical, and neurophysiological factors of both the pain stimulus and the memory of past pain experiences. Patients usually describe the pain with such adjectives as sharp, crushing, burning, electric-like, and persistent. This pain is usually exacerbated by any force or pressure directed at the local site. Residual limb pain is often associated with phantom limb sensation or pain and may be related to that etiology in the central nervous system.

CASE HISTORY #13

Sydney, a 26-year-old male soldier, was treated at Walter Reed Army Medical Center. This patient experienced severe residual limb pain in his right stump immediately after surgery five months earlier. His chronic pain felt like the presence of "a hot wire right up my leg," with spasms that resulted in intolerable agony. This pain became even more pronounced at night to the point that he had to scream in order to diminish his discomfort. He had difficulty falling asleep and staying asleep, resulting in severe fatigue. The condition also caused him to feel depressed, irritable, and angry. Upon examination, it was found that he had a red tongue with a thin, yellowish coating, and his pulses were wiry, slippery, and somewhat fast.

Chinese medical pattern discrimination: Qi stagnation and blood stasis in the channels

Scalp acupuncture treatment

Area selection
Primary area: Upper 1/5 Sensory Area, Foot Motor and Sensory Area
Secondary area: Motor Area

Manipulation
The Foot Motor and Sensory Area is known as a primary treatment center to treat lower limb pain. Needles should be inserted bilaterally even if the patient has pain in only one leg. The Sensory Area is another important site to treat opposing limb pain. Generally speaking, the painful extremity is treated by choosing the opposite side of the Sensory Area on the scalp. For instance, for a patient with pain in the right leg and foot, the left side of the

Sensory Area should be needled. However, for a patient who has had brain surgery due where part of the brain was removed, needle the same side of the scalp as the side of the limb pain. For example, if a patient had part of the brain removed and has pain in the left leg and foot, the left side of the Motor Area on the scalp should be needled. The upper 1/5 region is used to treat contralateral pain of the lower extremity, trunk, spinal cord, and neck. The middle 2/5 region is used to treat contralateral pain in the upper extremity. The direction of needling is usually from the upper part of the area downward, penetrating the entire area.

The upper 1/5 Sensory Area is unilaterally selected to treat opposing leg and foot pain. That was, for example, selected to treat opposing leg and foot pain for the patient in Case #12. The Motor Area is classified as a secondary area to treat limb pain and is bilaterally selected to treat spasm pain on the opposite side.

Proper manipulation techniques are crucial toward obtaining the desired results. Rotate the needles at least 200 times per minute with the thumb and index finger for 1–3 minutes, twirling them as vigorously as the patient can tolerate and repeating the stimulation every 10 minutes. Those patients with some sensations during treatment usually respond and improve more quickly. However, those who do not have sensations could still have immediate, positive results. Retain the needles for 30–45 minutes. Patients are treated two to three times a week depending upon the degree of pain and a therapeutic course consists of 10 treatments.

Results of Case #13

Needles were applied on Sydney's scalp at the Foot Motor and Sensory Area and upper 1/5 Sensory Area. Fifteen minutes after four needles were inserted, the patient felt a numb and tingling sensation in his leg. After that, the extreme tightness in his leg started to loosen and the pain gradually diminished. After five more minutes, the tight pain and leg spasms were almost completely gone. Sydney and his wife were happy to see these results so quickly.

Discussion

Whether in the upper or lower limb, scalp acupuncture can be extremely help-ful for patients with residual limb pain. For many patients with this condition, the initial response to scalp acupuncture treatment can be dramatic. Over time, however, the benefits of treatment may diminish or become less consis-tent, although symptoms can usually still be fairly well controlled. When this occurs, scalp acupuncture areas should be alternated with different treatments so that the patient's sensitivity to the stimulation of the needles is maintained. Some body acupuncture is very helpful for patients in the later treatments. The recommended points are He Gu (LI 4), Wai Guan (TB 5), and Qu Chi (LI 11) for upper limb, Tai Chong (Liv 3), Xue Hai (Sp 10), Zu Lin Qi (GB 41), Yang Ling Quan (GB-34) for lower limb, and Ashi points at the amputation sites. Commonly used ear points include Shen Men, Subcortex, Sympathetic Nerve, and corresponding limb points. Electrical acupuncture stimulation of ear points, Hua Tuo Jia Ji extra point), local Ashi points, and the sensory areas are also very good places for healing residual limb pain. However, electrical stim-ulation should not be applied at local Ashi points if the patient has experienced muscle spasm at the amputation site.

Plantar Fasciitis

Plantar fasciitis and heel spurs are commonly lumped together when patients are discussing their heel pain but they are not the same condition. Plantar fasciitis is an inflammation of the connective tissue surrounding the muscles of the sole of the foot and running from the heel to the ball of the foot. On the other hand, a heel spur is a soft, bendable deposit of calcium on the calcaneus or heel bone. While about 70% of patients with plantar fasciitis have heel spurs as well, 50% of patients with heel spurs do not have pain. Heel pain is most often caused by plantar fasciitis. A heel spur by itself does not cause pain. It is often difficult and unnecessary to distinguish between plantar fasciitis and heel spur because the treatment for the two conditions is the same. The causes of heel pain include inadequate flexibility in the calf muscles, lack of arch sup-port, obesity, sudden increase in physical activity, and standing on the feet too long. Patients with plantar fasciitis usually have heel pain on the front and bot-tom of their heel, although the pain may move around. Another factor of this pain is that it occurs with the first few steps in the morning and then may subside after a few minutes, but often will return after prolonged standing or walking. The pain can be mild or debilitating and it can last a few months or become permanent. The pain often increases gradually over weeks or months before patients seek help, and improvement is usually slow. Despite the claims of various product manufacturers, there is no cure for this condition in Western medicine at this time.

CASE HISTORY #14

Lucy, a 53-year-old first-grade teacher, came to our Santa Fe clinic for severe heel pain. Observing how painful it was for her to stand and teach, the parent of one of her students had suggested she come to our clinic. Lucy had been diagnosed with plantar fasciitis a year before. We told her that acupuncture is very effective for relieving heel pain, but sometimes the insertion of needles around the heel can hurt due to nerve-ending inflammation. Her desire for relief made her a willing patient for acupuncture, but not for surgery.

She had burning and stabbing pain in the bottom of her left heel and in the entire bottom area of her right foot. The pain was worse in the morning but then exacerbated as the day progressed in the classroom. Lucy had tried other treatments such as orthotics, steroid injections, physical therapy, and medication for inflammation, but with no lasting, positive results. Upon examination, we found that both her heels were swollen and were very sensitive to touch. Her tongue was red with a little coating, her pulses were wiry and fine, and her cubit (*chi*) position pulses lacked force bilaterally as well.

Chinese medical pattern discrimination: Qi stagnation and blood stasis in the channels, kidney yin deficiency

Scalp acupuncture treatment

Area selection

Primary area: Upper 1/5 Sensory Area and Foot Motor and Sensory Area

Manipulation

Needles should be inserted in both the upper 1/5 Sensory Area and Foot Motor and Sensory Area and stimulated bilaterally if the pain is in both heels. The opposite side of the scalp should be chosen for needling if the patient has only one affected heel. Rotate the needles at least 200 times per minute with thumb and index finger for 1–3 minutes, twirling them as vigorously as the patient can tolerate and repeating stimulation every 10 minutes. During the treatment, some patients may feel heat, cold, tingling, numbness, heaviness, distention, or the sensation of water or electricity moving along their spine, legs or feet. Patients who feel new sensations usually respond and improve more quickly. Retain the needles for 25–30 minutes. Treatment is given two to three times per week and a therapeutic course consists of 10 treatments.

Results of Case #14

During the first treatment, Lucy was very sensitive to the needles around her feet. However, we were able to insert all the needles for her treatment except for those in the bottom of her heels. Even so, she was very happy to leave our clinic with some relief from her heel pain. During the second treatment, although we did ear acupuncture and scalp acupuncture first to reduce her sensitivity to the needles in her heels, Lucy was still in quite a bit of pain from heel needles. When a needle was inserted in the bottom of her heel she screamed loudly enough to startle everyone else in the clinic. Fortunately, Lucy felt significant improvement after the second treatment and was able to stand and walk with a lower, more tolerable level of pain.

With each additional session, Lucy experienced gradual improvement and less sensitivity to the needles in her heels, though she still screamed at every session. Even though we hesitated to put needles in the bottom of her heels, Lucy would insist on their insertion, saying "no pain, no gain," to encourage both of us. By the eighth treatment, she reported no further pain in either foot and was even able to wear many pairs of shoes she had been unable to wear for some time. Because of acupuncture she has been free of pain for nine years now.

Discussion

Acupuncture has very positive results for heel pain. It can relax the connective tissue and muscles of the foot, reduce the inflammation, and promote the circulation of qi and blood in the feet, thus relieving the pain. Usually the heel pain diminishes gradually as treatments progress. Acupuncture is not only a good tool to treat heel pain, but also to balance the whole body and thus benefit the legs, hips, and low back as well. Patients often compensate for their heel pain by posturing or gaiting differently. In our practice, we have found that it is very helpful to use other acupuncture methods along with scalp acupuncture in order to enhance the effects. The most commonly used points for body acupuncture are Tai Xi (Ki 3), Zhao Hai (Ki 6), Kun Lun (Bl 62), Yang Ling Quan (GB 34), Cheng Shan (Bl 57), and Ashi points on the bottom of the feet. Electrical stimulation to the above points with high frequency and low intensity is also very helpful. Although acupuncture treatments are important to cure the heel pain, it is also necessary to recognize and adjust any lifestyle factors that may be contributing to the condition. For example, the patient may need to lose weight and limit the amount of time spent standing or walking on a daily basis.

Restless Leg Syndrome

Restless leg syndrome is a neurological movement disorder characterized by abnormal sensations in the legs and an uncontrollable urge to move them in order to relieve these unpleasant feelings. The sensations are often described as antsy, electric creeping, itching, pins and needles, pulling, tugging, painful, or like insects are crawling inside the legs.

The abnormal sensations and urge to move can occur in any part of the body, but the most cited location is the legs. Any inactivity such as lying down or sitting can trigger those sensations and the subsequent urge to move. Movement usually brings immediate relief, but often it is only temporary and partial. Most patients report that the symptoms are less noticeable during the day and more pronounced in the evening or night. The exact cause of restless leg syndrome is unknown and it can be a lifelong condition for which there is no cure in Western medicine.

While we know that, according to Chinese medicine, all involuntary movement in the body is due to the internal stirring of liver wind, there are many other patterns that lead to or exacerbate this pattern. These may include spleen qi vacuity, which leads to or worsens liver blood vacuity, as well as qi stagnation, blood stasis, and/or damp heat.

CASE HISTORY #15

Donna, a 92-year-old female, was referred to our clinic in Albuquerque by her primary care physician. She had suffered from restless leg syndrome for 15 years. Because Donna felt creeping and burning sensations in her legs, she could not keep them still day or night. This became even more pronounced at night, when she had to move around constantly to diminish the discomfort. She had difficulty falling asleep and staying asleep, which caused severe fatigue. She felt depressed, had a poor appetite, and constipation. Her tongue was red with a thin, yellowish coating. Her pulses were fine and wiry.

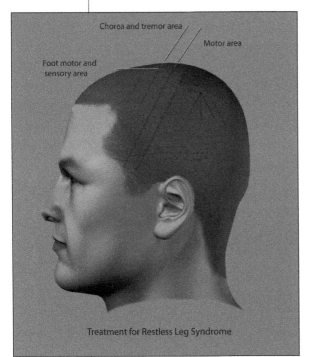

Chorea and tremor area

Motor area

Foot motor and sensory area

Treatment for Restless Leg Syndrome

Chinese medical pattern discrimination: Liver wind stirring internally, accompanied by transformative heat, liver blood deficiency, spleen qi deficiency

Scalp acupuncture treatment

Area selection

Primary area: Foot Motor and Sensory Area, Chorea and Tremor Area
Secondary area: Upper 1/5 Sensory Area

Manipulation

Needles should be inserted in the Foot Motor and Sensory Area and Chorea and Tremor Area and stimulated unilaterally. Rotate the needles at least 200 times per minute with the thumb and index finger for 1–3 minutes, twirling them as vigorously as the patient can tolerate and repeating this stimulation every 10 minutes. During the treatment, some patients may feel their restless legs becoming relaxed and feel less of an urge to move them. Some patients may experience their tremors becoming a little more severe. Patients with some or all of these sensations usually respond and improve more quickly. However, those who do not have such sensations could still have immediate, positive results. Retain the needles for 25–30 minutes. The treatment is given two to three times per week and a therapeutic course consists of 10 treatments.

Results of Case #15

Donna was very calm as the doctor inserted four needles in her scalp. A few minutes afterwards, she said there was a warm sensation moving from her head down to her legs. After that she was able to relax her legs and keep them still, which she had not been able to do for a long time. The abnormal leg sensations also improved somewhat, to a tolerable level. She was amazed that her legs stayed still for the entire 30 minutes of treatment, which she never could have done without scalp acupuncture. At the second treatment, Donna reported that, not having needed to walk around to ease the strange sensations in her legs at night, she had slept much better. She had more energy and less depression. The poor appetite and constipation remained unchanged. Needles were inserted in the Stomach Area as well as other scalp areas during her second treatment.

By the third treatment, Donna was sleeping through the night. By the sixth treatment, she had not had any restless leg symptoms for several weeks and her appetite and bowels had returned to normal. Examination showed that her tongue had become light red with a thin, white coating and her pulses had changed to fine. She needed no further acupuncture and was enjoying her senior years again.

Discussion

Scalp acupuncture has positive results with restless leg syndrome and usually produces some immediate response in the initial treatment, with significant and complete reduction of symptoms occurs in approximately 70% of patients receiving treatment. Although the norm has been that restless legs gradually improve with each treatment, it is not uncommon for some patients to experience the symptoms worsening during their treatments. If restless legs are not well-controlled by scalp acupuncture alone, patients may experience better results when combining it with body acupuncture. Commonly used points are Tai Chong (Liv 3), Yang Ling Quan (GB 34), San Yin Jiao (Sp 6), Feng Shi (GB 31), and Gan Shu (Bl 18). However, for patients with severe restless legs, it is not advisable to use body points in their legs because the constant movement while needles are inserted could cause severe leg pain and muscle spasm.

Fibromyalgia

Fibromyalgia is a chronic disorder characterized by pain in various muscles and their surrounding ligaments and tendons. Chronic pain can occur in joints and bones as well, but inflammation is not a factor. Multiple points are extremely tender. The pain causes fatigue, headache, and impaired sleep. The syndrome affects more females than males.

Symptoms and signs can vary depending on stress, physical activity, weather changes, or even the time of day. Common symptoms include widespread pain and stiffness, fatigue and sleep disturbances, heightened sensitivity of the skin, headache and facial pain, irritable bowel syndrome, weakness of limbs, muscle spasms, and impaired concentration and short-term memory. The degree of symptoms may also vary greatly from day to day with periods of flare-ups or remissions.

Fibromyalgia often starts as a result of some mental or physical trauma, major surgery, or disease. Symptoms are often aggravated by any unrelated illness. The cause of fibromyalgia is still unknown in Western medicine. One theory states that patients with fibromyalgia have a lower threshold for pain because of increased sensitivity in the brain to pain signals. Other theories include abnormalities of the autonomic nervous system, changes in muscle metabolism, injury, infection, psychological stress, or hormonal changes. There is no universal cure for fibromyalgia in Western medicine. In general, treatment for fibromyalgia emphasizes minimizing the symptoms and improving general health.

Fibromyalgia is described by Chinese medical literature as being most commonly due to liver-spleen disharmony plus blood deficiency as the basic presenting pattern. Many other patterns, however, usually complicate each individual case. These patterns can include damp heat, qi and yin deficiency with deficiency heat, spleen-kidney yang deficiency, and blood stasis.

CASE HISTORY #16

Judy was 48 when she came to our clinic in Santa Fe, having been diagnosed with fibromyalgia 10 years earlier. Previously, Judy had been a very physically active woman, participating in aerobics, skiing, jogging, and hiking. For the last 10 years these activities had to stop because the pain in her neck and back made simple tasks like washing the dishes nearly unbearable, much less exercise. Her legs hurt so severely that even walking a short distance left her in tears. Every morning her neck was so stiff and painful that she could not turn her head. Over time, the pain became worse and spread throughout her body. She began to gain weight and feel depressed.

The condition slowly worsened, bringing on insomnia, fatigue, mood swings, poor memory and concentration, and either diarrhea or constipation. Her immune system was so weak that she caught the flu or a cold frequently. Although she received many kinds of therapy, Judy showed little improvement. Examination showed that she had a red tongue with a thick white coating and teeth marks, and her pulses were fine and wiry.

Chinese medical pattern discrimination: Liver depression qi stagnation, with depressive liver heat, spleen qi/heart blood deficiency

Scalp acupuncture treatment

Area selection

Primary area: Sensory Area, Chorea and Tremor Area
Secondary area: Foot Motor and Sensory Area, Head Area

Manipulation

Needles should be inserted in both the Sensory Area and Chorea and Tremor Area bilaterally. Choose secondary areas based on symptoms in Western medicine and patterns in Chinese medicine. It is a good technique to put one needle in the ear point Shen Men to help the patient relax and reduce the sensitivity of the needle insertion and stimulation of the scalp. Use as few needles as possible in the scalp and rotate them at least 200 times per minute with the thumb and index finger for two minutes, twirling as gently as possible in the beginning so the patient can tolerate the sensations. Then gradually increase the intensity of the stimulation, repeating it every 10 minutes. Tell patients before the needles are inserted that unusual sensations are normal and patients who experience them typically respond and improve more quickly. If they do not have such sensations, they could still have immediate, positive results. Retain the needles in place for 10–20 minutes. Initially, treatment should be given two to three times per week. After a few weeks, reduce to once a week and then once a fortnight. The patient should be treated about once a month thereafter if noticeable improvement is obtained. A therapeutic course consists of 10 treatments.

Results of Case #16

During her first scalp acupuncture treatment, Judy felt her body totally relax. She fell deeply asleep just a few minutes after the needles were inserted and felt completely at ease when she awakened. After only six treatments, her pain and stiffness were reduced by about 70%. Her nighttime sleep refreshed her. She also no longer felt the searing pain in her neck, back, and legs that used to bring her to tears. By the tenth treatment, Judy had significantly overcome the insomnia and fatigue. She looked forward to resuming many of the physical activities she had once enjoyed. After 20 treatments Judy experienced almost no pain. She had lower back pain occasionally but it was definitely manageable, and receiving scalp acupuncture treatments every four to six weeks kept the pain under control. She no longer took painkillers. Judy reported that her immune system was stronger, and she rarely suffered from a cold or flu since she began receiving scalp acupuncture treatments.

Discussion

Scalp acupuncture has a very good track record for treating fibromyalgia. It is important to offer patients a hopeful and confident attitude toward the treatment, as the disease affects both mental and physical activities and is very frightening. It is also helpful to introduce new patients to former patients who have experienced treatment success. This will give new patients hope and encouragement, which in turn will produce better results.

It is very helpful if other acupuncture methods are added to scalp acupuncture treatments as adjunct therapies. It is reported that penetrating technique showed very effective for treating fibromyalgia.[41] Commonly used points are Wai Guan (TB 5) penetrating to Nei Guan (Per 6), He Gu (LI 4) to Lao Gong (Per 8), Yang Ling Quan (GB 34) to Yin Ling Quan (Sp 9), Kun Lun (Bl 60) to Tai Xi (Ki 3), and Feng Chi (GB 20) penetrating to Feng Fu (GV 16). The selection of body acupuncture points should be individualized based on the differentiation of patterns in Chinese medicine. For instance, Tai Chong (Liv 3), Yang Ling Quan (GB 34), Dan Shu (Bl 19), and He Gu (LI 4) are used for the stagnation of the liver qi, and Tai Xi (Ki 3), Zhao Hai (Ki 6) and Shen Shu (Bl 23) for deficiency of the kidneys. Cupping is another valuable method for patients with fibromyalgia. The area for cupping commonly applied is around the gallbladder and urinary bladder channels because the pain these patients have is usually located on those channels. The most frequently used points are Feng Chi (GB 20), Jian Jing (GB 21), Huan Tiao (GB 30), Feng Shi (GB 31), and Yang Ling Quan (GB 34), Fei Shu (Bl 13), Xin Shu (Bl 15), Gan Shu (Bl 18), Dan Shu (Bl 19) and Shen Shu (Bl 23). In the late stages of fibromyalgia the kidneys are often affected and the use of points to reinforce and supplement the kidneys, such as Tai Xi (Ki 3), Shen Shu (Bl 23), and Guan Yuan (CV 4) are useful.

In addition, fibromyalgia often becomes worse with stress, whether physical, emotional, or psychological. Therefore, scalp areas that have the function to relieve anxiety, irritability, worry, or depression should be combined with the Foot Motor and Sensory Area for the best results. Furthermore, other therapies that can promote relaxation and a sense of well-being may be helpful in relieving fibromyalgia symptoms or the distress it causes. Some effective therapies include meditation, hypnosis, yoga, and herbs.

Herpes Zoster

Herpes zoster, commonly referred to as shingles, is a skin infection resulting from reactivation of the varicella-zoster virus acquired during the primary varicella infection, or chicken pox. After an episode of chicken pox the virus lies dormant, sometimes for decades. It reappears when the immune system is weakened by age, stress, disease, and some medications such as chemotherapy or corticosteroids. Herpes zoster typically manifests as a vesicular rash in a unilateral dermatomal distribution associated with burning pain and itching. Burning pain often precedes the rash by several days and can persist for several months after the rash resolves. Post-herpetic neuralgia as a complication of herpes zoster can be highly debilitating. Although some medications can be effective, including antiviral, antispasmodics, painkillers, steroids, antidepressants, and anticonvulsants, up to 20% of herpes zoster patients experience prolonged and sometimes debilitating post-herpetic neuralgia. Conventional medicine has little to offer for such a condition.

In Chinese medicine, it is believed that a righteous qi deficiency plus, spleen dampness, depressive liver heat or fire, and heat toxins are the main patterns resulting in this condition. If it endures for a long time, qi stagnation and blood stasis will also be engendered.

CASE HISTORY #17

Robert was 89 years old with a complaint of shingles when he came to our clinic in Santa Fe. Two days before the eruption of shingles, he experienced strange pains on the left side of his chest and felt sick with fatigue and malaise. A week later Robert discovered that about half of his left trunk, from his chest around to his back, was covered with blisters and rash. The eruptions caused unbearable burning pain and itching day and night. He quickly became debilitated by such continuous pain and could barely eat or sleep. The deep stabbing caused him to be irritable, angry, and depressed, and he had lost 10 pounds. First he consulted a dermatologist, who gave him painkillers, antiviral and antidepressant medications, and three injections that had not relieved his pain. Upon examination, blisters and rash covered two-thirds of his left side of dermatome distribution. He screamed or moaned frequently, had feeble breathing, and was very sensitive to touch in the affected area. His tongue was deep red with a thin, yellow coating, and his pulses were wiry and fine.

Chinese medical pattern discrimination: Liver qi binding stagnation with stagnant heat sometimes transforming to liver fire, damp heat in the gallbladder

Scalp acupuncture treatment

Area selection

Primary area: Upper 1/5 Sensory Area and lower 1/5 Sensory Area

Manipulation

Needles should be inserted in the upper 1/5 Sensory Area and lower 1/5 Sensory Area and stimulated unilaterally. Rotate the needles at least 200 times per minute with the thumb and index finger for 1–3 minutes, twirling them as vigorously as the patient can tolerate and repeating the stimulation every 10 minutes. During treatment, some patients may feel sensations of pressure, fullness in their chest, back, or costal area. Those patients with some or all of these sensations usually respond and improve more quickly. Retain the needles for 25–30 minutes. Treatment is given two to three times per week and a therapeutic course consists of 10 treatments.

Results of Case #17

Robert felt the burning pain was diminished just a few minutes after two needles were inserted into his scalp. The pain was gradually reduced to the level that he could tolerate with no more screaming or moaning and his breathing returned to normal. He felt much better and fell asleep during the treatment. Upon awaking, he reported that the pain was 80% better and he felt hungry. After the first treatment, his sleep improved remarkably and his family was greatly relieved.

Robert felt much better after each additional treatment. By the fourth visit, the blisters on his chest and back had dried up and the intense burning pain had reduced to only 10%. At the end of the eighth treatment, the pain was completely gone and he could eat and sleep very well. Robert was still feeling well and had no pain one month after the last treatment.

Discussion

Scalp acupuncture usually provides immediate results for relieving post-herpetic neuraliga pain. In our practice, the best results occur by adding ear and body acupuncture and Chinese herbs. Commonly used ear points are Shen Men, Sympathetic Nerve, Liver, and the points corresponding to the pain area. The effective body points are Xing Jian (Liv 2), Zu Ling Qi (GB 41), Zhong Zhu (TB 3), Qu Chi (LI 11), and Xue Hai (Sp 10). The Chinese herbal formula for retention of damp heat in the liver and gallbladder *is Long Dan Xie Gan Tang.* It is also necessary to administer some antiviral herbal formulas for early stages of herpes zoster. Possible choices are *Chuan Xin Lian Pian*, or *Ban Lan Gen Chong Ji*.

Low Back Pain

Low back pain is a common musculoskeletal or neurological disorder that affects the lumbar segment of the spine. Back pain is the second most common ailment in the United States next to headache. Acute low back pain usually lasts from a few days to a few weeks and it often is the result of trauma, such as a sports injury or car accident. In acute cases, the structures damaged are more likely soft tissues such as muscles, ligaments, or tendons.

When low back pain persists for more than three months, it is considered chronic. This is often caused by osteoarthritis, rheumatoid arthritis, degeneration of a disc or disc herniation, vertebral fracture, a tumor, or infection. Some patients first feel low back pain just after lifting a heavy object, moving suddenly, or sitting in one position for a long time. Prior to the specific event, however, their back structure might have been losing strength or integrity, or become too stiff and tight. Low back pain may range from muscle aches to shooting and stabbing pain, often accompanied by limited flexibility or range of motion. Low back pain may travel to the buttocks, and sometimes it may go further down the leg and even into the foot. The pain may be worse on bending and is often worse from sitting. Sometimes turning over in bed and sitting up are agonizing. The muscles of the lower back may go into painful spasm as well. In Western medicine, treatment for acute or chronic low back pain involves a combination of prescription drugs and over-the-counter remedies. Lumbar surgery is another choice when conservative treatment is not effective or when the patient develops progressive neurological symptoms such as leg weakness, bladder or bowel incontinence. When people with low back pain do not respond to more conventional approaches, they should consider acupuncture treatment.

According to Chinese medicine, low back pain of a chronic nature is usually thought to relate to some type of kidney deficiency, whether of qi, yin, yang or a combination of these. However, other patterns may be present as well that hinder recovery, including spleen qi deficiency which leads to liver blood deficiency and also inhibits the proper transformation and transportation of fluids in the body. Furthermore, any chronic condition may also lead to local blood stasis if it endures for a long time.

CASE HISTORY #18

John, a 72-year-old retiree, came to our clinic from El Paso, Texas. John had suffered from severe lower back pain for more than fifteen years and had been previously diagnosed with central and lateral recess stenosis at L 2-3 and L 3-4 and bilateral foraminal stenosis at L 4-5. He was desperate and had tried many therapies that doctors recommended. He had undergone three surgeries and at least three epidural injections. John stated that the surgeries did not help much and each injection had not lasted as long as the previous one. The last injection seemed not to have helped at all.

His pain was localized primarily in the left and right gluteal region and radiated down both legs with sensations of numbness, tingling, and weakness. He could not find a comfortable position in which to sleep and he felt fatigued, depressed, irritable, angry, and hopeless. He was tired of having severe constipation due to painkillers. An MRI showed disc degeneration, mild loss of disc space height, mild-to-moderate broad-based disc bulge at L 2-3 and L 3-4, advanced disc space narrowing with disc degeneration, and moderate broad-based disc bulge. Upon examination, he had a purple tongue with a red tip and sides and a thick, yellow, dry coating. His pulses were wiry and fine.

Chinese medical pattern discrimination: Qi stagnation and blood stasis in the channels, liver qi binding stagnation with stagnant or depressive heat

Scalp acupuncture treatment

Area selection

Primary area: Upper 1/5 Sensory Area, Foot Motor and Sensory Area
Secondary area: Head Area

Manipulation

Needles should be inserted in both Sensory Area and Foot Motor and Sensory Area bilaterally. Choose secondary areas based on patterns in Chinese medicine. It is a good technique to put one needle in the ear point Shen Men to help patients relax and reduce the sensitivity of the needle insertion and stimulation of the scalp. Use as few needles as possible in the scalp and rotate them at least 200 times per minute with the thumb and index finger for two minutes, twirling them as gently as possible in the beginning so that the patient can tolerate the sensations and then gradually increasing the intensity of the stimulation. Repeat the stimulation every 10 minutes. Tell patients before the needles are inserted that some unusual sensations might occur, that they are normal, and that those who experience them usually respond and improve more quickly. Retain the needles in place for 10–20 minutes. Initially, treatment should be given two to three times per week. After a few weeks, it can be spaced out to once a week and then once a fortnight. A therapeutic course consists of 10 treatments.

Results of Case #18

John was very skeptical before his first treatment began, but his daughters had urged him to come. We told him that we had treated many patients with severe lower back pain and there were usually very effective outcomes. John felt much pain and yelled or moaned many times when the doctor sought tender points in his lower back, hips, and legs during the examination.

His back tenseness loosened and the pain diminished soon after a few needles were inserted into his scalp and legs. He fell soundly asleep, in contrast to his previous inability to lie in one position for long. When he woke up, John moved his back and legs many different ways to test that the pain was truly less. At the second treatment, he reported that the pain was about 80% better in his back, hips, and legs. With better sleep and less fatigue, his mood also improved, and the constipation was diminishing. After four treatments, the pain in John's lower back, legs, and hips had reduced by about 90%, and he was optimistic about further recovery.

When John returned for more treatments, he reported that the pain in his back, legs, and hips was less, he was sleeping well, had more energy, and had started to walk as exercise again. He took much less medication to control the pain and some days he took none. After eight acupuncture treatments, John had no pain in his lower back, hips, and legs. He stopped taking any pain medication and enjoyed a normal life again.

Discussion

Scalp acupuncture is very effective for treating low back pain and most patients have significant improvement in the first few treatments. Body acupuncture added to scalp acupuncture is also helpful. The selection of body acupuncture points should be individualized based on the differentiation of patterns in Chinese medicine. Commonly used points are Wei Zhong (Bl 40), Kun Lun (Bl 60), Tai Xi (KI 3), Shen Shu (Bl 23), Da Chang Shu (Bl 25), and Guan Yuan Shu (Bl 26). Cupping is another valuable method for patients with low back pain. The area for cupping is around the bladder channels because that is where the pain normally is located. In chronic low back pain the kidneys are often affected, requiring the use of points to reinforce the kidneys, such as Tai Xi (Ki 3), Shen Shu (Bl 23), Ming Men (GV 4), and Guan Yuan (CV 4).

In addition, some low back pain can become worse with stress, whether the source is physical, emotional, or psychological. Therefore, the scalp areas that have the function of relieving anxiety, irritability, worry, and depression should be combined with the Foot Motor and Sensory Area for the best results. Furthermore, other techniques that can promote relaxation and a sense of well-being may be helpful in relieving low back pain symptoms or the distress it causes. Patients may apply ice for the first 24-48 hours and use heat after that. Patients should not perform activities that involve heavy lifting or twisting their back for the first six to eight weeks after the pain begins. It is often helpful if patients lie in a curled-up, fetal position with a pillow between their legs or to place a pillow under their knees to relieve pressure if they usually sleep on their back.

CHAPTER SEVEN

Aphasia

Aphasia is a neurological disorder caused by damage to the portions of the brain that are responsible for language. Primary symptoms of the disorder include difficulty in expressing oneself when speaking, trouble understanding speech, and difficulty with reading and writing. The most common cause of aphasia is a stroke. It can also result from a head injury, brain tumor or infection, Parkinson's disease, or dementia that damages the brain. Aphasia usually occurs suddenly, such as the result of a stroke or head injury, but it also may develop slowly, such as in the case of a brain tumor.

Generally, aphasia can be divided into four types: expressive, receptive, anomic, and global aphasia. The type and severity of the language dysfunction depends on the precise location and extent of the damaged brain tissue. Expressive

153

aphasia, also known as Broca's aphasia, motor aphasia, and nonfluent aphasia, is caused by damage to the anterior regions of the brain known as Broca's area. This type of aphasia exhibits the common problem of agrammatism, in which case speech is difficult to initiate, nonfluent, labored, and halting. In extreme cases, patients may be unable to produce even a single word. Receptive aphasia, also known as Wernicke's aphasia, sensory aphasia, or fluent aphasia, is often caused by damage to the superior temporal gyrus, called the Wernicke's area. This aphasia involves difficulty understanding spoken or written language. Patients cannot make sense of words even though they hear the word or see it in print. Anomic aphasia, also called nominal aphasia, is essentially a difficulty with naming certain words linked by their grammatical type or semantic category, or it is a more general naming difficulty. Global aphasia results from damage to extensive portions of the language areas of the brain. Patients with global aphasia have severe communication difficulties and may be extremely limited in their abilities to speak or comprehend language. There is no specific treatment for aphasia in Western medicine. Treatment mostly focuses on the cause, such as intravenous tPA for acute stroke, or surgery for brain tumor, which may help to alleviate the deficit.

The outcome of aphasia treatment is difficult to predict given the wide range of variability of the condition. Generally, patients who are younger or have less extensive brain damage recover faster and more completely. The location of the damage is also important and is another clue to prognosis. Brain imaging techniques including PET (positron emission tomography), CT (computed tomography), MRI (magnetic resonance imaging), and fMRI (Functional magnetic resonance imaging) are helping to define brain function, determine the severity of brain damage, and predict the severity of the aphasia. New techniques such as these can identify areas of the brain that are used for speaking or listening. In-depth testing of the language ability of patients with various aphasic symptoms is helping to design more effective treatment strategies.

In general, patients treated with scalp acupuncture tend to recover more quickly if they have expressive aphasia compared to other types. Scalp acupuncture, however, offers fairly good results for patients with all types of aphasia. Several patients treated with scalp acupuncture at our clinics have shown some immediate improvement. That said, treating patients with aphasia is very challenging because patients cannot speak or report clearly about their condition. It requires the doctor to possess not only very good techniques of gentle insertion and manipulation of the needles, but also good communication skills.

Family involvement is also a crucial component of aphasia treatment. Family members need to learn the best ways to assist their loved ones in exercises in order to help them regain their speech functions. During treatment, quite often a helpful approach is for the doctor and family members to work together as a team with the patient in order to observe even the smallest changes in speech function.

Expressive Aphasia

CASE HISTORY #19

Maria, a 69-year-old female, sought scalp acupuncture treatment in 2007. Her left side had been partially paralyzed since her first stroke six years before. A second stroke three years later caused aphasia. Her daughter reported that the entire left side of Maria's body was completely paralyzed and she had severe spasms and pain in her left arm and leg that caused her to scream or yell frequently. After the second stroke, Maria had 20 acupuncture treatments on body points, which evoked little response or improvement. Upon examination, the patient's mind was clear when responding to the questionnaire. Although she could make sounds in response to questions, her speech was unintelligible. Maria's left limbs showed no positive movements at all, they were very stiff and tight and could hardly be moved by another person. Her tongue was red with a little coating, and her pulses were wiry and fine.

Chinese medical pattern discrimination: Kidney essence deficiency, phlegm and heat obstructing the orifices

Scalp acupuncture treatment

Area selection

Primary area: Upper 1/5 and middle 2/5 of Motor Area, Speech I Area
Secondary area: Upper 1/5 and middle 2/5 of Sensory Area

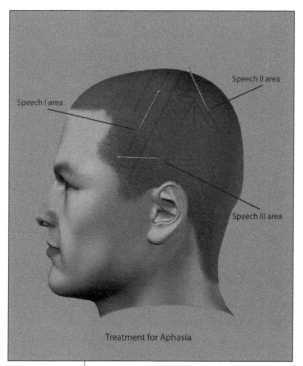

Treatment for Aphasia

Speech II area

Speech I area

Speech III area

Manipulation

Insert needles in the Motor Area, Sensory Area, and Speech I Area. These should be stimulated unilaterally according to the patient's symptoms. If paralysis is in the leg and foot, upper 1/5 Motor Area should be chosen; if in the upper limb, middle 2/5 should be the choice; if in the face, lower 2/5 should be selected. If there are some abnormal sensations in the leg and foot, arm and hand, or face, upper 1/5, middle 2/5, or lower 2/5 should be chosen respectively. The chosen insertion area should be on the side opposite the affected limb. For the patient with motor aphasia both sides of Speech I Area should be needled. Rotate the needles at least 200 times per minute with the thumb and index finger for 1–3 minutes, twirling them as vigorously as the patient can tolerate and having the patient move the affected limb actively and passively, if possible. Repeat the stimulation every 10 minutes. During treatment, some patients may experience sensations of heat, cold, tingling, numbness, heaviness, distention, or sensations of water or electricity moving down the affected limb. Those patients usually respond and show improvement more quickly. However, those who do not have such sensations could still have immediate positive results. Retain the needles for 30–45 minutes. The patient is given two to three treatments per week, and a therapeutic course consists of 10 treatments.

Results of Case #19

Maria had a very positive response to her first scalp acupuncture treatment. After the needles were inserted in her scalp, the spasms, stiffness, and tightness in her left arm and leg showed immediate improvement. Her left limb became looser, and her daughter was able to move the leg and arm up and down with little resistance. To her surprise, she answered "Maria" when being asked her name. Then she replied "69" to the question "How old are you?" Maria's eyes were full of tears as she answered questions with a strong, clear voice. She said, "Thank you so much, doctor. I am so glad I can now speak again." Several minutes later, Maria was able to move her left leg and arm on her own. She was able to pull and push her left leg so strongly that we encouraged her to try walking. She immediately and clearly said, "Yes, I would like to try." As she walked back and forth, exercising her leg with the help of an assistant, she kept saying, "Thank you so much for this miracle."

Discussion

In our practice, most patients with expressive aphasia have had a stroke in which the blood supply to language areas in the brain was interrupted, causing brain cells to die or be seriously damaged. Besides aphasia, stroke patients often experience paralysis, apraxia, altered coordination, difficulty swallowing, and mental and emotional changes.

Scalp acupuncture has been found to have a very good effect on expressive aphasia. The potential for functional recovery from expressive aphasia after a stroke is excellent. Patients should get acupuncture treatment as soon as their condition is stable. The earlier the treatment, the better the prognosis. Most aphasia patients treated at our clinic show improvement in the initial three treatments, and many of them appear better after the first session.

There are several different acupuncture techniques to treat expressive aphasia. Although scalp acupuncture gives the fastest response, other techniques are necessary for enhancing its efficacy. According to the individual's condition, regular body acupuncture, electrical acupuncture, and moxibustion can be combined with scalp acupuncture to speed up recovery. Treatments should be done at regular intervals, and common points are Ya Men (GV 15), Lian Quan (CV 23), Tong Li (Ht 5), and Tai Chong (Liv 3).[42] Electrical stimulation is very helpful if the practitioner has difficulty performing the rotation of the needle more than 200 times per minute. It is suggested that only two of the scalp needles be stimulated at any one session, or the brain can become too confused to respond. Moxibustion can enhance the therapeutic results of scalp acupuncture, especially for older or weaker patients. Because of its excellent outcome in most cases, the practitioner should consider scalp acupuncture as the primary approach, rather than a complementary approach, to the patient with expressive aphasia.

CASE HISTORY #20

Joe was 68 when he came by himself to our clinic for scalp acupuncture treatment of motor aphasia. He could not speak at all and had to write his chief complaints and medical history in order to communicate with us. After a stroke eight years prior, he had completely recovered from paralysis of his right leg and arm, but the aphasia remained unchanged. His tongue was red with a thin, yellow coating, and his pulses were wiry and fine.

Chinese medical pattern discrimination: Phlegm and heat obstructing the orifices

Scalp acupuncture treatment

Area selection
Primary area: Speech I Area
Secondary area: Head Area

Manipulation
Needles should be inserted in Speech I Area and stimulated bilaterally. Rotate the needles at least 200 times per minute with the thumb and index finger for 1–3 minutes, twirling them as vigorously as the patient can tolerate and having the patient move the affected limb actively and passively, if possible. Repeat the stimulation every 10 minutes. Regular acupuncture treatment has been found to enhance recovery from expressive aphasia. Common points are Ya Men (GV 15), Lian Quan (CV 23), Tong Li (Ht 5), and Tai Chong (Liv 3). During the treatment, some patients may feel heat, cold, tingling, numbness, heaviness, distention, or sensations of water or electricity in their

mouth, tongue, or throat. Those patients usually respond and show improvement more quickly. However, those who do not have such sensations could still have immediate positive results. Retain the needles for 30–45 minutes. Patients are given two to three treatments per week, and a therapeutic course consists of 10 treatments.

Results of Case #20

After we inserted two needles in Speech I Area of the temple region on each side of the head, Joe tried to talk with some sounds that were unintelligible. After we placed a needle in the point She Xia (extra point) under Joe's tongue, however, he immediately could count from one to 10. He was surprised when he was able to say "68" when asked his age. During this treatment he was able to say words of one or two syllables easily but still had difficulty with words of more than three syllables.

At the beginning of his second treatment, Joe told the doctor very slowly, "I am able to speak and tell you my name now." He could speak more clearly and faster when two needles were inserted on Speech I Area of his scalp again and with three more needles inserted in Ya Men (GV 15) on his neck and Tong Li (Ht 5) on his wrists. Joe was given the same treatment two more times and gradually experienced more improvement in his speech. He was completely cured after the fifth treatment with scalp acupuncture.

Research on the effect of scalp acupuncture for aphasia

- Chen Dao-yi reported the treatment of 109 cases of aphasia due to stroke using scalp acupuncture in 1987. All 109 patients were diagnosed through MRI to have had an infarction or hemorrhage in the brain. Patients were treated at Speech I Area and Speech III Area. Treatments were given once a day, a total of 15 treatments making a course. The results showed that 67 cases were cured, 19 cases were markedly improved, 15 cases showed some improvement, and 8 cases showed no improvement, yielding a total effective rate of 92.7%.[43]

Receptive Aphasia

Charles, a 36-year-old male, came to our clinic in Albuquerque, NM. Three months prior, he had been diagnosed with cerebral thrombosis in the left side of his brain. After the stroke, Charles had aphasia and was completely paralyzed on the right side of his body. Moving his right side had gradually improved. He could walk with a cane, but still had difficulty lifting his right leg and foot. Charles could only move his right arm a little but could hardly move his right hand and fingers at all. He had sensory aphasia, meaning that he could respond when questioned, but the answer did not make sense. For example, when asked what his name was, he said "Mary," and he replied "19" when asked his age. When counting, he could say the numbers one to five correctly, but then jumped to 16 and then to 20. In addition, he had trouble holding urine. His tongue was purple with a thick, white coating, and his pulses were wiry and slippery.

Chinese medical pattern discrimination: Phlegm and blood stasis obstructing the mind and orifices, kidney qi deficiency

Scalp acupuncture treatment

Area selection
Primary area: Speech III Area
Secondary area: Upper 1/5 Motor Area, middle 2/5 Motor Area

Manipulation

Needles should be inserted in the Speech III Area and stimulated bilaterally depending on the affected areas of the patient's brain. Since most aphasia is accompanied by paralysis, Motor Area should be needled accordingly. If paralysis is in the upper limb, the middle 2/5 Motor Area should be chosen; if in the leg and foot, the upper 1/5 should be the choice; if in the face, the lower 2/5 should be selected. If there are some abnormal sensations in the leg and foot, arm, and hand or face, the upper 1/5, middle 2/5, or lower 2/5 should be chosen respectively. The chosen insertion area should be the opposite of the affected limb. Rotate the needles at least 200 times per minute with the thumb and index finger for 1–3 minutes, twirling them as vigorously as the patient can tolerate and having the patient move the affected limb actively and passively during treatment. Repeat the stimulation every 10 minutes. During treatment, some patients may feel heat, cold, tingling, numbness, heaviness, distention, or sensations of water or electricity moving down the affected limb. Those patients usually respond and show improvement more quickly. Encourage patients to talk, read, or make conversation during treatments. This is necessary not only to exercise their speech function, but also to evaluate the degree to which they are recovering. Retain the needles for 30–45 minutes. Patients are given two to three treatments per week, and a therapeutic course consists of 10 treatments.

Results of Case #21

Charles had very quick, positive responses during his first scalp acupuncture treatment. He felt tingling sensations in his right arm, hand, and fingers and a hot sensation in his right leg and foot after the needles were inserted in his scalp. Five minutes later, he was able to lift his right leg and foot while walking, and the right side of his body was less heavy. After another few minutes, he was able to raise his right arm above his shoulder and his right hand and fingers started to move, enabling him to close his right hand and shake hands. However, the sensory aphasia remained unchanged. During the second treatment, Charles correctly replied "Charles" when asked his first name. He was able to count from one to 10 without a mistake, and then counted from one to 20. At the beginning of the sixth treatment, Charles reported that he had little trouble finding correct words when speaking and had no problem holding urine. He was able to move his right arm and hand slowly due to initial stiffness, but the right arm and leg felt tight. His walking was almost normal but slow. His tongue had changed to slightly purple with a thin white coating; his pulses were slippery and slightly wiry. The treatment strategy was modified according to his clinical manifestations. Chorea and Tremor Area in the scalp was added bilaterally to address the tenseness in his right upper and lower limbs. Body point Nei Guan (Per 6) in the right arm, San Yin Jiao (Sp 6) in the right leg, and Lian Quan (CV 23) in the neck were added to enhance the scalp acupuncture stimulation. During the sixth treatment Charles demonstrated that he had no problem with speaking and the right upper and lower limbs became much looser while he was exercising. He had started to drive again and was returning to a more normal life.

Discussion

Scalp acupuncture for treatment of aphasia strives to improve a patient's ability to communicate by helping the person restore language abilities as much as possible and by using remaining abilities to compensate for language problems. The potential for functional recovery from receptive aphasia after a stroke is not as good as for expressive aphasia, but most patients show some improvement and some make a full recovery. Patients should get scalp acupuncture treatment as soon as their condition is stable, the earlier, the better the prognosis. Most aphasia patients treated at our clinic show some improvement within five scalp acupuncture treatments, and some of them appear better at the first session. For patients who are extremely sensitive to needles, stimulation by twirling should be avoided in the first one or two sessions. When treating patients with aphasia it is important to observe their responses and reactions while inserting, stimulating, and withdrawing the needles and to adjust techniques accordingly. Also body acupuncture can enhance the therapeutic results of scalp acupuncture, especially for those who have less positive responses to treatment via the scalp in early sessions. Commonly used points are Lian Quan (CV 23), Nei Guan (Per 6), Zhao Hai (Ki 6), San Yin Jiao (Sp 6) and Ya Men (GV 15) for moving energy and opening orifices.

Learning other methods of communication is also an important goal. Speech therapy may rehabilitate patient's language skills and provide them with better communication experiences. However, recovery of language skills is usually a relatively slow process and few patients regain pre-damage communication levels. Speech therapy should begin as soon as possible and be tailored to the individual needs of the patient. For most cases of aphasia treated by speech therapy alone, language recovery is not as rapid or as complete as it is when combined with scalp acupuncture. Together, these two modalities allow those with aphasia to have brighter hopes for recovery in the future.

Anomic Aphasia

Teresa was 58 when she came to our scalp acupuncture seminar in Washington, DC, accompanied by her daughter, who gave a brief medical history. A year before Teresa had a stroke that affected the left side of her brain. Initially she was totally paralyzed on the right side and could not speak. Starting two weeks later, she started receiving physical therapy and speech therapy. The aphasia gradually improved and Teresa was able to say simple things, but could not speak in long sentences, nor could she name objects. Luckily, her right arm and hand completely recovered, but she still dragged her right foot while walking. Because the aphasia and paralysis of the right foot had shown no further improvement during the past three months, her primary care physician recommended that she try acupuncture treatment. Upon examination, her tongue was purple with a thin, white coating, and her pulses were fine and wiry.

Chinese medical pattern discrimination: Qi stagnation and blood stasis obstructing the orifices

Scalp acupuncture treatment

Area selection
Primary area: Speech II
Secondary area: Speech III, upper 1/5 Motor Area

Manipulation
For treating anomic aphasia, insert the needles in Speech III and Speech II Areas bilaterally and rotate them at least 200 revolutions per minute for 1–3 minutes every 10 minutes for a total of 30–45 minutes. For treating right foot paralysis, insert needles in the upper 1/5 Motor Area. Generally speaking, the paralyzed extremity is treated by choosing the opposite side of the Motor Area in the scalp. However, for patients where part of the brain was removed by surgery, needle the same side of the scalp as the paralyzed limb. Twirl the needles as vigorously as patients can tolerate, and if possible, have

patients move their affected limb actively and passively. It is helpful to have the patient talk or walk, with or without assistance, between stimulations. During treatment, some patients may have sensations of heat, cold, tingling, numbness, heaviness, distention, or water or electricity moving in their throat and tongue or affected limb. Those patients usually respond and show improvement more quickly. Initially, the treatment should be two to three times a week until major improvements are achieved, then once weekly, every two weeks, and then spaced out as indicated by the patient's condition. A therapeutic course consists of 10 treatments.

Results of Case #22

Teresa was instructed to do some passive exercise, having her daughter move her right leg and foot during the treatment. Then she was instructed to walk by concentrating the energy flow from her brain to her right foot. The audience was surprised to observe that Teresa could lift her right foot normally. When asked what a cup was, she replied, "It is something for holding water for drinking." Asked what a pen was, she said, "It is something for writing." Although she was able to answer questions from the audience, still she could not give the exact names for objects. At the end of Teresa's treatment, we inserted two more needles in the Speech I Area of her scalp, one on each side. When a pen was held up and we asked her what it was, she responded, "It is a pen." The audience applauded.

Discussion

Patients with anomic aphasia usually have fluent speech, intact auditory and writing comprehension, but an inability to name objects. Anomic or "not naming" often is an initial presentation of aphasia and sometimes it may follow recovery from another type. It is less specific in lesion location than other aphasias previously discussed. It may occur with lesions in the parietal lobe, the dorso-lateral frontal cortex, or the thalamus. This may be the reason that Teresa showed significant improvement after all of her Speech areas were stimulated.

Scalp acupuncture has a fairly good effect on anomic aphasia. It can stimulate and restore affected brain tissue or retrain unaffected brain tissue to take over the lost functions of damaged brain areas. In this case, anomic aphasia was caused by stroke, which has the best prognosis compared to head injury or brain tumor. It is necessary to mention that this patient got only one scalp acupuncture treatment and recovered completely, but this is quite unusual. In our practice it often takes from several weeks to several months for stroke patients to improve and recover. The timeframe is important. The earlier that stroke patients get treatment, the better the prognosis. The longer the duration of the impairment, the more gradual will be the improvement.

Spasmodic Dysphonia

CASE HISTORY #23

Judy was 38 and a high school physical education teacher when she returned to our clinic in Albuquerque, NM, after being successfully treated for low back pain by acupuncture 10 years previously. She returned seeking help for dysphonia, or difficulty in speaking associated with noticeable hoarseness. Her dysphonia started after trying a new medication for anxiety brought on by major stress at work. She also developed nervousness, insomnia, and fatigue. Judy could not say any words starting with 'S' or 'R' after she took the new anti-anxiety medication. Although her physician declared that her dysphonia had nothing to do with the medication, Judy decided to stop taking it right away. Unfortunately, the dysphonia did not disappear and she could no longer keep her job. Her speech worsened and sometimes disappeared completely. Her voice began with hoarseness and some cracking but worsened to the point where she could barely make herself understood. Judy saw a few physicians and speech therapists but showed no improvement. A surgeon could not guarantee to cure the problem. In addition to dysphonia, she became progressively more sensitive to stress and developed depression, headache, poor memory and concentration, plus increased frequency of anxiety attacks. All her symptoms worsened. Examination showed that her face was stiff and her jaws and throat became visibly tense and strained when she attempted to speak. Her tongue was red with teeth marks and a thin, white coating, and her pulses were wiry and fine.

Chinese medical pattern discrimination: Kidney yin and essence deficiency, liver qi binding stagnation

Scalp acupuncture treatment

Area selection

Primary area: Speech I Area, Chorea and Tremor Area
Secondary area: Head Area

Manipulation

Needles should be inserted in Speech I and Chorea and Tremor Areas and stimulated bilaterally. Since most patients with dysphonia are accompanied by emotional changes, the Head Area should be chosen. Rotate the needles at least 200 times per minute with the thumb and index finger for 1–3 minutes, twirling them as vigorously as the patient can tolerate and having the patient move his/her tongue and practice speech actively during treatment. Repeat the stimulation every 10 minutes. During treatment, some have sensations of twitching, tingling, numbness, heaviness, distention, or sensations of water or electricity around their throat or vocal cords. Those patients usually respond and show improvement more quickly. Encourage patients to speak, read aloud, or make conversation during treatments. This is necessary not only to exercise their speech function, but also to evaluate the degree to which they are recovering. Retain the needles for 30–45 minutes. Patients are given two to three treatments per week, and a therapeutic course consists of 10 treatments.

Results of Case #23

Judy felt a twitching and tingling sensation in her throat and tongue after needles were inserted in her scalp. During her first scalp acupuncture treatment, the tenseness in her face and jaws considerably diminished. She was gradually able to speak more words beginning with "S" and "R," but still had some difficulty a third of the time. Judy's speech showed steady progress with each additional treatment. Also her general well-being including sleep, energy, mental activity, and emotions noticeably improved. After the fifth treatment, her speech was much clearer and sometimes she was able to clearly enunciate a long sentence without making a mistake. After eight treatments, Judy's speech was completely restored to normal.

Discussion

Spasmodic dysphonia is a voice disorder caused by involuntary movement of one or more muscles of the larynx. There are three types of spasmodic dysphonia: adductor, abductor, and mixed spasmodic dysphonia. Adductor spasmodic dysphonia is characterized by words that are often cut off or difficult to start because of muscle spasms. Speech may be choppy and sound similar to stuttering. Patients with abductor spasmodic dysphonia often sound weak, quiet, breathy, or whispery. Mixed spasmodic dysphonia has characteristics of both adductor and abductor spasmodic dysphonia. The cause of this disorder remains a medical mystery. Some scholars believe that it results from a neurohormonal imbalance that involves the basal ganglia in the central nervous system, which ultimately manifests peripherally in the throat through the extrapyramidal motor system. Because currently accepted theories lack any appreciation of the underlying disordered energetic functioning, current Western medical treatments remain necessarily mechanistic and pragmatic such as speech therapy, psychotherapy, injection of Botox, medication, or surgery. In Western medicine, there is not any specific effective treatment, and there is presently no cure for spasmodic dysphonia.

In contrast, Chinese scalp acupuncture offers very good results for patients with spasmodic dysphonia. Several patients treated with scalp acupuncture at our clinics have shown some immediate improvement. However, treating patients with spasmodic dysphonia is challenging because they cannot speak or report clearly, and it requires good communication skills.

Family members need to learn the best ways to assist their loved ones with exercises in order to help them regain their speech function. A helpful approach is for the doctor and family members to work together in order to observe even the finest changes of speech function during the treatment. For patients who are extremely sensitive to needles, stimulation should be avoided in the first one or two sessions. When treating patients with dysphonia, it is important to observe their responses and reactions while inserting, stimulating, and withdrawing the needles, and adjust the techniques accordingly.

Body acupuncture can enhance the therapeutic results of scalp acupuncture, especially for those who have less positive responses to scalp acupuncture in early treatments. Commonly used points are Lie Que (Lu 7), Tai Chong (Liv 3), and Yang Ling Quan (GB 34) for moving qi, relieving spasm, and opening orifices.

Speech therapy may rehabilitate patients' language skills and provide them with positive communication experiences. Speech therapy should begin as soon as possible and be tailored to the individual needs of the patient. However, for most cases of dysphonia treated by speech therapy alone, language recovery is not as rapid or as complete as when combined with scalp acupuncture. Together, these two modalities give those with dysphonia brighter hopes for recovery.

Vocal Cord Paralysis

CASE HISTORY #24

Sherry, a 36-year-old female, came to our clinic in Santa Fe, NM. She had lost her voice after a surgical procedure for a thyroid tumor that paralyzed the right side of her vocal cords. She had tried many different therapies, including speech therapy for two months, with no positive results. It was impossible for her to keep her job, where typically she gave a speech every day. At first, Sherry was frustrated and worried, but then developed anxiety and depression. She could not sleep at night, felt constant fatigue, and could not concentrate. Her tongue was red with teeth marks and a thin, white coating, and her pulses were fine and wiry.

Chinese medical pattern discrimination: Liver qi binding stagnation, heart and kidney qi deficiency

Scalp acupuncture treatment

Area selection

Primary area: Speech I Area
Secondary area: Head Area

Manipulation

Insert needles in the Speech I and Chorea and Tremor Areas and stimulate bilaterally. Since most dysphonia is accompanied by emotional changes, the Head Area should be chosen unilaterally. Rotate the needles at least 200 times per minute with the thumb and index finger for 1–3 minutes, twirling them as vigorously as the patient can tolerate and having the patient move his/her tongue and practice speech actively during treatment. Repeat the stimulation every 10 minutes. During treatment, some patients may sensations of twitching, tingling, numbness, heaviness, or distention around their throat or vocal cords. Those patients usually respond and show improvement more quickly. Encourage patients to talk, read aloud, or converse with them during treatment. This is necessary not only to exercise their speech function, but also to evaluate the degree to which they are recovering. Patients with dysphonia from vocal cord paralysis should avoid hot and spicy food, which often irritates the throat and affects the results of acupuncture treatment. Retain the needles for 30–45 minutes. Patients are given two to three treatments per week, and a therapeutic course consists of 10 treatments.

Results of Case #24

Sherry felt a twitching sensation in her vocal cords after needles were inserted in her scalp. During her first treatment she was able to speak, but in such a low voice that it was inaudible farther than one foot away. Her voice improved a little with each additional treatment. At the same time, her general well-being including sleep, energy, mental activity, and emotion noticeably improved. After the fifth treatment, Sherry's voice was much louder, and sometimes she was able to clearly enunciate a long sentence by changing the volume of her voice. After 12 scalp acupuncture treatments, Sherry's voice was completely restored. Her neurosurgeon said she had never before seen a patient with vocal cord impairment speak so clearly.

Discussion

Dysphonia is a voice disorder characterized by hoarseness, weakness, or even loss of voice. This can occur if the nerves controlling the functions of the larynx are impaired as a result of an accident, a surgical procedure, or a viral infection. Overuse and emotional stress can cause loss of voice as well. Sometimes the trouble stems from paralysis that damages the nerves that move the vocal cords. Essentially, airflow from the lungs generates voice. The vocal folds vibrate when air is pushed past them with sufficient pressure. Without normal vibration of the vocal folds in the larynx, the sound of speech is not present.

Scalp acupuncture has a good effect on dysphonia due to vocal cord paralysis resulting from different reasons. Patients should receive treatment as soon as possible. The earlier the patient gets treatment, the better the prognosis. Most aphasia patients at our clinic show some improvement within three scalp acupuncture sessions and some improve at the first session. When treating patients with aphasia or dysphonia, it is important to observe their responses and reactions while inserting, stimulating, and withdrawing the needles and adjust the techniques accordingly. Also body acupuncture can enhance the therapeutic results of scalp acupuncture, especially for those who have less positive responses in early treatments. Commonly used points are He Gu (LI 4), Lian Quan (CV 23), Nei Guan (Per 6), and Feng Chi (GB 20) moving energy and opening orifices.

CHAPTER EIGHT

Sense Organ Disorders

The part of the central nervous system that processes sensory information comprises the sensory system, which consists of sensory receptors, neural pathways, and parts of the brain involved in sensory perception. Traditionally, there are five senses: sight, smell, taste, touch, and hearing. All sensation must be processed in the brain by a normally functioning central nervous system for proper perception.

In addition, each sensation is perceived through a specific sense organ. Each of these consists of specialized cells that have receptors for specific stimuli such as sound or taste. From these special sensory receptors, 12 pairs of cranial nerves transmit information about the senses of balance, smell, sight, taste, touch, and hearing. This information is processed in the central nervous system and thus sent to the brain. There, instructions are formulated that travel through the cranial nerves to the skeletal muscles. In the face and throat, for example, these muscles control movements for smiling and swallowing.

A brief review of the sense organs will be given here. The eye is the organ of vision. Sight is the most developed sense in humans, followed closely by hearing. The ear is the organ of hearing. The receptors for taste, called taste buds, are situated chiefly on the tongue, but they are also found in the roof of the mouth and near the pharynx. They are able to detect four basic tastes: sweet, salty, bitter, and sour. The nose is the organ responsible for the sense of smell. The sense of touch is spread throughout the body. Nerve endings in the skin and other parts of the body transmit touch sensations to the brain. Four kinds of touch sensations can be identified: cold, heat, contact, and pain. In addition to sight, smell, taste, touch, and hearing, humans also sense balance, pressure, temperature, pain, and motion that may involve the coordinated use of multiple sensory organs. For example, the sense of balance is maintained by a complex interaction of visual inputs, the proprioceptive sensors, the inner ear vestibular system, and the central nervous system.

The disorders of the sense organs discussed in this chapter are a group of neurological disorders that involve the central nervous system. They involve neurological diseases or injury that cause impairments to vision, hearing, taste, smell, or touch. Sense organs are vulnerable to various disorders and can be damaged by trauma, infections, degeneration, structural defects, tumors, blood flow disruption, and autoimmune disorders. Diseases of the brain, such as multiple sclerosis, stroke, tumors, and Parkinson's disease can often result in dysfunctions of vision, hearing, taste, smell, and touch.

Any sudden or gradual changes in the five senses should be brought to a physician's attention promptly, since early diagnosis and treatment are usually effective and can prevent serious deterioration. Scalp acupuncture has been proven to have very effective results in treating many types of sensory disorders due to brain damage. It usually brings about improvement immediately, sometimes taking only one to two treatments. The disorders discussed in this chapter are commonly seen in our practice of scalp acupuncture.

Ménière's Syndrome

Ménière's syndrome is characterized by the buildup of fluid volume in the semi-circular canals causing elevated pressure in the ear. The pattern and incidence of the symptoms may vary from patient to patient, but the general symptoms are the same: dizziness, vertigo, headache, tinnitus, and the sensation of pressure in the ear. There may also be severe nausea and vomiting and profuse sweating during an acute episode. In some cases, there is progressive deafness in the affected ear, often leading to a permanent hearing disability or entire hearing loss. The cause of Ménière's syndrome, as defined by Western medicine, is unknown, so there is no specific treatment in conventional medicine.

CASE HISTORY #25

Larry was 41 when he came to our clinic in Albuquerque, NM. He had been suffering from constant dizziness and vertigo for more than two weeks. He was diagnosed with Ménière's syndrome. The vertigo was so severe that he felt the whole room was violently spinning and he fell down easily if standing by himself. He had to spend whole days flat on his back with his eyes closed in order to avoid head movement that aggravated the vertigo. Larry experienced nausea, vomiting, temporal headaches, and a sensation of fullness in his ears. All symptoms were exacerbated due to severe stress at work. Other symptoms included constipation, dry mouth, excessive thirst, blurring of vision, and tinnitus at a high pitch. He had become quite irritable, angry, and frustrated. His complexion was red and urine was yellow. His tongue was red with a thick, yellow coating, and he had large, tight, and slippery pulses.

Chinese medical pattern discrimination: Hyperactivity of liver yang with liver wind stirring internally, damp heat in the middle burner

Scalp acupuncture treatment

Area selection

Primary area: Vertigo and Hearing Area
Secondary area: Liver Area

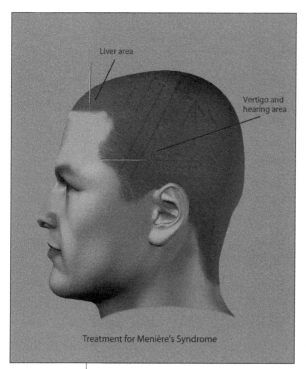

Liver area

Vertigo and
hearing area

Treatment for Menière's Syndrome

Manipulation

Needles should be inserted in the Vertigo and Hearing Area and stimulated bilaterally. The Vertigo and Hearing Area is relatively sensitive to scalp acupuncture because of the temporalis muscle under the skin, which has more blood vessels than other nearby tissue. Always put one needle in ear point Shen Men to help patients relax and reduce the sensitivity of needle insertion and stimulation of the scalp. Pay attention to the angle of needle insertion and make sure it is 15–25 degrees from the skin of the scalp. If needles are inserted in the wrong layer of the scalp, especially into the muscle, it is painful enough that some patients cannot tolerate it and must stop treatment. Rotate the needles at least 200 times per minute with the thumb and index finger for 1–3 minutes, twirling them as vigorously as the patient can tolerate and repeating stimulation every 10 minutes. During treatment, some patients may feel their vision change or have sensations of pressure, fullness, or tic in their eye or ear. Patients with some or all of these sensations usually respond and improve more quickly. Retain the needles for 25–30 minutes. Treatment is given two to three times per week, and a therapeutic course consists of 10 treatments.

Results of Case #25

During the first scalp acupuncture treatment, Larry reported that a "curtain" in front of his eyes felt like it was liftiing. This sensation cleared his mind, and the blurred vision and headache disappeared. Quickly following these results, the vertigo and dizziness diminished significantly. After this first treatment, he was able to walk to the secretary's desk to pay his bill and make another appointment without assistance. Larry had not had any episodes of dizziness and vertigo since the first treatment and had resumed driving to work. The anger and frustration diminished dramatically, and he did not experience tinnitus or constipation anymore. After the fifth and last treatment, his urine cleared, his tongue changed to slightly red with a thin, white coating, and the pulses softened. In the following 12 years, the patient had only one episode of vertigo and dizziness, due to high stress at work. After two scalp acupuncture sessions, Larry recovered again.

Discussion

Scalp acupuncture has a remarkable effect on Ménière's syndrome as well as dizziness and vertigo from other causes such as hypertension, hypotension, anemia, and hypoglycemia. About 85% of the patients we have treated with scalp acupuncture due to these conditions show immediate positive results during the initial visit. Most only need four to eight treatments to be free of symptoms, which is fewer sessions than with regular body acupuncture and ear acupuncture. In our practice, however, we have found that it is very helpful to use other acupuncture methods along with scalp acupuncture. The selection of body acupuncture points should be individualized based on the differentiation of patterns in Chinese medicine. For instance, Xing Jian (Liv 2) and Zu Lin Qi (GB 41) are for hyperactivity for liver yang, Feng Long (St 40) and Yin Ling Quan (Sp 9) for retention of dampness and phlegm, Zu San Li (St 36) and San Yin Jiao (Sp 6) for deficiency of qi and blood, and Tai Xi (Ki 3) and Zhao Hai (Ki 6) for depletion of kidneys. Body acupuncture can enhance the results of scalp acupuncture and address underlying constitutional disorders. When combined, scalp and body acupuncture treat root problems of dizziness and vertigo and prevent them from reoccurring.

Tinnitus

Tinnitus is a perception of sound in the absence of an acoustic stimulus. The sound may be high-pitched like whistling, roaring, or hissing, or low pitched such as buzzing, ringing, and humming. Tinnitus may be intermittent, continuous, or pulsatile, and it can be in one or both ears. The mechanisms causing tinnitus are obscure. The common causes are ear infections and inflammation, Menière's syndrome, acoustic neuroma, benign tumors, anemia, hypertension, hypothyroidism, head trauma, and side effects of some drugs. So far there is no specific medical or surgical therapy for tinnitus in Western medicine.

CASE HISTORY #26

Mary came to our clinic at age 48 having suffered from tinnitus for two and a half years. She reported that the onset came from battling emotional stress for a long time. She said the constant ringing in her ears was very high-pitched like a hissing teakettle. Sometimes it sounded like fingernails scratching on metal. She tried to relax through meditation, yoga, and other exercises, as well as changing her diet, but the intrusive noises in her ears remained. There was an increase in intense anxiety, irritability, and depression, and Mary suffered from fatigue due to lack of sleep. Other symptoms included no appetite, diarrhea, and an inability to relax. An otolaryngologist and an audiologist offered medications to treat anxiety, depression, and insomnia, but no relief for tinnitus. The initial examination revealed that the tongue was red with a thick, white coating. There was tremor on the tongue and teethmarks on the front and sides of the tongue. Her pulses were wiry and fine, and the cubit (*chi*) positions were noticeably weaker bilaterally than the other positions.

Chinese medical pattern discrimination: Liver qi binding stagnation with occasional flaring of liver heat, spleen qi deficiency

Scalp acupuncture treatment

Area selection
Primary area: Vertigo and Hearing Area
Secondary area: Head Area and Thoracic Cavity Area

Manipulation
For tinnitus and dizziness, needles should be inserted in the Thoracic Cavity Area and stimulated bilaterally, while the Head Area should be stimulated

unilaterally. Vertigo and Hearing Area is relatively sensitive to scalp acupuncture treatments because of the temporalis muscle with its many blood vessels just under the skin. Always insert one needle in ear point Shen Men to help patients relax and reduce the sensitivity of needle insertion and stimulation of the scalp. Pay attention to the angle of needle insertion and make sure it is at an oblique or acute angle of about 15–25 degrees. If needles are inserted in the wrong layer of the scalp, especially in the muscle, it is painful enough that sometimes treatment must stop. Rotate the needles at least 200 times per minute with the thumb and index finger for 1–3 minutes, twirling them as vigorously as the patient can tolerate and repeating the stimulation every 10 minutes. During treatment, some patients may feel sensations of pressure or fullness in their ears. Patients who experience these responses usually improve more quickly. Retain the needles for 25–30 minutes. Give treatment two to three times per week; a therapeutic course consists of 10 treatments.

Results of Case #26

During the initial session, Mary felt relaxed and then fell asleep. When she awoke she reported that the pressure and sensation of fullness in her ears were greatly relieved, and the ringing sensation seemed a little diminished as well. At the beginning of the second treatment, she reported that she had slept much better for several nights, and the ringing in her ears had changed from a high pitch to a low pitch like a buzzing or humming sound, which she could tolerate much better. The mood swings including depression, anxiety, and irritability were better, the loss of appetite was significantly improved, and she had not had diarrhea since the last treatment. The tinnitus and other symptoms continued to improve in the following sessions. At the sixth treatment, the ringing in her ears had become intermittent, and noises in her ears seemed to be moving away from her head and fading into the background. Other symptoms had almost completely disappeared. Her tongue had turned a light red with a thin, white coating, and the tremor was gone. The teethmarks on the tongue were better, and the pulses had become softer and only slightly wiry. By the tenth visit, the tinnitus was completely gone, allowing Mary to enjoy her life again.

Discussion

Scalp acupuncture has a fairly good track record for controlling tinnitus. However, treatment should be directed at the underlying cause if that is known. In addition to scalp acupuncture, the selection of body acupuncture points should be individualized, based on the differentiation of patterns in Chinese medicine. For instance, Xing Jian (Liv 2), Tai Chong (Liv 3), and Zhong Zhu (TB 3) would be selected for retention of damp heat in the liver and gallbladder, and Tai Xi (Ki 3), Zhao Hai (Ki 6), and Fu Liu (Ki 7) would be used for kidney weakness and deficiency.

The types of sound heard by those with tinnitus do not necessarily indicate what the underlying causes are, in terms of Western medicine. They do, however, provide clues for the treatment strategy in Chinese medicine. Generally speaking, sounds with high pitch indicate an excessive condition that requires reducing or draining techniques, while lowpitched sounds indicate a deficient condition that requires reinforcing or supplementing techniques. In addition, tinnitus often gets worse with any type of stress. Therefore the scalp areas that have the function of relieving anxiety, irritability, or depression should be combined with the Vertigo and Hearing area for best results. Other therapies that promote relaxation and a sense of well-being such as meditation, hypnosis, yoga, and herbs may be helpful in relieving tinnitus or the distress it causes.

Hearing Loss

Loss of hearing refers to conditions in which individuals are fully or partially unable to detect or perceive sound. Ordinarily, sound travels as waves, which are collected by the external ear and cause the tympanic membrane to vibrate. Sound energy passes through the air of the external ear, the bones of the middle ear, and the liquid of the inner ear. Then it is translated into nerve impulses and sent to the brain. There may be a dysfunction in hearing if any of the above-mentioned processes are interrupted. It is known as conductive hearing loss when interruption occurs in the external or middle ear, and it is called sensory hearing loss when there is damage to the cortex and acoustic nerve. Neural hearing loss is mostly caused by damage to the acoustic nerve and the parts of the brain that control hearing. Removing the blockages, such as earwax, infection, or tumor, usually solves conductive hearing loss. However, there is no effective treatment in Western medicine for hearing loss due to sensory or neural causes.

In Chinese medicine, hearing loss is usually believed to be due to a decline in kidney function.

Judy was 44 when she came to our clinic in Santa Fe, NM, in 2000 with a complaint of hearing loss in the left ear that occurred after an ear infection a few months before. Her physician had said that the hearing loss was permanent. Since the infection, she also had experienced constant congestion and pressure in the left ear. Examination revealed a red tongue with teethmarks and a thin, white coating. The pulses were wiry and slippery with less strength in the cubit (*chi*) positions bilaterally.

Chinese medical pattern discrimination: Kidney yin and yang deficiency

Scalp acupuncture treatment

Area selection

Primary area: Vertigo and Hearing Area
Secondary area: Reproductive Area

Manipulation

Needles should be inserted in the Vertigo and Hearing Area and stimulated bilaterally. Rotate the needles at least 200 times per minute with the thumb and index finger for 1–3 minutes. Vertigo and Hearing Area is relatively sensitive to scalp acupuncture treatment because of the temporalis muscle with its many blood vessels just under the skin. Always place a needle in the ear point Shen Men to help the patient relax and reduce the sensitivity of needle insertion and stimulation of the scalp. Pay attention to the angle of needle insertion and make sure it is at an oblique angle of about 15–25 degrees. Twirl the needles as vigorously as the patient can tolerate and repeat stimulation every 10 minutes. During treatment, some patients may feel sensations of pressure, fullness, or tics in their ears, and those patients may improve more quickly. Retain the needles for 25–30 minutes. Treatment should be given two to three times per week, and a therapeutic course consists of 10 treatments.

Results of Case #27

During the first scalp acupuncture treatment, Judy experienced very positive results. After two needles were inserted she felt the pressure and congestion in her ear gradually subside and her hearing improved. At the second treatment, Judy reported her hearing had increased by about three-quarters and the pressure and congestion were gone from the left ear. The second treatment caused total improvement in her hearing, and treatment was complete.

Discussion

Scalp acupuncture may help patients with sensory and neural hearing loss to improve the circulation of fluids in the head that lead to chronic congestion and noises or restore the ear function involved in transmitting signals from the inner ear to the brain. In our practice we have found that it is helpful also to use body acupuncture in these cases. The points should be individualized based on the differentiation of patterns in Chinese medicine. For instance, Xing Jian (Liv 2), Zhu Lin Qi (GB 41), Zhong Zhu (TW 3) are for retention of damp-heat in the liver and gallbladder, and Tai Xi (Ki 3), Shen Shu (Bl 23), and Zhao Hai (Ki 6) for depletion of the kidneys.

Vision Loss

Blindness is the condition of losing visual perception due to physiological or neurological factors. Total blindness is the complete lack of visual light perception and is clinically recorded as NLP, an abbreviation for no light perception. Blindness sometimes refers to severe visual impairment with only light perception. In those cases, the person has no more sight than the ability to tell light from dark and the general direction of a light source. Serious visual impairment has a variety of causes. The most common causes of blindness are diabetes, glaucoma, macular degeneration, accidents, cataracts, onchocerciasis, trachoma, and leprosy. People with injuries to the occipital lobe of the brain may still be partially or totally blind despite having undamaged eyes and optic nerves.

CASE HISTORY #28

Terry, a 46-year-old male in a wheelchair, was brought to our clinic in Albuquerque, NM. He had paralysis and pain in the left arm and leg and was blind since having a stroke three months before. He had received physical therapy for two months with no improvement. Upon examination, it was found that the left hand and foot had no movement at all, and the left arm showed a little movement. Terry could see some very bright light occasionally. His tongue was red with a thin, white coating, and his pulses were bilaterally wiry and slippery.

Chinese medical pattern discrimination: Qi stagnation with phlegm obstructing the channels

Scalp acupuncture treatment

Area selection
Primary area: Vision Area
Secondary area: Liver Area

Manipulation
The Vision Area is the primary center to treat blindness and other eye disorders. The Liver Area is another important treatment site. Needles should be inserted in both areas and stimulated bilaterally. Proper manipulation techniques are crucial in obtaining the desired results. Rotate the needles at least 200 times per minute with the thumb and index finger for 1–3 minutes, twirling them as vigorously as the patient can tolerate and repeating the stimulation every 10 minutes. As mentioned previously, during treatment some patients have sensations of heat, cold, tingling, numbness, heaviness,

distention, or the feeling of water or electricity moving along their spine, legs, or feet. Patients with some or all of these sensations usually respond and improve more quickly. Retain the needles for 30–45 minutes. Patients are treated two to three times a week depending upon the degree of blindness or paralysis. A therapeutic course consists of 10 treatments.

Results of Case #28

During the first consultation, we told Terry that he had a good chance to regain movement in his left arm and leg, but restoring vision was not certain. According to Western medical literature, blindness is not usually reversible. With the first scalp acupuncture treatment, Terry had a positive response. He was able to lift his left arm and move his left leg 10 minutes after the needles were inserted. His vision, however, showed no change. During the second treatment, Terry showed more improvement with the formerly paralyzed left arm and leg. He reported seeing flashing lights as the needle in his scalp on the occipital area was stimulated. We held up different numbers of fingers to test if Terry's vision had actually changed, but he got the correct response only half the time. The results were the same during the following two treatments.

A change occurred during the fifth treatment, when Terry noticed that the doctor had a mustache. When asked why he could correctly identify the number of fingers held up only half the time, Terry replied that his flash visions turned on and off by chance outside of his control.

Another unusual occurrence came during the eighth treatment. Terry said the scalp acupuncture worked like an electrical switch; his sight turned on when we inserted the needles and turned off when we removed them. He wanted more treatments and of a longer duration. After the eighteenth session, though his vision was still only present when there were needles in his scalp, Terry walked out of our clinic without assistance. He could lift his left arm above his head and use his left hand for many functions.

We also used other acupuncture techniques, such as putting needles in the local point Jing Ming (Bl 1) and at some distal points such as Tai Chong (Liv

3) and Guang Ming (GB 37), which have proven effective for eye disorders, but Terry's vision stayed unchanged. He could see everything when the needles were in his scalp and was blind as soon as the needles were removed.

At the nineteenth treatment, we suggested trying *qi gong* therapy for blindness. After inserting two needles in the Vision Area of the occipital region, we held the needle handles and performed *qi gong* therapy for 10 minutes. Although there was no immediate improvement, the family was told to pay attention to Terry's vision because it might improve within a few hours or a day after *qi gong* therapy. The next morning, we received a phone report that Terry's vision had returned early that day. Since then his vision has been permanently restored.

Discussion

Scalp acupuncture has been used to treat several eye disorders in our practice, but Terry is the only patient with blindness whom we have treated. Although good results were achieved in this case, the treatment of blindness is very challenging. Other acupuncture techniques for blindness have been proven effective as well, especially body acupuncture. Commonly used body points are: Jing Ming (Bl 1), Qiu Hou (extra point), Guang Ming (GB 37), and Tai Chong (Liv 3). Based on our clinical experience, electrical stimulation to the above points with high frequency and low intensity is also very helpful.

Qi gong is an ancient breathing technique combined with gentle movement and meditation to cleanse, strengthen, and circulate the life energy (qi) of the body. It is a powerful system originating in China to promote health and vitality and a tranquil state of mind. Many people practice *qi gong* for themselves the same way one might do a daily yoga practice, both for its preventative and self-healing value and as a type of deep breathing exercise. When a trained person uses *qi gong* to do health assessment and noncontact treatment, it is called external qi healing. While it can increase the efficacy of other treatments, extensive practice and meditation is required in order to achieve this type of healing power. External qi healing techniques may be used alone for wellness and treatment or may be combined with massage and acupuncture. It is necessary to mention that there are many people practicing external qi healing in the world, but few actually have mastered this powerful technique. This is the only case where the author (Jason Hao) has applied external qi healing because he is still training in this method.

Diplopia (Double Vision)

Diplopia (double vision) is the perception of two images from a single object. The double images may be horizontal, vertical, or diagonal in relationship to each other. When double vision occurs because the two eyes are not correctly aligned while they are aiming at an object, this is called binocular diplopia. It is called monocular diplopia when double vision occurs while viewing with only one eye. Alcohol intoxication or head injury such as concussion can cause temporary diplopia. The most common causes of double vision are misalignment of the two eyes due to functional problems in the visual system. Any problem that affects one or more of the muscles around the eyeball that control the direction of the gaze can cause binocular diplopia, especially damage to nerves controlling the extraocular muscles. Nerves can be injured by brain damage caused by multiple sclerosis, stroke, head trauma, a brain tumor, or infection. Western medical treatment for binocular diplopia includes surgical straightening of the eye, prism lenses, and vision therapy.

CASE HISTORY #29

Samuel, a 59-year-old male, came to our seminar in Pittsburgh, PA, in 2007. Since a car accident in 1970, he had suffered from double vision. Though he had seen many doctors, there was still no solution for it. He wore glasses to correct the double vision, but still, when looking a certain way, he experienced the problem. Samuel also suffered from headaches on the right side rated 6 on a scale of 1–10; the left side of his low back was in pain and rated an 8 out of 10. He also suffered from neck stiffness and often experienced tingling and numbness in his feet. His tongue had a red tip and was otherwise slightly purple with a thin, white coating. His pulses were slippery and wiry and, the cubit (*chi*) position pulses were bilaterally weaker than the other positions.

Chinese medical pattern discrimination: Liver blood-kidney yin and essence deficiency

Scalp acupuncture treatment

Area selection

Primary area: Vision Area, Foot Motor and Sensory Area, and lower 2/5 Motor Area
Secondary area: Liver Area

Manipulation

Vision Area, Foot Motor and Sensory Area, and Liver Area should be treated with needles bilaterally. Also, upper 1/5 Sensory Area should be needled on the left side of the scalp only. Because the Vision Area is one of the most sensitive, always insert a needle in ear point Shen Men to help the patient relax and to reduce the sensitivity of the needle insertions and stimulation of the scalp. Use the fewest number of needles possible in the scalp and rotate them at least 200 times per minute with the thumb and index finger for two minutes, twirling as gently as possible at the beginning so that the patient can tolerate the sensations better, and repeating the stimulation every 10 minutes. During treatment, patients may experience sensations of heat, cold, tingling, numbness, heaviness, distention, tears, or the sensation of water or electricity moving around the eyes or face. Keep the needles in place for 10–20 minutes. The treatment is given two times per week at the beginning and then gradually reduced to fewer sessions as the patient experiences improvement. A therapeutic course consists of 10 treatments.

Results of Case #29

Samuel had a very positive response to his first scalp acupuncture treatment. He felt more tingling sensations in his feet just a few minutes after the needles were inserted in his scalp. The pain in the left side of his lower back started to diminish five minutes later. After 15 minutes had passed, his headache disappeared and the numbness and tingling sensations in his feet showed some improvement as well. At the beginning of treatment he removed his glasses and experienced double vision immediately. At the end of the treatment, he reported that the double vision as well as the tingling and numbness in his feet were all completely gone. He was very happy that he did not need to wear glasses to correct his vision any more.

Discussion

Scalp acupuncture has a fairly good track record for controlling double vision. However, the treatment of double vision should be directed at the appropriate underlying condition if the cause is clear, such as in neurological disease. The selection of body acupuncture points should be individualized based on the differentiation of patterns in Chinese medicine. For instance, Qu Quan (Liv 8), Tai Chong (Liv 3), and Gong Sun (Sp 4) are chosen for deficiency of liver blood, and Gan Shu (Bl 18), Shen Shu (Bl 23), and Zhao Hai (Ki 6) for deficiency of kidney and liver yin.

CHAPTER NINE

Female and Male Disorders

Uterine Bleeding

Dysfunctional uterine bleeding is defined in three ways: abnormal, excessive uterine bleeding exceeding 80 ml daily, a woman having to change pads or tampons more than every one to two hours, or a period that lasts longer than seven days. According to Western medicine, excessive uterine bleeding is usually caused by disorders of the uterus, hormone imbalance, at-risk pregnancy, or approaching menopause. Mild uterine bleeding may cause anemia, but severe uterine bleeding may be life-threatening. The goals of treatment are to control the bleeding, reduce morbidity, and prevent complications.

In Chinese medicine, there are only four disease mechanisms for pathological bleeding. These are heat forcing the blood out of the channels, qi deficiency not holding the blood in its channels, blood stasis blocking the channels, or trauma cutting the channels. Most cases involve at least two of these disease mechanisms.

When traveling in China, I always carry acupuncture needles with me. Some time ago, while traveling by train from Harbin to Beijing, an announcement was made that a female traveler was in critical condition and any doctors on board were asked to attend her immediately. Responding to this summons, I found a woman in her early thirties suffering from severe uterine bleeding. She was semiconscious, manifested shortness of breath, and was extremely pale. Although several other doctors were present, they could not help her without coagulants or surgery. I was unsure if scalp acupuncture could help such a severe condition, but there were no better options available. The patient's tongue was very pale, and her pulses were faint.

Chinese medical pattern discrimination: Qi and blood deficiency

Scalp acupuncture treatment

Area selection
Primary area: Foot Motor and Sensory Area
Secondary area: Reproductive Area

Manipulation
Both Foot Motor and Sensory Area and the Reproductive Area should be needled and stimulated bilaterally. Throughout treatment, rotate the needles at least 200 times per minute for 1–3 minutes, twirling them as strongly as the patient can stand and repeating stimulation every 10 minutes. During treatment, patients may experience heat, cold, tingling, numbness, heaviness, distention, or the sensation of water or electricity moving along their chest and abdomen. Patients experiencing some or all of the sensations usually respond and improve more quickly. Retain the needles for 30–40 minutes.

Under normal circumstances, treatment is given two to three times per week. A therapeutic course consists of 10 treatments.

Results of Case #30

Although there was not time to determine a pattern discrimination, I immediately applied the scalp acupuncture and also inserted needles at San Yin Jiao (Sp 6) and Xue Hai (Sp 10). Two to three minutes after the needles were inserted and stimulated, the woman's complexion slowly regained some color, the shortness of breath improved, and the uterine bleeding had stopped. She soon opened her eyes and feebly thanked me. I continued to stimulate the needles every five minutes until the train reached its next destination three hours later. At that time the woman was in stable condition and was transferred to a local hospital.

Discussion

Scalp acupuncture at the Foot Motor and Sensory Area and Reproductive Area effectively controls uterine bleeding. To achieve even more striking results, combine scalp acupuncture with body acupuncture and moxibustion at San Yin Jiao (Sp 6) and Xue Hai (Sp 10). As documented, Chinese herbs are also very useful in controlling uterine bleeding. When bleeding is acute, in order to save the patient's life the doctor should administer *Yunnan Baiyao*. This is an ancient Chinese prepared medicine, which, if given immediately, stops bleeding very effectively. A patient with signs of hypovolemia should be hospitalized and undergo volume resuscitation. While treating a patient with chronic, recurrent bleeding, the Chinese herbs should be given based on the individual's pattern discrimination.

Impotence or Erectile Dysfunction

Impotence is a sexual dysfunction characterized by the inability to achieve or maintain an erection of the penis sufficient for sexual performance. The process of an erection is most often initiated as a result of sexual arousal, when signals are transmitted from the brain to nerves in the penis. Erectile dysfunction occurs when there is lack of the normal hydraulic effect of blood entering and being retained in the penis.

According to Western medicine, there may be either or both psychological and physical causes for impotence. The psychological causes are usually anxiety or depression. Physical reasons for impotence often include disease such as diabetes, spinal cord and brain injuries, Parkinson's disease, Alzheimer's disease, multiple sclerosis, stroke, prostate and bladder cancer surgery, or side effects of certain drugs, such as antidepressants or drugs for hypertension. In addition, Chinese medicine considers that excessive indulgence in sex and/or masturbation, which brings about the decline of *ming men* fire and the exhaustion of the kidneys, are other main causes for impotence. Western medical treatments for impotence depend on the cause and often work on a temporary basis. Testosterone supplementation may be used for cases due to hormonal deficiency.

Chinese medicine has much to say about erectile dysfunction, and there are at least eight distinct patterns of disharmony that can present in these cases, some being replete or excess patterns and some being of a vacuous and deficient nature. For details about all types of male reproductive and sexual dysfunction and Chinese medicine, see the reference listed.[44]

CASE HISTORY #31

Tom, a 54-year-old male in a wheelchair, was brought to our clinic with paralysis of the left arm and leg caused by a stroke eight months previously. The left side of his body had decreased sensation of touch, temperature, and pain. Tom also experienced weakness and pain in his lower back, frequent urination three to five times during the night, and fatigue. His wife mentioned that he had often been irritable, angry, and impatient before the stroke but now his moods had gotten worse. Examination revealed that the muscular tone in his left arm was 1 out of 5, where some contractions occurred in the muscle but without movement. His left leg registered 3 out of 5, with some movement in the leg and none in the left foot. His tongue was pale and slightly purple with a thin, white coating, and his pulses were wiry and fine. The pulse was not detectable in the cubit (*chi*) positions.

Chinese medical pattern discrimination: Kidney qi deficiency, liver qi binding stagnation

Scalp acupuncture treatment

Area selection

Primary area: Foot Motor and Sensory Area
Secondary area: Reproductive Area

Manipulation

Both Foot Motor & Sensory Area and Reproductive Area should be needled and stimulated bilaterally. Twist the needles at least 200 times per minute with the thumb and index finger for 1–3 minutes, twirling the needles as energetically as the patient can tolerate. Repeat stimulation every 10 minutes. During treatment, some patients have sensations of tingling, numbness, heaviness, or distention through the sex organ area; these patients usually experience quicker response and improvement. However, those who do not have such sensations may still have immediate, positive effects. Retain the needles for 25–30 minutes and give the treatment two to three times per week. A therapeutic course consists of 10 treatments.

Results of Case #31

Tom had a very good response to the initial scalp acupuncture treatment. He was able to lift his left arm above his shoulder and he showed some movement in the left hand and fingers. He experienced some tingling sensations in the left leg and was also able to move it. He could stand with assistance and walk a few steps while dragging his left foot.

During the interview prior to the second treatment, Tom's wife told us that he was able to have an erection the evening after his first acupuncture treatment. Tom had been impotent for more than 10 years. Over the preceding decade his erections had gradually gotten weaker until he could no longer perform at all. He had stopped trying five years ago and refused his wife's urging to get medical help because he felt ashamed. He took vacations with his wife and changed diets hoping for improvement, but with no effect. Tom thought the impotence was due to his highly stressful lifestyle and pressures in the workplace. Additionally, he had high blood pressure for which he was on beta-blockers, smoked 30 cigarettes a day, and drank quite heavily.

Tom showed steady improvement with every session of scalp acupuncture. For the sixth session, he walked into our clinic with a cane. He reported that his erectile function was still good and he had more energy than he had had in a long time. He had no more low back pain after 20 years of that afflic-tion. Some nights he slept through without waking up to urinate. By the fif-teenth session, Tom could move the entire left side of his body almost nor-mally with slight movement in his left hand. The abnormal sensations on the left side of his body had completely disappeared. He had quit smoking, drank alcohol only occasionally, and had started routine exercise. The impotence disappeared with scalp acupuncture treatment. At the end of his therapy at our clinic, his wife reported that the acupuncture had changed her husband both physically and mentally.

Discussion

For many years, body acupuncture has been used to treat impotence success-fully. Acupuncture or moxibustion are applied on regular body points such as Guan Yuan (CV 4), Tai Xi (Ki 3), Shen Shu (Bl 23), Ming Men (GV 4), and Bai Hui (GV 20). However, scalp acupuncture has a faster effect for curing impo-tence. The Foot Motor and Sensory Area is used, which has the function of treating paralysis and sensations in the lower limbs, low back pain, hip and leg pain. This area also has other uses, and promoting and restoring sexual func-tion is one of them. When treating impotence as a chief complaint, the scalp acupuncture Reproductive Area should be added in order to achieve a better outcome. It is also very helpful to combine scalp acupuncture with body acupuncture and moxibustion.

Male Infertility

Infertility refers to the inability either to conceive or to carry a pregnancy to term after 12 months of trying. Most people aren't aware that male infertility is as common as female infertility. About 30% of infertility can be attributed to male factors, and 30% can be attributed to female factors. In about 20% of cases infertility is unexplained, and the remaining 20% of infertility is caused by a combination of problems in both partners.

According to Western medicine, factors that can cause both male and female infertility include diabetes mellitus, thyroid disorders, adrenal disease, hypopituitarism, and some genetic disorders. Common causes of specifically female infertility include ovulation problems, fallopian tube blockage, uterine problems, and age-related factors. The most common causes of male infertility include abnormal sperm production or function, impaired delivery of sperm, varicocele, undescended testicle, testosterone deficiency, chlamydia, and gonorrhea. Treatment methods for infertility may be grouped into medical or complementary-and-alternative treatments. Some methods may be used in concert with others. Treatment of infertility by Western medicine generally involves the use of fertility medication, medical devices, and surgery.

In Chinese medicine, many patterns may be discriminated in both male and female patients suffering from infertility. Most Chinese medical sources always include kidney qi, yin, and/or yang deficiency as one of the presenting patterns in all cases of infertility, but many other patterns may be present as well.

CASE HISTORY #32

Matt was 39 when he visited our clinic with complaints of severe low back pain after a car accident 18 months prior. The accompanying symptoms were leg pain, insomnia, dream-disturbed sleep, and depression. Matt could not straighten his back and was walking quite bent over like a very old man. His tongue was deep red and purple with a thin, white coating. His pulses were fine and wiry, and both cubit (*chi*) position pulses were very forceful.

Chinese medical pattern discrimination: Kidney qi deficiency, liver depression with transformative heat, blood stasis

Scalp acupuncture treatment

Area selection

Primary area: Foot Motor and Sensory Area
Secondary area: Reproductive Area

Manipulation

Both Foot Motor and Sensory Area and Reproductive Area should be needled and stimulated bilaterally. Rotate the needles at least 200 times per minute for 1–3 minutes, manipulating them as vigorously as the patient can tolerate. Repeat the stimulation every 10 minutes. During treatment, some patients have sensations of heat, cold, tingling, numbness, heaviness, distention, or the feeling of water or electricity moving through the affected area. These patients usually experience a quicker response and improvement. Retain the needles for 25–30 minutes, and give the treatment two to three times per week. A therapeutic course consists of 10 treatments.

Results of Case #32

After being needled on his scalp, Matt experienced a warm sensation that traveled from his head through his spinal cord and then down to his testicles. He was very happy to leave the clinic with his low back pain immediately better after the first treatment. After seven sessions, his low back pain was completely gone and the other symptoms showed remarkable improvement as well. During our consultation at the end of his eighth treatment, Matt reported excitedly that his wife was now pregnant. The couple had been married for 15 years, but Matt had been told he was infertile because his right testicle was very small and undeveloped since birth. He felt the pregnancy was a miracle.

Discussion

The above-mentioned scalp acupuncture protocol is helpful for infertility in both male and female patients. The treatment that this patient received, scalp acupuncture on the Foot Motor and Sensory Area, also has the ability to treat low back pain due to accidents and has other indications such as promoting and restoring sexual function. Body acupuncture is very useful for male and female infertility as well. Body acupuncture should be individualized according to patient's pattern discrimination. Commonly used points for both male and female infertility are Qi Hai (CV 6), Guan Yuan (CV 4), Tai Xi (Ki 3), Shen Shu (Bl 23), and Bai Hui (GV 20). Quite often in our practice we have relieved problems that patients did not even complain about, because acupuncture is not just for relieving pain and curing paralysis but also for balancing the whole human system.

CHAPTER TEN

Pediatric Disorders

Attention Deficit Hyperactivity Disorder

Attention deficit hyperactivity disorder (ADHD) is a common neurobehavioral disorder of childhood characterized by signs of inattention, hyperactivity, and impulsivity. Children with ADHD are unable to focus and concentrate on a task or purpose, unable to be productive, and unable to physically settle down and be still. They are impulsive, disruptive, and even aggressive in the classroom, at home, or in other social settings. They have difficulty organizing tasks or play activities. It is said that they seem as if driven by a motor because they fidget with their hands or feet, squirm in their seats, and interrupt or intrude on others. They also seem unable to curb their immediate reactions or think before they act. Consequently, they blurt out inappropriate comments or display their emotions without restraint. The behaviors of children with ADHD often lead to significant academic and social difficulties.

The severity of symptoms varies greatly. It depends on the degree of abnormality in the brain, the presence of related conditions, and the individual's environment and response to that environment. Although the causes of ADHD are still unknown in Western medicine, most substantiated sources appear to fall in the realm of neurobiology and genetics. Specifically, the brains of individuals with or without ADHD may differ with respect to the balance of neurotransmitters, as well as the size and operation of specific functions of the frontal lobes of the cerebrum. The functions of the frontal lobes are to solve problems, plan ahead, understand the behavior of others, and restrain impulses. There is no cure for ADHD in Western medicine. Thus, most treatments are for reducing the symptomatic behaviors by medication for the central nervous system, as well as psychotherapy.

According to Chinese medical pattern discrimination, ADHD may be attributed to at least six different patterns or combinations of those patterns, most often involving some type of pathological heat, wind, or hyperactivity of yang harassing the heart spirit.[45]

CASE HISTORY #33

Mike, a 12-year-old seventh-grade student, was brought to our acupuncture clinic in Santa Fe. Mike was diagnosed with attention deficit hyperactivity disorder when he was in the second grade and experienced chronic difficulties with inattention, impulsiveness, and highly active behavior throughout most of his school years. His teacher described him as disruptive and oppositional in class, and he had difficulty paying attention during structured or unstructured activities. His math and reading skills were two to three years below grade level. At home Mike was rebellious, and his parents were overwhelmed by the task of raising him. He refused to go to bed at night, did not want to get up for school in the morning, never helped out with housework or yard work, and wet the bed frequently. Upon initial examination, Mike was so hyperactive that he was hardly still for a minute. His tongue was red with a deep crack in the center, and it was covered with a thick, white coating. His pulses were slippery and wiry.

Chinese medical pattern discrimination: Phlegm fire obstructing the orifices of the heart

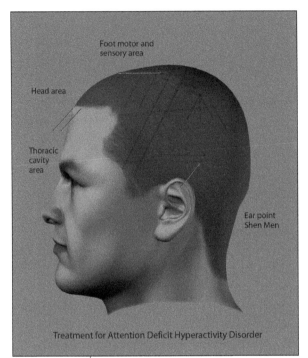

Foot motor and sensory area

Head area

Thoracic cavity area

Ear point Shen Men

Treatment for Attention Deficit Hyperactivity Disorder

Scalp acupuncture treatment

Area selection:

Primary area: Foot Motor and Sensory Area, Head Area
Secondary area: Thoracic Cavity Area

Manipulation

Insert needles bilaterally in both the Foot Motor and Sensory Area and Thoracic Cavity Area and in the Head Area unilaterally. Select the finest gauge needles that you can insert into the scalp. Always put one needle in ear point Shen Men to help a young patient relax and to reduce the sensitivity of the needle insertion and stimulation of the scalp. Use as few needles as possible, rotating them at least 200 times per minute with the thumb and index finger for one minute, but twirling them as gently as possible in the beginning so the child can tolerate the intense sensations. Repeat stimulation every 10 minutes.

Communicate with children and their parents more often than with adult patients in order to reduce their fear and anxiety. During treatment, some patients may experience sensations of heat, cold, tingling, numbness, heaviness, distention, or the sensation of water or electricity moving along their spine, legs, or arms. Tell the child before the needles are inserted that those sensations are normal, and patients who experience some or all of these sensations usually respond and improve more quickly. This encourages the child and parents to come back for additional treatments. However, it's important to also convey that patients who do not have such sensations could still have immediate positive results. Retain the needles in place for

10-to-20 minutes. Treatment is given two to three times per week. A therapeutic course consists of 10 treatments.

Results of Case #33

At the beginning of his first treatment, Mike acted out terribly with crying, kicking, and flailing against the acupuncture needles' insertion. His parents had to hold him down in order for him to receive the needles. However, he was quite cooperative after the needles were inserted. He looked very calm and relaxed when he finished his first session of treatment. His parents reported at the second appointment that Mike's hyperactivity and attention deficit had improved somewhat. He was able to read a book for a while without fidgeting with his hands and squirming in his seat. He began to like treatments and said he enjoyed the feeling of relaxation of his whole body.

By the fifth session, his parents said he was more attentive and less hyperactive, and his impulsiveness at both school and home had diminished. Mike was getting along better with other children and had stopped wetting the bed. After the tenth session, Mike's grades and behavior in school and behavior at home had significantly improved. His attention span had increased from less than one minute to approximately 50 minutes. He improved so quickly that his treatments went from twice a week to once a week, and then to once every other week. Mike continued to make progress in school and at home, but he had occasional setbacks when he missed a treatment. More intense treatments were given at following appointments when this occurred. After his twentieth session he had become a happy, communicative, and responsive boy who could control his emotions and express his feelings instead of acting them out. His parents were very happy to report that his math and reading scores had progressed to a grade level higher.

Discussion

Scalp acupuncture has fairly good effects on patients with ADHD. The patient should begin acupuncture treatment as soon as he or she has a clear diagnosis. The earlier the patient gets treatment, the better the prognosis. There are many different acupuncture techniques to treat ADHD. Although scalp acupuncture has the fastest response, other techniques are necessary for further treatment. Ear acupuncture can increase the results of scalp acupuncture for ADHD patients. Commonly used points are Shen Men, Heart, Liver, and Sympathetic Point. Regular body acupuncture can enhance the results of scalp acupuncture. Commonly used points are Tong Li (Ht 5), Shen Men (Ht 7), Nei Guan (Per 6), Xing Shu (Bl 15), Shen Tang (Bl 43), and Tai Chong (Liv 3). The points on the feet and hands are very sensitive to needling and are thus not advisable during the early sessions of treatment.

Down's Syndrome

Down's syndrome is a genetic disorder characterized by impairment of cognitive ability, physical growth, and facial appearance. Patients often have mild to moderate mental retardation that limits intellectual abilities and adaptive behaviors including conceptual, social, and practical skills. They also may have delayed language and physical development. Down's syndrome patients share some common physical traits, including a flat face with an upward slant to their eyes, a large tongue protruding from the mouth, a short neck, a deep crease in the palms of their hands, white spots on the iris of their eyes, poor muscle tone, loose ligaments, and small hands and feet. Some patients may also have congenital heart disease, ear or eye problems, intestinal problems, thyroid dysfunction, skeletal problems, or dementia. Down's syndrome is also called trisomy 21 because the disorder is caused by the presence of an extra twenty-first chromosome. There is no cure for Down's syndrome. However, early childhood intervention, screening for common problems, a supportive family environment, and vocational training can improve the overall development of children with Down's syndrome.

The Chinese medical assessment of Down's syndrome and all types of mental or developmental retardation is usually described as being due to prenatal kidney essence insufficiency, although other patterns may also present.

CASE HISTORY #34

Judy was 13 when she started scalp acupuncture treatment at her home in Albuquerque. When she was four, her parents had noticed that Judy's speech and mental and physical development were slower than other children of her age. She started to stand and walk late; she had very little facial expression; and her speech never sounded like that of a normal child. Soon after she was diagnosed with Down's syndrome. At the age of five, Judy was enrolled in a special education program for students with developmental disabilities. Judy had problems interacting with children and adults due to poor social skills. She was very shy and did not like to talk to others. She had difficulty enunciating words so that her speech was extremely hard to understand; often she said only yes or no. In addition, she had trouble understanding questions, which had to be repeated several times. Besides her cognitive disabilities, she had physical limitations as well. She was unable to jump, stand on one leg, or run. Judy's math and reading levels were equivalent to a six-year-old. Upon physical examination, she had a flat face, a large, protruding tongue, and deep creases in her palms. Her tongue was red with a thick, white coating. Her pulses were fine and wiry and notably weaker in the cubit (*chi*) positions.

Chinese medical pattern discrimination: Kidney essence insufficiency, phlegm obstructing the orifices of the heart

Scalp acupuncture treatment

Area selection

Primary area: Foot Motor and Sensory Area, Head Area
Secondary area: Chorea and Tremor Area

Manipulation

Both the Foot Motor and Sensory Area and the Chorea and Tremor Area should be needled bilaterally and the Head Area unilaterally. Select the finest gauge needles that you can insert into the scalp. Always put one needle in the ear point Shen Men to help the young patient relax and reduce the sensitivity of the needle insertion and stimulation. Use the fewest number of needles possible in the scalp, rotating them at least 200 times per minute with thumb and index finger for just 1 minute. Twirl the needles gently at the beginning so the child can tolerate the sensation better, and repeat the stimulation every 10 minutes. Communicate with children and their parents more often than with adult patients in order to reduce their fear and anxiety. During treatment, some patients experience sensations of heat, cold, tingling, numbness, heaviness, distention, or the sensation of water or electricity moving along their spine, legs, or arms. Because it is very difficult to communicate with patients who suffer from mental retardation or disability, doctors should pay close attention to their facial expressions, since most children with Down's syndrome have difficulty expressing emotions and giving verbal responses. Retain the needles in place for 10–20 minutes. Treatment is given two times per week at the beginning and then gradually reduced to fewer sessions after patients show improvement. A therapeutic course consists of 10 treatments.

Results of Case #34

Judy cried when the needles were first inserted in her ear and scalp, but then she was quite cooperative during the few minutes of needle stimulation. Surprisingly, she shouted, "Don't take out the needles" when Dr. Hao removed the needles from her head and ear. At the second session she came out of her room to greet the doctor, which her parents said was highly unusual. She was able to stay calm for the needle insertion, and she appeared angry again when the needles were withdrawn from her head. After six sessions, her parents reported that her physical activities showed remarkable improvement. She started to jump, jump rope, and run with her sister and other children. Her teachers also noticed that she had made more progress in her social skills and interaction with other students. By the tenth treatment, Judy's behavior had changed significantly. She now liked most family activities, participated in some conversations, and had improved in the clarity of her speech. Her teachers reported that she was working harder to catch up, and her math and reading scores had jumped almost two levels in a very short period of time. Unfortunately, follow-up was impossible as her family moved to another state and her treatment had to be terminated.

Discussion

Scalp acupuncture offers fairly good results for children with Down's syndrome. Several children treated with scalp acupuncture at our clinic have shown some improvement in both their mental and physical abilities.

However, to treat children with scalp acupuncture is very challenging because both children and their parents are not always willing to participate in pediatric needling as a therapeutic method. The doctor needs to have very good needling skills for both insertion and manipulation, as well as excellent communication skills. It is helpful to play or chat with young patients as if they are old friends or family members before the treatment. It is also a good strategy to ask the parents to talk, play with, or feed young patients during the insertion and stimulation of needles. These act as a diversion to take their attention away from the needles and make them less sensitive. For a child who is extra sensitive to needles, stimulation should be avoided in the first one or two sessions. Compared to adult patients, generally speaking, young patients should receive fewer needles, milder stimulation, and a shorter time of needle retention. When treating a child with Down's syndrome, it is important to observe the responses and reactions while inserting, stimulating, and withdrawing the needles and adjust the techniques accordingly. Although some of the mental and physical limitations of children with Down's syndrome cannot be overcome, scalp acupuncture will definitely improve the health and the quality of their lives.

Seizure

Seizure is a central nervous system disorder involving periodic disturbances of the brain due to excessive electrical discharges. Clinical manifestations of seizure vary depending on the areas of the brain affected by the abnormal electrical discharge. Some patients may present symptoms such as eye staring, involuntary movements of limbs or head, confusion, and uttering meaningless sounds. Other symptoms include an inability to understand conversation, speech lacking in spontaneity, or sparsity of language. In resisting help during a seizure event, some may experience jerking or spasm of the limbs, frothing at the mouth, loss of bladder control, teeth clenching, tongue biting, convulsions, or loss of consciousness. A seizure can last from just a few seconds up to severe epileptic status, which is a continuous seizure that does not stop without intervention. About 20% of patients have some pre-seizure symptoms, called an aura, such as unusual sensations of smell, taste, and vision, or an intense emotional feeling. When seizures stop, patients may have headaches, sore muscles, some abnormal sensations, confusion, and profound fatigue.

While many types of seizure that begin in early childhood have no known cause in Western medicine, Chinese medicine does have pattern discriminations for most types of seizures. While some patients present with deficiency patterns, most exhibit signs and symptoms of heat, wind, phlegm, and possibly blood stasis. If the cause can be identified and eliminated, no additional treatment is necessary. If patients have less positive responses to conventional medications or severe reactions from the side effects of medications, scalp acupuncture is a very good alternative treatment.

CASE HISTORY #35

Sam was seven when he was first brought to our clinic in Santa Fe, NM. Sam had a history of seizures starting when he was three years of age. The first episode occurred when he was playing with his mother and jumping in the back yard. He suddenly stopped, his left arm twitched a little, and he seemed disoriented for several seconds. Afterward, his mother observed that he was quieter than usual, although he said he was fine. A few days later he had two more episodes of muscle twitching and weakness accompanied with staring blankly, moving his head slightly back and forth, and for a minute or two being unable to respond to his parents. The seizures gradually increased until they occurred numerous times each day. Soon after that he was diagnosed with epilepsy and he began having seizure episodes that were characterized by eye twitching, jerking of his arms and legs, and occasional loss of consciousness. These events occurred two to four times a week despite anti-seizure medications. Sam also began wetting the bed and having frequent nightmares. Upon examination, his tongue had a red tip with a thin, white coating. His pulses were overall soft or soggy.

Chinese medical pattern discrimination: Liver wind stirring internally, kidney qi and possible essence deficiency

Scalp acupuncture treatment

Area selection

Primary area: Foot Motor and Sensory Area, Head Area
Secondary area: Chorea and Tremor Area

Manipulation

Both Foot Motor and Sensory Area and Chorea and Tremor Area should be needled bilaterally and the Head Area unilaterally. Select the finest gauge needles that you are able to insert into the scalp. Always put one needle in the ear point Shen Men to help a young patient relax and reduce their sensitivity to needle insertion and stimulation. Use as few needles as possible, rotating them at least 200 times per minute with the thumb and index finger for 1 minute. Twirl the needles as gently as possible at the beginning so that young patients can tolerate the sensations, and repeat the stimulation every 10 minutes. Communicate with children and their parents more often than with adult patients in order to reduce their fear and anxiety. During treatment, some patients may have sensations of heat, cold, tingling, numbness, heaviness, distention, or the sensation of water or electricity moving along their spine, legs, or arms. Tell the child that these are normal, and people who experience any of these sensations usually respond and improve more quickly, which may encourage them to come back for additional treatments. However, those who do not have such sensations could still have immediate positive results. Retain the needles in place for 10–20 minutes. Treatment is given two times per week at the beginning, then gradually reduced to fewer sessions according to the number of seizure episodes. A therapeutic course consists of 10 treatments.

Results of Case #35

Sam just smiled when he was told there was a needle inserted in his ear, and he did not notice or feel the needle at all at the beginning of the treatment. He was quite cooperative and stayed calm in spite of a little twitching reaction as one of the needles was inserted. After his initial scalp acupuncture treatment, Sam had fewer episodes of seizure, and his bed-wetting and nightmares diminished significantly. Also, his parents reported that Sam said he liked to come to our clinic for treatment because the bed-wetting had bothered and embarrassed him in the past. After five treatments, the number of seizures dropped substantially with only a few reported. He also slept better without any bed-wetting or nightmares. By the tenth treatment, he had had no more seizure episodes for a few weeks. In addition, his teachers noticed that he was happier, more playful, and paid better attention in class. Subsequently, Sam had one treatment every other week or once a month for five more visits and then did not need further treatment.

Discussion

Scalp acupuncture offers fairly good results for seizures in both adults and children. However, to treat children with acupuncture, let alone scalp acupuncture, is very challenging because both children and their parents can be hesitant to participate in pediatric acupuncture as a therapeutic method. The doctor needs to have very good needling technique for both insertion and manipulation, as well as excellent communication skills. Sometimes it is necessary to show a patient how tiny the needles are or to demonstrate the insertion of a needle in the doctor's body. This helps to reduce fear and anxiety in both patient and parents. It is very helpful to play or chat with young patients as if they were old friends or family members before the treatment. It is also a good strategy to ask the parents to talk, play with, or feed young patients during the insertion and stimulation of needles. These activities act to divert the child's attention away from the needles and make them less sensitive. For a child who is extra-sensitive to needles, stimulation should be avoided in the first one or two treatments. For children less than two years old, an effective technique is to hide the needle from their sight while inserting and stimulating it. Compared to adult patients, in general, young patients should receive fewer needles, milder stimulation, and shorter needle retention. Whether treating a child or an adult, it is important to observe the responses and reaction of the patient while inserting, stimulating, or withdrawing the needles, and adjust the techniques accordingly.

Research on the effect of scalp acupuncture for seizure and nocturnal enuresis

- Shen Xiu-lian and colleagues reported on the treatment of 240 cases of seizure using scalp electro-acupuncture in 1989. The patients were treated at Foot Motor and Sensory Area, Head Area, and Balance Area. Treatments were given once a day for a total of 20 treatments. The results showed 51 cases cured, marked improvement in 103 cases, some improvement in 69 cases, and no improvement in 17 cases, yielding a total effective rate of 92.92%.[46]

• Wang Tai-dong and colleagues reported on the treatment of 163 cases of nocturnal enuresis using scalp electro-acupuncture in 1987. The patients were divided into a group that received scalp acupuncture combined with herbs (87 cases) and a group that received only scalp acupuncture (76 cases). Both groups were treated at Foot Motor and Sensory Area. Treatment was given once a day for a total of 20 treatments. The results for the combined group showed that 29 cases were cured, improvement was shown in 35 cases, and no improvement in 23, yielding a total effective rate of 73.6%. In the group that received only scalp acupuncture, 46 cases were cured, improvement was shown in 20 cases, and no improvement in 10, yielding a total effective rate of 90%.[47]

Pediatric Aphasia

Disorders of language affect children and adults differently. For children who have not used language from birth, the disorder often occurs in the context of a language system that is not fully developed or acquired. However, for an adult with aphasia, the loss of speech and language abilities is commonly caused by a stroke. An individual with aphasia may hear or see a word but may not be able to understand its meaning and may have trouble getting others to understand what he or she is trying to communicate.

As the speech mechanism and voice mature, an infant is able to make controlled sounds; this begins in the first few months of life with cooing. By six months, an infant usually babbles or produces repetitive syllables such as "mama" and "papa." Babbling soon turns into a type of nonsense speech that often has the tone and cadence of human speech but does not contain real words. By the end of their first year, most children have mastered the ability to say a few simple words. By 18 months of age, most children can say eight to 10 words. By age two, most are putting words together in crude sentences such as "more milk." During this period, children rapidly learn that words symbolize or represent objects, actions, and thoughts. At ages three, four, and five, children's vocabulary rapidly increases and they begin to master the rules of language. If parents have concerns about their child's speech or language development, they should consult their child's doctor or a speech-language pathologist before the age of five. A child with aphasia since birth has a better response from scalp acupuncture if he or she is treated before five years old.

In Chinese medicine, developmental disorders are usually attributed either to insufficient pre-natal kidney essence, liver/kidney depletion and deficiency, or heart blood/spleen qi insufficiency.

CASE HISTORY #36

Tony, a four-year-old with aphasia, came from Houston, TX, with his parents to our office in Santa Fe. An acupuncturist in Texas had referred him to our clinic for scalp acupuncture therapy. His mother reported that he had never spoken a word since birth and he was having seizures every two or three weeks. The parents had taken him to many ear and throat specialists and neurologists with no clear diagnosis or explanation as to the cause of these symptoms. Several intensive examinations, including magnetic resonance imaging (MRI) and electroencephalography (EEG), showed unremarkable results. Tony had been receiving speech therapy for one year without any positive outcome. Although Tony had aphasia, Dr. Hao's examination showed no abnormal findings of his mental activities, his coordination, physical development, or hearing. His tongue showed a red tip with a thin, white coating, and his pulses were slippery.

Chinese medical pattern discrimination: Kidney essence deficiency

Scalp acupuncture treatment

Area selection
Primary area: Speech I, Speech III
Secondary area: Foot Motor and Sensory Area

Manipulation
For treating child aphasia, insert the needles in Speech I and Speech III areas bilaterally. Select the finest gauge needles that you are able to insert into the

scalp. Always put one needle in the ear point Shen Men to help a young patient relax and reduce sensitivity to needle insertion and stimulation of the scalp. Use the least number of needles possible in the scalp, and rotate them at least 200 times per minute with the thumb and index finger for 1 minute. Twirl the needles as gently as possible so that the child can tolerate the sensation, and repeat stimulation every 10 minutes. Communicate with children and their parents more often than with adult patients in order to reduce their fear and anxiety. Encourage the child with aphasia to talk, count, or sing in order to exercise his speech. During treatment, some patients may have sensations of heat, cold, tingling, numbness, heaviness, distention, or the sensation of water or electricity moving along their spine, legs, or arms. Tell the parents and child that these are normal and patients who experience these sensations usually respond and improve more quickly, which encourages patients to come back for additional treatments. However, those who do not have such sensations could still have immediate positive results. Include the Foot Motor and Sensory Area in cases where the patient has other retardation symptoms and signs. Retain the needles in place for 10–20 minutes. The treatment is given two to three times per week. A therapeutic course consists of 10 treatments.

Results of Case #36

Although Tony was afraid and crying before the beginning of treatment, he was quiet and cooperative during the insertion of the needles. The ear point Shen Men was selected for the first needle in order to help him relax and to reduce his sensitivity to scalp acupuncture. However, he did not notice that there was a needle inserted in his ear and showed no negative reaction at all. Next, four needles were put in the Speech I Area and the Foot Motor and Sensory Area of his scalp. The needles were retained without any stimulation. He did not show any improvement during and after the first treatment.

During the second session, Tony was not afraid. He said, "I love you" and "thank you" to us in sign language. He felt a little pain but was distracted by a new toy his mother showed him as the last needle was inserted. He tried very hard to make some sounds in order to get the new toy, and this was a positive response. Tony attempted to repeat the conversation the doctor and his parents were having and continued to make many kinds of sounds although he could not be understood.

Prior to the third session, his mother reported that Tony had started to talk in clearer sentences, some of which she could understand. She had found him already dressed when she went to wake him up to go to the acupuncture clinic. The fourth treatment was the same as the third, and four needles were inserted without any pain. The treatment room was filled with laughter and talk, as Tony was speaking like a normal child. At the fifth and last session, his mother said they couldn't stop Tony from talking now. At a consultation three months later, his parents reported that Tony was still speaking like a normal child and that he had not experienced any more seizures.

Discussion

Scalp acupuncture has been found to have a good effect for children with expressive aphasia. Patients should get acupuncture treatment as soon as their condition is diagnosed. The earlier the child gets treatment, the better the prognosis. Most aphasia patients treated at our clinic show some improvement in the first three scalp acupuncture treatments, and many appear better after the first session. Although scalp acupuncture has the fastest response, other techniques are helpful. Regular body acupuncture has been found to have a positive therapeutic effect on recovery from expressive aphasia. Common points for a child with aphasia are Ya Men (GV 15) and Nei Guan (Per 6).

CHAPTER ELEVEN

Additional Neuro-psychological Disorders

Post-traumatic Stress Disorder

Post-traumatic stress disorder (PTSD) is a severe anxiety disorder that is triggered by a shocking or painful event. One can develop post-traumatic stress disorder from experiencing or witnessing an event that causes intense fear, helplessness, or horror, overwhelming the individual's ability to cope. Post-traumatic stress disorder symptoms are commonly grouped into three types: intrusive memories, avoidance and numbing, and increased emotional arousal. Symptoms of intrusive memories may include flashbacks, intrusive emotions and memories, and nightmares or night terrors. Symptoms of avoidance and emotional numbing may include avoiding emotions, relationships, responsibility for others, and situations that are reminiscent of the traumatic event. Symptoms of increased emotional arousal may include irritability or anger, overwhelming guilt or shame, sleep disturbance, extreme vigilance, exaggerated startle reaction, and vision and auditory hallucinations.

Post-traumatic stress disorder is caused by either physical or psychological trauma or, more frequently, a combination of both. Symptoms may result when a traumatic event causes an overactive adrenaline response, which creates deep neurological patterns in the brain. Three areas of the brain whose function may be altered in PTSD have been identified: the prefrontal cortex, amygdala, and hippocampus. Western medical treatment usually includes both medication and psychotherapy. A variety of medications have shown an adjunctive benefit in reducing PTSD symptoms, but there is no clear drug treatment for PTSD. Several forms of therapy may be used to treat both children and adults with PTSD, including cognitive therapy, exposure therapy, and cognitive behavior therapy.

According to Chinese medicine, all psychological or spirit-essence disorders are due to one or a combination of malnourishment and nonconstruction of the heart qi, harassment of the spirit by pathological heat, or blockage of the heart spirit function by some pathologic qi such as phlegm or blood stasis. These three may combine and also be complicated by liver depression qi stagnation.

CASE HISTORY #37

Charles, a 59-year-old veteran, had suffered from PTSD and major depression for more than 30 years before he came to our Albuquerque, NM, clinic. He reported feeling extremely aroused both cognitively and behaviorally. He often experienced flashbacks and nightmares, and his symptoms included feeling as if the events in the past were recurring. He was too nervous and anxious to drive a car. He had constant low back pain and headaches. He slept poorly, waking up many times during the night. He also experienced severe fatigue, poor appetite, and abdominal distention. His memory and concentration were severely impaired, rendering him disabled and unable to work for almost 20 years. He had irritability, anger, anxiety, depression, fear, and startle reactions. He had constipation and a burning sensation when urinating. His tongue was red with a thin, yellow coating, and his pulses were wiry and slippery.

Chinese medical pattern discrimination: Ascendant heart fire hyperactivity, liver spleen disharmony, kidney qi and yin deficiency

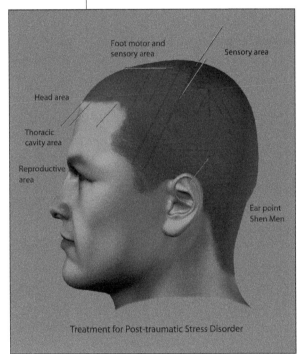

Foot motor and sensory area
Sensory area
Head area
Thoracic cavity area
Reproductive area
Ear point Shen Men

Treatment for Post-traumatic Stress Disorder

Scalp acupuncture treatment

Area selection

Primary area: Foot Motor and Sensory Area, Head Area
Secondary area: Thoracic Cavity Area, Reproductive Area, and Sensory Area

Manipulation

Insert needles bilaterally in the Foot Motor and Sensory Area, Head Area, Thoracic Cavity Area, and Reproductive Area and stimulate bilaterally. The Sensory Area is needled unilaterally according to the patient's symptoms. Put needles in the Shen Men and Heart points on the ear to help a PTSD patient relax and reduce sensitivity to needle insertion and stimulation of the scalp. At the initial session, insert only two to four needles in the scalp, aimed at the main complaint. Rotate the needles at least 200 times per minute for 1–3 minutes, twirling them as vigorously as the patient can tolerate and repeating the stimulation every 10 minutes. During treatment, some patients may have sensations of increasing tingling or numbness, heat, cold, heaviness, distention, or the sensation of water or electricity moving along their spine, legs, or arms. Patients with some or all of these sensations usually respond and improve more quickly. However, those who do not have such sensations could still have immediate positive results. Select the Sensory Area on the scalp according to the patient's symptoms of pain or other abnormal sensations. Keep the needles in place for 30–40 minutes. Treatment is given two to three times per week. A therapeutic course consists of 10 treatments.

Results of Case #37

Charles felt deeply relaxed and fell asleep 10 minutes after a few needles were inserted into his ear and scalp during the first session. When he awoke, he was significantly less anxious than usual. At the second session he reported his sleep much improved and he had not had any nightmares. He had more energy and felt calmer. His wife added that he had begun to do a few chores around the house, something he hadn't done for a long time. By the fifth session, his digestion was functioning almost normally. He had no constipation or abdominal distention, and his appetite had returned to normal. His bowel movements were normal, and urination occurred without the burning sensation. Charles no longer had low back pain and only occasional headaches. His sleep was less disturbed by nightmares or awakening during the night. He reported emotional improvement, with no anger or irritability since the fourth session. After the eighth treatment, his memory and concentration were improved and his energy level was almost normal. The redness of his tongue had receded to the tip and the coating was now thin and white. His pulses were now slippery and only slightly wiry. After three months and 19 treatments he was able to drive, had completed some household improvement projects, and planned to return to work. He no longer exhibited any symptoms of PTSD.

Discussion

Scalp acupuncture has positive results in treating post-traumatic stress disorder. It usually takes three to five sessions for patients to show noteworthy improvements cognitively, behaviorally, physically, and psychologically. However, PTSD patients have multiple symptoms and signs involving physical activities, psychological changes, and cognitive functions. Therefore, it could take 20–30 treatments for complete recovery. The patient should get acupuncture treatment as soon as possible. The earlier the better the prognosis will be. Scalp acupuncture treatment for PTSD has had much success in reducing anxiety, depression, irritability, and anger, and improving sleep and reducing fatigue. Many patients also have reported improvements in bladder and bowel control and in their overall sense of well-being after treatment.

Although scalp acupuncture has a better track record for improving symptoms, other techniques can enhance recovery. Ear acupuncture has been found to have a good effect on the recovery from PTSD. Commonly used ear points are Shen Men, Heart, Liver, Kidney, Sympathetic Point, and Brain. Body acupuncture can have a positive therapeutic effect as well. Commonly used points are Xin Shu (Bl 15), Jue Yin Shu (Bl 14), Gan Shu (Bl 19), and Shen Shu (Bl 23) on the back, and Tai Chong (Liv 3), Tai Xi (Ki 3), and Nei Guan (Per 6) on the limbs. Electrical stimulation is helpful if the practitioner has difficulty performing the needle rotation more than 200 times per minute. It is suggested that no more than two scalp needles be stimulated at any session so the brain does not become too confused to respond. Moxibustion can enhance the therapeutic results of scalp acupuncture, especially for older or weaker patients. Recommended points are Zu San Li (St 36), Guan Yuan (CV 4), and Yong Quan (Ki 1). The authors of this book believe that scalp acupuncture should be considered as the primary approach rather than as a complementary one or a last choice for the patient with PTSD. Our results demonstrate that PTSD patients can have very good responses both subjectively and biologically.

Post-concussion Syndrome

Post-concussion syndrome consists of a specific set of neuropsychological disorders caused by a traumatic injury to the brain. Its clinical manifestations include physical, mental, or emotional symptoms. Common physical symptoms are headache, dizziness and vertigo, fatigue, insomnia, and impaired balance. Emotional symptoms include depression, anxiety, irritability, restlessness, or mood swings. Mental symptoms include amnesia, confusion or impaired cognition, difficulty concentrating, or difficulty with abstract thinking. The symptoms usually appear in groups or clusters, and they may persist for months, years, or sometimes for life. Memory loss, mood changes, and attention deficit are the three chief complaints of patients with post-concussion syndrome. In many cases, the impairments are widespread and disrupt several brain systems. The overall effect can be profoundly disabling.

Leading causes of post-concussion syndrome are automobile accidents, work-place injuries, acts of violence, falls, or sports and recreational injuries. When the head receives a sudden, sharp blow, movement between the brain and the skull produce extreme forces that cause the brain to be torn, contused, dis-placed, crushed, or shaken, which in turn results in traumatic brain injury. The maximum injury is often at the point of impact. However, the frontal and tem-poral areas of the brain are consistently vulnerable to contusions regardless of the direction or the point of impact. This is due to percussion and shearing forces on brain tissue. Conventional medical treatments may help relieve some symptoms of post-concussion syndrome, but they often do not address the root of the problem. Medication may provide temporary relief from pain, and counseling may help some patients understand the need to control their impulses and emotions. However, there is no evidence in the medical literature that medication or rehabilitation can effectively restore impaired functions of the brain in post-concussion syndrome.

According to the statements of fact in Chinese medicine, any tissue or system of the body requires the nourishment of blood to perform its normal func-tion. If a traumatic injury causes blood stasis and stagnation of qi to an area of the brain, fresh blood cannot circulate to nourish that area. Thus the nor-mal functions of the brain are disrupted. This situation will commonly be complicated by whatever other patterns patients may have presented prior to their trauma.

CASE HISTORY #38

At his first visit to our acupuncture clinic, Miguel, a 26-year-old graduate student, reported that his chief complaint was loss of short-term memory after an auto accident three months before. He also experienced poor con-centration, headaches, loss of balance, and fatigue. He went from having excellent grades to not being able to remember what he read and being unable to focus in class. This made him angry, anxious, and depressed. Although Miguel had received several acupuncture treatments in a student clinic, he had shown little improvement. After he failed all of his midterm exams, the dean of the college told him that he had two options. One was to quit school; the other was to see Dr. Hao, who specialized in acupuncture for brain injury. He chose the latter. The examination revealed a red tongue covered by a thick, white coating. His pulses were wiry and slippery.

Chinese medical pattern discrimination: Heart and liver blood deficiency, liver qi binding stagnation with flaring of liver fire

Scalp acupuncture treatment

Area selection

Primary area: Foot Motor and Sensory Area, Head Area
Secondary area: Balance Area and Vertigo and Hearing Area

Manipulation

Foot Motor and Sensory Area should be needled and stimulated bilaterally, and the Head Area stimulated unilaterally. Rotate the needles at least 200 times per minute for 1–3 minutes, twirling them as strongly as the patient can stand and repeating the stimulation every 10 minutes. During treatment, some patients may experience sensations of heat, tingling, numbness, heaviness, distention, or the sensation of water or electricity moving along their spine, legs, or arms. Patients with some or all of these sensations usually respond and improve more quickly. Select the Balance Area or Vertigo and Hearing Area if the patient presents symptoms related to balance, dizziness, or vertigo. Retain the needles for 25–30 minutes. Treatment is given two to three times per week, and a therapeutic course consists of 10 treatments.

Results of Case #38

As soon as five needles were inserted into his scalp, Miguel felt a hot sensation moving from his head, through his spinal cord, and down his legs. Marked improvement of his balance and headaches were observed after the first session. A week later he reported that his mind seemed less confused. He could remember things better, and his attention span in class was greatly improved. Also Miguel's headaches, balance, and fatigue were much better since treatment. After six treatments his symptoms had dramatically disappeared. He could remember all that he read after only scanning the material one time. Miguel's physical and mental activities all returned to normal after eight visits and he received all 'A's on his final examinations.

Discussion

In our practice, scalp acupuncture has been used as a very effective treatment to restore the impaired functions of the brain, improve neurological damage, relieve psychosocial problems, and enhance mental performance. Scalp acupuncture has a remarkable effect on post-concussion syndrome; about 80% of patients we treat show immediate positive results during the first session. Most patients need only six to 12 treatments to free them from symptoms. This is dramatically fewer treatments when compared to the number needed using regular body and ear acupuncture. In our practice, however, we have found that it is very helpful to use other acupuncture methods along with scalp acupuncture to enhance the effects. The selection of body acupuncture points should be individualized based on the differentiation of patterns in Chinese medicine. For instance, one may choose Shen Men (Ht 7) and Xin Shu (Bl 15) for deficiencies of the heart, Zu San Li (St 36) and San Yin Jiao (Sp 6) for deficiencies of qi and blood, Tai Xi (Ki 3) and Zhao Hai (Ki 6) for deficiencies in the kidneys, or other points as suggested by the presenting patterns.

Parkinson's Disease

Parkinson's disease is a progressive neurological disease with a gradual exacerbation of the four primary symptoms of tremor, muscle rigidity, slowness of movement (bradykinesia), and impaired balance and coordination. As these symptoms become more pronounced, patients may develop stooped posture, speech problems such as softness of voice and slurred speech, and festination, or the acceleration of forward gait. Other symptoms may include depression and other emotional changes, difficulty in swallowing or chewing, urinary problems, constipation, sleep disruption, fatigue, and skin problems. One out of every three patients with Parkinson's disease has Alzheimer's disease as well. Parkinson's disease results from a progressive loss of cells in the brain's motor control center, called the *substantia nigra*. These cells produce dopamine, a neurotransmitter that relays signals for normal movement. When dopamine is deficient, an overly active part of the brain in another area appears to compensate for the dopamine-deficient chemical imbalance. As a result, patients develop stiff muscles, severe shaking, stooped posture, bradykinesia, and festination. Often there is no specific cause. Some patients, however, seem to have genetic, environmental toxicity, head trauma, virus, or drug-induced causes of Parkinson's disease. At present there is no cure, although a variety of medications or brain surgery may provide some relief from the symptoms.

In Chinese medical pattern differentiation, Parkinson's disease is usually due to consumption and damage to liver blood and kidney yin complicated by yang hyperactivity leading to internal stirring of liver wind, as well as blood stasis and/or phlegm and dampness obstructing the channels and network vessels resulting in tremors or shaking.

CASE HISTORY #39

Richard had been experiencing motor dysfunction symptoms for nine years before he came to our Santa Fe clinic at the age of 70. He first noticed the problem while skiing, when his legs became very stiff and heavy and would not move on command. Soon after he was diagnosed with Parkinson's disease. His condition gradually worsened; he felt very tired, his legs felt heavy, and his balance suffered. Richard had used a cane for the past six years because the disease had undermined his ability to walk. The trembling in his hands and arms had become so severe that he was unable to hold his one-year-old grandson. Richard frequently experienced difficulty rising from a bed or couch, sometimes falling backward onto the floor while attempting to rise. Once standing or walking, he might fall because of gait abnormality. He could barely lift his feet from the ground and shuffled along, often tripping over small objects on the ground and sometimes losing his balance when turning or attempting to walk because his feet felt glued to the floor. In addition, he complained of frequent urination at night, as much as four to six times. Visual examination showed that he walked mostly on the forepart of his feet and would have fallen with every step if he had not been supported by his cane. Richard was not able to walk backward at all and could only turn by walking in a circle. His tongue was deep red with a slightly thick, white coating. His pulses were wiry and fine.

Chinese medical pattern discrimination: Liver wind stirring internally, liver qi binding stagnation, kidney qi deficiency

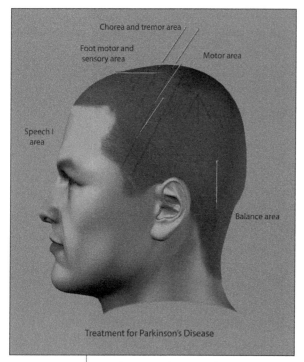

Chorea and tremor area

Foot motor and
sensory area

Motor area

Speech I
area

Balance area

Treatment for Parkinson's Disease

Scalp acupuncture treatment

Area selection

Primary area: Chorea and Tremor Area, Motor Area, Balance Area
Secondary area: Foot Motor and Sensory Area, and Sensory Area

Manipulation

Chorea and Tremor Area and Balance Area should be needled and stimulated unilaterally. Sensory Area, Motor Area, and Foot Motor and Sensory Area should be unilaterally or bilaterally stimulated according to signs and symptoms. Rotate the needles at least 200 times per minute with the thumb and index finger for 1–3 minutes, twirling them as vigorously as the patient can bear and repeating the stimulation every 10 minutes. During treatment, some patients may experience sensations of heat, tingling, numbness, heaviness, distention, or the sensation of water or electricity moving along their spine, legs, or arms. Retain the needles for 25–30 minutes. Treatment is given two to three times per week, and a therapeutic course consists of 10 treatments.

Results of Case #39

Richard had a very positive response during his first scalp acupuncture treatment. He felt hot sensations along his spine to his legs just a few minutes after the needles were inserted. Afterward, the tremors in his hands and arms were remarkably diminished, and he felt the tightness and stiffness in his body relax. He could stand up straighter without losing his balance, lift his feet with big steps, and walk steadily. The major improvement was that he could now turn around freely and abruptly instead of walking around in a circle. He actually walked out of our clinic having forgotten his cane. At the second session Richard said his energy had improved, and he did not need to arise at night to urinate very frequently. However, his tremor and walking problems had improved for only two days after the first treatment. With more treatment his improvement continued, with longer-lasting results. After two months of scalp acupuncture Richard had no more tremor or difficulty in walking and needed no more treatment at that time.

Discussion

This patient's improvements were quite remarkable, and scalp acupuncture can be extremely helpful for patients with Parkinson's disease, whether in the early or later stages. It can improve mobility, range of motion, muscle tone, gait, and ability to swallow and balance. Although scalp acupuncture cannot stop the progression of the disease, it can improve patients' symptoms and help them to feel more confident, thus improving the quality of their lives. For some patients with Parkinson's disease, the initial response to scalp acupuncture treatment can be dramatic. Over time, however, the benefits of treatment frequently diminish or become less consistent, although symptoms can usually still be fairly well controlled. When this occurs, scalp acupuncture areas should be alternated with different treatments so that patients can increase their sensitivity to the stimulation of the needles. Certain body acupuncture treatments are very helpful for patients in the later stages. The recommended points are Tai Chong (Liv 3), Yang Ling Quan (GB 34), Tai Xi (Ki 3), Wai Guan (TB 5), Shen Shu (Bl 23), and Gan Shu (Bl 18). In addition to acupuncture treatments, patients should try to change their lifestyle by adding activities such as physical therapy, *Tai Ji, Qi Gong*, yoga, and other exercise, and adhering to a healthy diet.

Chorea

Chorea refers to an abnormal involuntary movement disorder. It is characterized by excessive, spontaneous movements of an irregular and abrupt nature. These movements may vary in severity from restlessness with mild intermittent exaggeration of gesture and expression, fidgeting movements of the hands and legs, and an unstable dance-like gait, to a continuous flow of disabling, violent movements. The pathophysiology of this condition is understood by Western medicine to be an overactivity of the neurotransmitter dopamine in the areas of the brain that control movement. Chorea is a primary feature of Huntington's disease, Syndenham's chorea, ataxia telangiectasia, and Ballism. Chorea can also be induced by drugs such as levodopa, anticonvulsants, and antipsychotics, as well as by metabolic and endocrine disorders and vascular incidents. In Western medicine there is no standard course of treatment for chorea, because it depends on the type of chorea and any associated disease. Although there are several drugs that may control it, there is no known cure so far in Western medicine.

According to Chinese medicine, all involuntary movement is due to pathological wind. Many other patterns may either lead to the development of internal wind and/or complicate the way in which it manifests.

CASE HISTORY #40

Lucy had a three-year history of involuntary movements when she came to our seminar in Washington, DC, at the age of 56. At first the involuntary movements affected only the left side of her body, but gradually they took over her whole body and made her disabled. An initial Western medical diagnosis of chorea had been made two years prior. She had no difficulty with speech, balance, or autonomic function, and there was no history of psychiatric illness or cognitive deterioration. There was also no history of involuntary movements during childhood or pregnancy. Neurological examination revealed normal extra-ocular movements and normal motor sensory and cerebellar function. Reflexes were physiologically normal and symmetrical. The patient's chorea movements were moderate to severe and predominantly distal, affecting the left arm and leg and, to a lesser extent, the right arm and leg. Facial chorea was also noted. Lucy displayed severe involuntary movements of her whole body. She constantly twisted her head, arms, legs, and trunk so that she could not stand or walk. She also experienced insomnia, fatigue, constipation, anxiety, and depression. She had tried many kinds of medications with little help. Her tongue was red with little coating, and her pulses were wiry and fine.

Chinese medical pattern discrimination: Liver wind stirring internally, heart yin deficiency

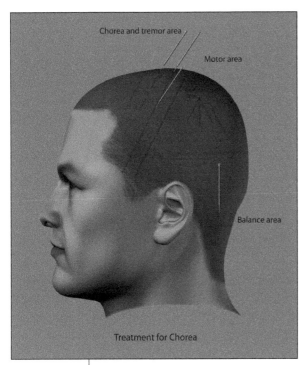

Chorea and tremor area

Motor area

Balance area

Treatment for Chorea

Scalp acupuncture treatment

Area selection

Primary area: Chorea and Tremor Area

Secondary area: Motor Area, Balance Area

Manipulation

The Chorea and Tremor Area is the primary center to treat this condition and should be needled first and bilaterally. The Motor Area and Balance Area are other important treatment sites. Motor Area and Balance Area are classified as secondary areas to treat chorea. The upper 1/5 Motor Area is unilaterally selected to treat involuntary movements of the opposing leg and foot. The middle 2/5 Motor Area is unilaterally selected to treat chorea of opposing arm and hand. The lower 2/5 Motor Area is unilaterally selected to treat chorea of the same side of the neck and head. Balance Area is bilaterally added only after the Chorea and Tremor Area and Motor Area are needled and if there are not positive results.

Proper manipulation techniques are important in obtaining the desired results. Rotate the needles at least 200 times per minute with the thumb and index finger for 2–3 minutes, twirling them as forcefully as the patient can tolerate and repeating the stimulation every 10 minutes. As mentioned previously, during treatment some patients may experience sensations of heat, cold, tingling, numbness, heaviness, distention, or the sensation of water or electricity moving along their spine, legs, or feet. Those patients with some or all of these sensations usually respond and improve more quickly. However, those who do not have such sensations could still have immediate, positive results. Retain the needles for 30–45 minutes. Patients are treated two or three times a week depending upon the degree of tremor, spasm, and pain. A therapeutic course consists of 10 treatments.

Results of Case #40

Lucy had a very positive response to the scalp acupuncture treatments. Within three minutes after several needles were inserted into her scalp the chorea dramatically decreased. Her head stopped involuntary movements first, then her upper limbs, and then her lower limbs. She liked seeing her whole body stay still. The seminar audience asked Lucy to stand up. She stood up with no difficulty and started to walk. Half an hour later, the chorea had completely left her body. Lucy stayed in the seminar room another hour without experiencing any chorea symptoms and left very happy.

Discussion

Acupuncture has very positive results for chorea and other involuntary movement disorders such as tic and essential tremor. Most patients with chorea whom we have treated have showed some improvement in the first three treatments. In our practice we have found that it is very helpful to use other acupuncture methods along with scalp acupuncture in order to enhance the effects. The most commonly used points for body acupuncture are Tai Chong (Liv 3), Yang Ling Quan (GB 34), and Tai Xi (Ki 3). Electrical stimulation at the above points with high frequency and low intensity is also helpful. Quite often we use ear acupuncture as well, commonly choosing ear points Shen Men, Liver, and Kidney.

Ataxia

Ataxia is a neurological symptom described as a lack of muscle coordination and poor coordination during voluntary movements such as walking or picking up an object. Ataxia can affect the eye, body, and limb movements, speech, and the ability to swallow. Signs and symptoms may include poor coordination, unsteady walking with a tendency to stumble, difficulty with fine movements such as eating, writing, or buttoning a shirt, slurred speech, abnormal eye movements, and difficulty swallowing. Ataxia is described by Western medicine as a nonspecific clinical manifestation, which implies that it is a dysfunction of the parts of the nervous system that coordinate movement, such as the cerebellum. Several possible causes exist for these types of neurological dysfunction including head trauma, alcohol abuse, stroke, tumor, cerebral palsy, multiple sclerosis, and transient ischemic attack. It is also possible to inherit a defective gene that can cause one of many ataxia variants. There is no Western medical treatment specifically for ataxia. In some cases, treating the underlying cause may resolve the problem. Ataxia patients may also benefit from physical therapy, occupational therapy, and speech therapy.

In Chinese medicine, diseases characterized by loss of muscular strength and coordination are called wilting conditions. The patterns that account for these types of conditions are usually deficiency or vacuity patterns, which may be complicated by liver depression qi stagnation and the development of phlegm, blood stasis, and/or internally engendered wind.

CASE HISTORY #41

Glen was 59 when he came to our Albuquerque clinic from Arizona, and he needed a cane to walk. He had been diagnosed with ataxia at age 45 and it had progressively worsened. His gait became broad-based, and spastic weakness had developed in his legs, making it difficult to stand and walk without support. As his balance and walking became more impaired, Glen was unable to work. Ten years from the disease onset, spastic weakness of the legs had become permanent. Cerebellar features of ataxic leg movements and a broad-based gait were more pronounced. In order to walk around his house he had to hang on to furniture or walls. In the past two years Glen also experienced dizziness, vertigo, mental confusion, poor concentration, and sometimes double vision. On examination, his mental status and language were normal. Rapid alternating movements were slow and clumsy, and there was mild finger-to-nose and considerable heel-to-shin ataxia. Deep tendon reflexes were uniformly brisk, and his gait was ataxic like a drunken swagger. His tongue was red with a thin, yellow coating, and his pulse was wiry and fine on the left side and forceless and fine on the right side.

Chinese medical pattern discrimination: Liver wind stirring internally, liver blood deficiency, spleen qi deficiency

Scalp acupuncture treatment

Area selection

Primary area: Balance Area, Vertigo and Hearing Area
Secondary area: Foot Motor and Sensory Area, Vision Area

Manipulation

The Balance Area and Vertigo and Hearing Area should be needled and stimulated bilaterally. Rotate the needles at least 200 times per minute for 2–3 minutes. The Balance Area and Vertigo and Hearing Area are relatively sensitive, so it is good strategy to put a needle in ear point Shen Men first to reduce the sensitivity of needle insertion and stimulation. Manipulate the needles as strongly as the patient can tolerate and repeat the stimulation every 10 minutes. During treatment, some patients may experience sensations of heat, cold, tingling, numbness, heaviness, distention, or the sensation of water or electricity moving along their neck, spine, or limbs. Those patients usually respond and improve more quickly. It is important to instruct patients to exercise their affected areas actively, if possible, during the treatment. Select the Foot Motor and Sensory Area as well if the patient has muscular spasms, weakness, or other abnormal sensations such as pain or numbness. Choose Vision Area bilaterally if patients have double vision, blurring of vision, or an eye focus problem. Retain the needles for 30–45 minutes. Treatment is given two or three times per week, and a therapeutic course consists of 10 treatments.

Results of Case #41

Glen had a very positive response to the first scalp acupuncture treatment. A couple of minutes after a few needles were inserted into his scalp he felt that the dizziness and vertigo were reduced and his head felt much clearer. Following a tingling sensation in both eyes the double vision was gone. Ten minutes later he was able to perform the finger-to-nose test much faster and almost like a normal person. He could stand steadily and even stood on one foot without difficulty, and he could walk without the cane and showed no problem with balance. At the second session, Glen reported that his balance was good most of the time and he was able to walk without a cane at home. He had not experienced dizziness, vertigo, or double vision since the first session. His sleep, concentration, and memory were better, too. After five weekly sessions, Glen had no more signs and symptoms of ataxia. Several months later, Glen came to our clinic and reported that the ataxia symptoms recurred after he had had an extremely emotional event in his life. He received two more sessions of scalp acupuncture and the symptoms again disappeared.

Discussion

Scalp acupuncture has been found to have very good effects on ataxia due to various causes including multiple sclerosis, Parkinson's disease, stroke, and traumatic brain injury. About 85% of our patients show immediate improvement in symptoms of disequilibrium at the initial session. Although scalp acupuncture has the best and fastest response, other techniques are needed for accelerating recovery. According to the individual's condition and pattern discrimination regular body acupuncture, electrical acupuncture, and moxibustion, as well as physical therapy and massage can combine with scalp acupuncture to speed the time of recovery. Regular acupuncture treatment has been found to have positive therapeutic effects on the recovery of symptoms of ataxia. Commonly used points are Gan Shu (Bl 19), Shen Shu (Bl 23), Tai Chong (Liv 3), Tai Xi (Ki 3), Feng Fu (GV 16), and Feng Chi (GB 20). Electrical stimulation may be helpful if the practitioner has difficulty performing the needle rotation more than 200 times per minute. If used, it is suggested that no more than two of the scalp needles be stimulated at any session so the brain does not become too confused to respond. However, the authors of this book feel that hand manipulation produces best results for scalp acupuncture treatment. The faster a practitioner can rotate the needles, the better the outcome will be. Moxibustion can also enhance the therapeutic results of scalp acupuncture, especially for older or weaker patients. Recommended points are Zu San Li (St 36), Guan Yuan (CV 4), and Tai Xi (Ki 3).

Research on the effect of scalp acupuncture for ataxia

• Zhang Yu-lian and colleagues reported on the treatment of 102 cases of ataxia due to stroke using scalp acupuncture in 2003. The patients were divided into a body acupuncture group (34 cases) and a scalp acupuncture group (68 cases). All 102 patients were diagnosed through CT scan or MRI to have had an infarction or hemorrhage in the cerebellum or the brainstem. The body acupuncture group was treated with needling from Bai Hui (GV 20), Feng Chi (GB 20), Jian Yu (LI 15), Qu Chi (LI 11), Wai Guan (TB 5), He Gu (LI 4), Zu San Li (St 36), Yang Ling Quan (GB 34), Feng Long (St 40), and Tai Chong (Liv 3). The scalp acupuncture group was treated at the Balance Area and Motor Area. Treatments were given once a day for a total of 20 sessions. The results showed that two cases were cured, seven showed marked improvement, 17 showed some improvement, yielding a total effective rate of 75% (26/34) in the body acupuncture group. In the scalp acupuncture group, 24 cases were cured, 32 showed marked improvement, and 12 showed some improvement, yielding a total effective rate of 100% (68/68).[48]

Alzheimer's Disease

Alzheimer's disease is a progressive, neurodegenerative brain disorder characterized by cognitive deterioration, declining activities of daily living, neuropsychiatric symptoms, and behavioral changes. Alzheimer's disease is the most common type of dementia. Signs of the disease are a general decline in mental ability such as loss of memory, language skills, reason, judgment, and concentration. The earliest symptom is minor forgetfulness, leading to amnesia (loss of short-term memory) when the condition becomes steadily more pronounced. As the disease progresses, cognitive impairments extend to aphasia (loss of speech), apraxia (loss of fine movement), agnosia (loss of recognition), disorientation, and disinhibition that leads to mental disability. Patients may also have some behavioral changes such as outbursts of violence or excessive passivity. In the later stages, some patients may present incontinence of urine or bowel and deterioration of musculature and motility that cause them physical disability. Although the ultimate cause of Alzheimer's disease is unknown in Western medicine, it is found that the impaired brain functions are closely related to the frontal and temporal areas and to the parietal cortex of the brain, which consists principally of neuronal loss or atrophy. Alzheimer's disease is an extremely difficult condition to treat. However, scalp acupuncture is always worth trying as Western medicine cannot prevent or cure this condition. It is observed that the older the patient is and the longer the problem lasts, the more difficult it is to treat.

The disease mechanisms that lead to Alzheimer's disease according to Chinese medicine are complex, and usually several mutually-engendering patterns are involved at the same time. See the suggested reference for a complete discussion of disease causes, patterns, and treatments suggested by Chinese medicine for this illness.[49]

CASE HISTORY #42

Chris, a 67-year-old male artist with significant memory problems and deficits in functional ability, came to our clinic in Albuquerque, New Mexico. The patient's wife mentioned that his memory problems had been occurring for about four years, although Chris thought it had been only one year. According to his wife, his memory loss was gradually getting worse. At first, he had trouble remembering the names of familiar people and he misplaced personal belongings such as his keys or toothbrush. As the disease progressed, there was dramatic deterioration of his communication abilities, memory, and life skills. He often forgot to put on his clothes to walk around his house. He even did not recognize himself in the mirror and asked his wife, "Who is that old man there?" Chris was depressed, angry, irritable, and also had lower back pain. He was completely disabled and needed a full-time caregiver. However, he could still recognize his paintings and talked a lot about them. Neuropsychological tests showed that he had moderate memory impairment, mild impairment of language comprehension, orientation, and attention. The PET scan findings showed that the distribution of FDG (flurodeoxyglucose) within the brain revealed significant hypometabolism in the parietal and temporal regions, and that frontal metabolism was significantly reduced. A CT scan showed that his brain was slightly atrophied. He was diagnosed with senile dementia of the Alzheimer's type. Most of his answers to our clinic's questionnaire were incorrect, and he asked why he had been brought to our clinic. He had a deep red tongue with a thick, white coating, and his pulses were wiry and fine.

Chinese medical pattern discrimination: Kidney essence deficiency, phlegm and heat obstructing the orifices of the heart

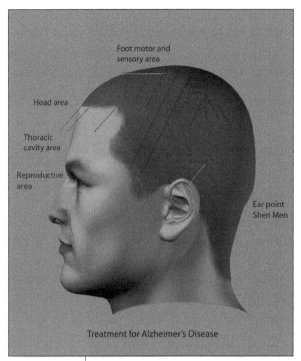

Foot motor and sensory area

Head area

Thoracic cavity area

Reproductive area

Ear point Shen Men

Treatment for Alzheimer's Disease

Scalp acupuncture treatment

Area selection:

Primary area: Foot Motor and Sensory Area, Head Area
Secondary area: Chorea and Tremor Area

Manipulation

Foot Motor and Sensory Area should be needled bilaterally and the Head Area unilaterally. Select the finest gauge needles that you are able to insert into the scalp at the initial treatment. Always put one needle in the ear point Shen Men to help the patient relax and reduce the sensitivity of the needle insertion and stimulation of the scalp. Use the fewest number of needles possible in the scalp, and rotate them at least 200 times per minute for 2 minutes, twirling as gently as possible at the beginning so that the patient can tolerate the sensation better, and repeating stimulation every 10 minutes.

Communicate with Alzheimer's patients more often than with others in order to reduce their fear and anxiety. During treatment, some patients may experience sensations of heat, cold, tingling, numbness, heaviness, distention, or the sensation of water or electricity moving along their spine, legs, or arms. Because it is difficult to communicate with Alzheimer's patients due to their mental confusion and inability to express themselves, doctors should pay close attention to their facial expressions and their overall responses. Retain the needles in place for 20–30 minutes. Request another person who is with the patient to stay in the treatment room for the entire session because most patients cannot remember that there are needles in their scalp and body, and it is very dangerous for them to move around during the sessions. The treatment is given two times per week at the beginning and then gradually reduced to fewer sessions after patients have experienced some improvement. A therapeutic course consists of 10 treatments.

Results of Case #42

Chris was quite cooperative and had no bad reactions to the needles in his scalp during the initial session. At the second treatment he said, "How are you, doctor?" which surprised his wife that he had remembered. She reported that he had not complained of lower back pain and appeared calmer during the week with less anger and irritability. At the fifth treatment, both he and his wife felt that he had improved remarkably. He was better able to perform normal functions of daily life such as remembering to put his clothes on and brush his teeth without being reminded. He regained an ability to understand his favorite TV shows and had much less difficulty with orientation. He was also more active and resumed some routine activities. He could answer the questions on our questionnaire correctly. Chris and his wife were extremely pleased by his improved ability to function. After three months of scalp acupuncture, Chris had showed significant improvements in mental activities and regained much of his routine life.

Discussion

Scalp acupuncture offers fairly good results for the patients with Alzheimer's disease. Several patients treated at our clinics have shown some improvement in both their mental and physical abilities. However, treating patients with memory loss is very challenging because patients cannot remember the simple things that you tell them during treatment sessions. It requires both very good, gentle needle technique as well as good communication skills. The practitioner should chat with Alzheimer's patients during treatment as if they were old friends or family members. For a patient who is extra sensitive to needles, stimulation should be avoided during the first one or two sessions. Compared to other patients, generally speaking Alzheimer's patients should receive fewer needles, milder stimulation, and shorter duration of needle retention. When treating such patients it is important to observe their responses and reactions while inserting, stimulating, and withdrawing the needles, and adjust the techniques accordingly.

Moxibustion can also enhance the therapeutic results of scalp acupuncture, especially for older or weaker patients who have less positive response to scalp acupuncture in the early sessions. Commonly used points for moxa therapy include Guan Yuan (CV 4), Tai Xi (Ki 3), Yong Quan (Ki 1), Zu San Li (St 36), San Yin Jiao (Sp 6), and Shen Shu (Bl 23) for supplementing and boosting their energy and essence. Although some of the mental limitations of patients with Alzheimer's disease cannot be overcome, scalp acupuncture will definitely improve their health and the quality of their lives.

Essential Tremor

Essential tremor, called familial or hereditary tremor when there is a positive family history of tremor, can be accurately diagnosed by Western medicine on the basis of the symptoms and a neurological examination. It may first appear at any age, often in early adult life, but it may also begin in childhood. The clinical manifestations are coarse, rhythmic and symmetric tremor, persisting throughout the range of motion of voluntary activity, increasing in amplitude as the limb approaches an object, or in handling or bringing food to the mouth. The tremor subsides during rest but is often exacerbated by physical or emotional stress. Currently there is no cure for essential tremor in Western medicine, and most available therapies focus on symptomatic treatment only. There are, however, some oral medications that may reduce the tremor severity and therefore decrease the social handicap or stigma.

Chinese medicine considers all involuntary movement of the body as a result of wind, usually internally engendered. Other patterns or disease mechanisms are also invariably involved, such as blood deficiency, phlegm and dampness, or blood stasis, for example.

CASE HISTORY #43

Charles was 53 when he came to our Santa Fe clinic with the complaint of tremors, but he remembered having tremors in his hands and body since the age of five. He had a phobic response to eating or speaking in public and noted that his condition became more pronounced in stressful situations.

Acupuncture treatments from other practitioners during the previous 20 years had not alleviated his symptoms. He also had an internal tremor in his body, which he could feel but no one else was able to see. Upon examination, Charles' arms and hands presented several tremors, but there was no visible tremor in his body. His tongue was red with a thin, white coating, and his tremor was present there as well. His pulses were wiry and fine.

Chinese medical pattern discrimination: Liver wind stirring internally, kidney essence deficiency

Scalp acupuncture treatment

Area selection
Primary area: Chorea and Tremor Area
Secondary area: Middle 2/5 Motor Area, Balance Area

Manipulation
The Chorea and Tremor Area, middle 2/5 Motor Area, and Balance Area should be needled and stimulated unilaterally. Insertion of needles in ear points Shen Men and Liver often enhance the function of scalp acupuncture for tremor patients. Rotate the needles at least 200 times per minute with the thumb and index finger for 1–3 minutes, twirling them as energetically as the patient can stand and repeating this stimulation every 10 minutes. During treatment, some patients may feel a sensation of pressure or fullness in the Chorea and Tremor Area on the head, or may experience their tremors becoming a little more severe. Patients with some or all of these sensations usually respond and improve more quickly. Retain the needles for 25–30 minutes. Treatment is given two or three times per week, and a therapeutic course consists of 10 treatments.

Results of Case #43

A few minutes after four needles were inserted in his scalp, Charles was amazed to see steadiness in his hands, which he had not experienced since early childhood. He felt calm and peaceful and fell asleep during the treatment. At the end of the first session Charles was very excited to see dramatically diminished tremors in his arms and hands as he raised them to shoulder level. After two additional sessions, the arm and hand tremors as well as the internal tremor were completely gone. At the fourth session, when asked why he spoke so slowly, Charles said he had learned to do this in order to cover the lifelong tremor in his voice. The stimulation areas were modified to include the Speech I Area in the fourth treatment because of this speech disorder.

Charles was able to talk faster and more clearly after the Speech I Area was needled and stimulated during the fourth visit. Within a week the voice tremor was gone, which friends and family noticed at once. Even after his tremors were completely gone, Charles preferred to receive a maintenance treatment once a month, especially when his stress level increased.

Discussion

Scalp acupuncture has fairly good results with essential tremor and usually produces some immediate positive responses. Significant and complete tremor reduction occurs in approximately 80% of people receiving scalp acupuncture. Although the norm has been that tremors gradually decrease with each session, some patients experience the symptoms becoming worse during treatment. If tremors are not well controlled by scalp acupuncture alone, patients may experience better results when combining it with body acupuncture or ear acupuncture. Commonly used body points are Tai Chong (Liv 3), Tai Xi (Ki 3), Yang Ling Quan (GB 34), and Wai Guan (TB 5). On the ear the commonly used points are Shen Men, Liver, Kidney, and Sympathetic point.

Research on the effects of scalp acupuncture for essential tremor

- Sui Kang-min and colleagues treated 60 patients with essential tremor in 2009. The patients were randomly divided into 30 cases in the combined acupuncture and medication group and 30 cases in the medication-only group. The combined group was treated at Bai Hui (GV 20), Si Shen Zhong (extra point), and Tai Xi (Ki 3), and both groups were administrated with Propranolol. Comprehensive effects and records of tremor were observed after 30 days of treatment in both groups. The results showed that the total effective rate was 90.0% (27/30) in the combined acupuncture and medication group. It was 56.7% (17/30) in the medication-only group (P < 0.01). The tremor score of the combined group was less than that of the medication-only group (P < 0.05).[50]

Coma

Coma is a state of prolonged unconsciousness in which a person is unable to awaken and does not respond purposefully to physical or verbal stimulation. There are four levels of unconsciousness: somnolence, stupor, semi-coma, and deep coma. When a patient is in the stage of deep coma (Grade 4), he or she has little or no response to any stimulus, including deep pain. The patient has flaccid musculature and incontinence. Stretch reflex and corneal reflex disappear, respiration is periodic, and the pulse is rapid. At the stage of semi-coma (Grade 3), the patient is able to withdraw from painful stimuli, has similar responses to persistent tactile stimuli, and has other stimulus-bound responses. The patient also experiences incontinence, the presence of reflexes, and spontaneous movements. At the stage of stupor (Grade 2), the patient presents considerable spontaneous movement, responds to pain and intense stimuli, and may give a combative response or withdrawal. And at the stage of somnolence (Grade 1), the patient may be clear mentally, but often confused, roused by various stimuli and may make appropriate motor and verbal responses, but also experience illusions, delusions, hallucinations, or delirium.

A coma patient typically has signs and symptoms of closed eyes, lack of consciousness, no response to stimuli, inability to be aroused, and a lack of sleep-wake cycles. There are many causes that can result in coma or other states of unconsciousness. They are divided into two general categories: anatomic causes and metabolic causes. Anatomic causes such as stroke, brain tumor, and brain injury result in disruption of the normal physical structure of the brain that is responsible for consciousness. Metabolic causes are those that adversely affect brain function by changing the chemical environment of the brain such as diabetes, infections, and liver or kidney failure. A coma is a medical emergency that can quickly become life-threatening, so seeking Western medical assistance immediately is extremely important.

Stroke is an acute neurological disease in which the blood supply to the brain is interrupted causing brain cells to die or be seriously damaged, thus impairing brain functions. Stroke is one of the common causes of coma and other types of unconsciousness. The degree of coma depends on the type of stroke and the area of the brain affected. Most patients in a coma are at a high risk of death. A person may stay in a coma for weeks, months, or even years. Sometimes the cause of a coma can be completely reversed, such as a drug overdose, and the person can regain normal function. However, some patients who recover from a coma may be permanently disabled.

According to Chinese medicine, coma is described as a state where the essence spirit cannot communicate with the outside world. This is either due to non-construction and malnourishment of the spirit by qi and blood or to blockage and obstruction by some pathologic qi such as phlegm or blood stasis.

CASE HISTORY #44

Paul was carried into our clinic in Santa Fe, New Mexico. Paul had suffered a stroke during brain tumor surgery six weeks before at age 65 and had been in a semi-coma ever since. He was kept in a local hospital for four weeks with little mental or physical improvement. Then he was sent to a rehabilitation center that deals with semi-coma patients. There he underwent physiotherapy, aromatherapy, and physical therapy. Unfortunately, his improvements were minimal and soon after he was sent home. Neurological examination revealed semi-coma, his pupils were fixed, light reflexes were intact, and corneal reflexes were sluggish. He had somnolence, mental confusion, tearful outbreaks, and dysphasia. Paul's slurred speech was barely understandable. His right arm and leg were completely paralyzed and he had incontinence of urine, constipation, and restless sleep. He had a deep red tongue with scant coating. His pulses were wiry and slippery.

Chinese medical pattern discrimination: Phlegm fire obstructing the orifices of the heart

Scalp acupuncture treatment

Area selection

Primary area: Head Area, Foot Motor and Sensory Area, upper 1/5 and middle 2/5 of Motor Area, and Speech I Area
Secondary area: Upper 1/5 and middle 2/5 of Sensory Area, and Speech III Area

Manipulation

Head Area and Foot Motor and Sensory Area should be chosen together for all kinds of unconsciousness issues. Motor Area, Sensory Area, and Speech Area I or III should be needled and stimulated unilaterally, according to the patient's symptoms. For a patient with aphasia, choose Speech I Area first if the patient cannot speak at all. Speech III Area should be chosen if the patient has comprehension problems. If paralysis is in the upper limbs, the middle 2/5 Motor Area should be chosen. If paralysis is in the leg and foot, the upper 1/5 should be the choice. If in the face the lower 2/5 should be selected. If there are some abnormal sensations in the leg, foot, arm, hand, or face, the upper 1/5, middle 2/5 or lower 2/5 should be chosen respectively. The chosen insertion area should be the opposite of the affected limb. For example, if there is paralysis in the right arm, the left middle 2/5 Motor Area should be selected. Rotate the needles at least 200 times per minute for 1–3 minutes, twirling them as strongly as the patient can tolerate and repeating the stimulation every 10 minutes. Retain the needles for 30–45 minutes. The patient is given two or three treatments per week, and a therapeutic course consists of 10 treatments.

Results of Case #44

About 40 seconds after the insertion and stimulation of needles to his scalp and Ren Zhong area (CV 26), Paul's consciousness improved dramatically. He opened his eyes and made good eye contact. Tears appeared when he was called by his name. He had a positive response to needle stimulation and gave a normal handshake. However, he returned to a semi-coma only five minutes after exhibiting these improvements. Paul started to respond again to tickling of the bottoms of his feet. Sometimes he was also able to blink his eyes as a response, hold his head up on his own for a while, and was able to focus on objects. On the first post-treatment day, he progressively recovered consciousness and was able to follow commands and move some muscles in his extremities. At the second session, his consciousness improved from semi-coma to drowsiness and somnolence. Paul's mental activities showed more alertness, and he was able to respond to some questions by saying yes or no. Ten days later during his third treatment, his speech had noticeably improved and he could respond to most questions correctly. Flaccid paralysis of the right extremities, however, became apparent as consciousness improved. He started to move his right leg and was able to sit up for a while as he gradually recovered. That night he was able to sleep for six hours peacefully for the first time since the stroke.

During his fourth visit he was fully alert, talked a lot, and made some jokes. Both his right arm and right leg moved better; and he started to have some movement in his fingers. He reported that he had more energy and did not have trouble sleeping any more. During the fifth session, Paul was walking again with a walker, his balance was much improved, and he had started to urinate by himself. He could have normal conversations most of the time, although he still had difficulty with certain words. By the seventh treatment he had started to walk with a cane, and urination and bowel movements had both returned to normal. By the tenth visit, he was able to move his right fingers and hold a glass with both of his hands for the first time since the stroke. Paul felt much stronger and was able to walk for a long time without exhaustion. By the twentieth treatment, he could walk with little support and had regained normal speech function. He was able to use his right hand almost normally. Because of all these dramatic changes, he had been able to start more routine exercise sessions. The only residual symptom was a weakness in his right leg. His tongue had changed to slightly red with a thin, white (normal) coating, and his pulses were slippery and only slightly wiry.

Discussion

It is advisable for a coma patient to receive emergency treatment in Western medicine rather than to receive acupuncture treatment at first. It is important to identify a stroke as early as possible because patients who are treated early have less chance of lapsing into a coma and are, therefore, more likely to survive with fewer disabilities. Stroke survivors usually have some degree of sequelae of symptoms, depending primarily on the location in the brain and the amount of brain tissue damaged. Disability affects about 75% of stroke survivors and can affect patients physically, mentally, emotionally, or a combination of all three. Because one side of the brain controls the opposite side of the body, a stroke affecting one side of the brain results in neurological symptoms on the other side of the body. Although there is no cure for stroke, most stroke patients now have a good chance for survival and recovery. When stroke patients pass the acute stage they should start scalp acupuncture as soon as possible. This can help them return to their normal life more quickly by regaining and relearning the skills of everyday living such as speaking or walking.

Scalp acupuncture has been found to have good results on the sequelae of stroke, including hemiplegia, aphasia, various grades of coma, and abnormal sensations in the limbs. According to advanced stroke research and brain imaging technology, physicians are continuing to gain new understanding of how the brain can adapt after stroke in order to regain its ability to function. New research suggests that normal brain cells are highly adaptable and can undergo changes, not only in function and shape, but also that allow them to take over the functions of nearby damaged cells. As a result, scalp acupuncture is geared toward stimulating and restoring affected brain tissue or retraining unaffected brain tissue to compensate for the lost functions of damaged brain tissue.

Although scalp acupuncture has the fastest response to help patients with coma, other techniques are necessary for a full recovery. According to the individual's condition, regular body acupuncture and moxibustion can combine with scalp acupuncture to speed up the time of recovery. Some regular acupuncture treatment has been found to have a positive therapeutic effect on recovery from unconsciousness. Commonly used points are Ren Zhong (CV 26), Yong Quan (Ki 1), Tai Chong (Liv 3), He Gu (LI 4), and Tong Li (Ht 5). Moxibustion can enhance the therapeutic results of scalp acupuncture as well, especially for older or weaker patients. Commonly used points are Zu San Li (St 36), San Yin Jiao (Sp 6), Guan Yuan (CV 4), and Yong Quan (Ki 1).

Chronic Fatigue Syndrome

Chronic fatigue syndrome (CFS), also known as myalgic encephalomyelitis (inflammation of the brain and spinal cord with muscle pain) or chronic fatigue immune deficiency syndrome (CFIDS), is a complicated disorder affecting the central nervous system, immune system, and organs. It is characterized by extreme fatigue that does not abate with rest, worsens with physical or mental activities, and it persists in duration for six months or longer. In addition to fatigue, CFS may include any or all of the following symptoms: impairment of short-term memory and concentration, muscle pain or pain in multiple joints, sore throat, headache, swollen lymph nodes in the neck or armpits, unrefreshing sleep or insomnia, shortness of breath, palpitation, diarrhea, dizziness, weight loss or gain, depression, irritability, mood swings, and anxiety.

Chronic fatigue syndrome is at present largely an exclusionary diagnosis in Western medicine because there is no accepted conclusive test or series of tests for it. While some patients are able to lead a relatively normal life, others are totally bed-bound and unable to care for themselves. Recently, stress and genetics have been found to be factors in the development of chronic fatigue syndrome. Some research suggests that this condition is linked to an impaired stress response and emotional instability, and it may involve subtle dysfunctions of the hypothalamus-pituitary-adrenal axis. The majority of patients with CFS begin experiencing it after a period of extreme stress in the year preceding the illness. It starts suddenly and often is triggered by a flu-like viral or similar illness. For some patients the disease starts gradually and slowly, without a clear history of illness and sometimes it is spread out over years. There is no specific treatment for chronic fatigue syndrome in Western medicine. In general, treatments are aimed at relieving symptoms. Some dietary supplements and herbal remedies have been recognized as having potential benefits for patients with CFS.

Since the over-riding complaint in CFS is debilitating fatigue that has often been triggered by extreme stress, in Chinese medicine the core disease mechanism is believed to be a liver-spleen disharmony with severely depleted spleen qi. There will, however, be many other disease mechanisms and consequent patterns present as well in most patients. See Flaws and Sionneau for a thorough discussion of this condition according to Chinese medicine.[51]

John was referred to our Santa Fe clinic by his primary physician when he was 45. Formerly, he had exercised numerous hours every week, being especially fond of hiking and swimming. He had first experienced extreme fatigue after having the flu three years previously. His fatigue never improved and gradually worsened to the point where he feared he might have to quit work. John was finally diagnosed with chronic fatigue syndrome a year later after having seen many doctors and undergoing many different kinds of tests. His symptoms included headaches, musculoskeletal pain, palpitations, shortness of breath, and insomnia. He also had trouble concentrating and remembering, had tinnitus, and often experienced diarrhea. The continual bone-weary exhaustion he suffered was hard for others to comprehend because he did not look sick and most of his lab tests were within normal ranges. John had tried many kinds of therapies and taken quite a lot of supplements, none of which helped. He was very depressed, could barely work half a day, collapsed when he got home, and had no energy to do any housework. Upon examination, John had a dull facial complexion. His tongue was pale and slightly purple with a thick, white coating. There were teethmarks on his tongue and it had a tremor as well. His pulses were fine and wiry overall, but fine, forceless, and deep in both of his cubit (*chi*) positions.

Chinese medical pattern discrimination: Heart blood/spleen qi dual deficiency, kidney qi deficiency

Scalp acupuncture treatment

Area selection
Primary area: Foot Motor and Sensory Area, Head Area
Secondary area: Sensory Area, Thoracic Cavity Area, Liver and Gallbladder Area, Stomach Area, and Reproductive Area

Manipulation
Insert needles in the Foot Motor and Sensory Area bilaterally and the Head Area unilaterally. Choose secondary areas based upon symptoms in Western medicine and patterns in Chinese medicine. It is a good technique to put

one needle in the ear point Shen Men to help the patient relax and reduce the sensitivity of the needle insertion and stimulation of the scalp. Use as few needles as possible in the scalp and rotate them at least 200 times per minute with the thumb and index finger for two minutes, twirling as gently as possible in the beginning so the patient can tolerate the intense sensations and repeating the stimulation every 10 minutes. During treatment, some patients may experience sensations of heat, cold, tingling, numbness, heaviness, distention, or the sensation of water or electricity moving along their spine, legs, or arms. Tell patients before the needles are inserted that those sensations are normal, and patients who experience them usually respond and improve more quickly. This encourages patients to come back for additional treatments. However, it is important to also convey that patients who do not have such sensations could still have immediate, positive results. Retain the needles in place for 10–20 minutes. Treatment is given two or three times per week, and a therapeutic course consists of 10 treatments.

Results of Case #45

John had a very positive response during his first scalp acupuncture treatment. The headache and general body aches were diminished and the palpitations were completely gone just a few minutes after the needles were inserted in his scalp. Later, John reported he had a new and pleasant feeling and he fell asleep. He was excited to explain that the headache was entirely gone and the ringing in his ears had subsided after his nap. At the second session interview, he reported sleeping better and having a bit more energy after work with no headaches or palpitations. After the fifth session, John had more energy and his sleep was much better. The diarrhea had ceased, his musculoskeletal pain showed remarkable improvement, and his memory and concentration were better as well. By the tenth session, John claimed that his energy had improved to 70% of its normal level. He was able to hike about 20–30 minutes and swim 10 laps without shortness of breath, he had no more tinnitus, and his memory and concentration had almost returned to normal. After 20 sessions he was normal mentally and physically, with no further symptoms of chronic fatigue.

Discussion

Scalp acupuncture has a fairly good track record for treating chronic fatigue syndrome. However, it usually requires long periods of treatment, and most patents need 20–30 visits. It is very helpful if other acupuncture methods are utilized along with scalp acupuncture, such as body acupuncture and moxibustion. The selection of body points should be individualized based on the differentiation of patterns in Chinese medicine. For instance, Zu San Li (St 36), San Yin Jiao (Sp 6), and Zhong Wan (CV 12) are used for spleen and stomach deficiency, and Yong Quan (Ki 1), Tai Xi (Ki 3), Zhao Hai (Ki 6), and Fu Liu (Ki 7) for kidney deficiency.

Reports show that chronic fatigue syndrome may worsen with increased stress whether from physical, emotional, or psychological sources. Therefore, the scalp areas that have the function of relieving anxiety, irritability, or depression should be combined with the Foot Motor and Sensory Area for best results. Other therapies that can promote relaxation and a sense of well-being may be helpful in relieving chronic fatigue syndrome, such as meditation, hypnosis, yoga, and herbs.

Conclusion

Chinese scalp acupuncture has greatly enhanced the practice of acupuncture in the last 38 years. This newer method successfully integrates traditional Chinese needling techniques with Western medical knowledge, based on areas of the cerebral cortex. As a modern medical technique, Chinese scalp acupuncture has been proven to be superior to other acupuncture methods and most Western modalities, particularly in its immediate effect in treating central nervous system disorders.

Scalp acupuncture is a dynamic component of acupuncture practice. In the past, the use of scalp acupuncture among Western practitioners has been unsatisfactory, largely because of the very limited number of highly experienced teachers and the absence of an authoritative and practical text for scalp acupuncture in English. It is our hope that this situation will begin to change after our book is studied and its principles and protocols are applied by acupuncture practitioners.

Further, we believe that the material presented here will be a valuable contribution to the advancement of acupuncture worldwide and will fill a major gap in both the literature and practice of this medicine in the West. The book provides acupuncture practitioners with new, effective techniques to treat central nervous system disorders for which other therapies have limited solutions.

Since its original innovation in the early 1970s, significant developments in treating central nervous system disorders with scalp acupuncture have taken place. As a result of these advances, the authors of this book are increasingly being called upon to study and explain the mechanisms of scalp acupuncture. Although there have been some papers focusing on the mechanisms and clinical applications, there is limited research of sufficient quality to evaluate the results of this method. There are very few studies published in China employing control groups using Western research standards, and many of the studies that have been done have only analyzed one or two changes in neurophysiology and biochemistry. There have also been a wide variety of techniques and treatment protocols used, which makes it extremely hard to evaluate the results critically. Some research findings suggest that scalp acupuncture improves the viscosity of the blood, improves vascular elasticity, reinforces cardiac contraction, and increases cerebral blood flow.[52]

For these reasons, it is very difficult to provide readers with a reasonable and comprehensive explanation using a Western biomedical viewpoint. However, what we do know is that scalp acupuncture has shown remarkable effects on central nervous system disorders, based on both the large amount of clinical evidence presented here as well as findings in the references listed (see pages 255-259).

The success of scalp acupuncture with central nervous system disorders is attractive to neurologists, who are always seeking effective ways to help patients. Both the authors and other practitioners who use scalp acupuncture are seeking to understand the mechanisms of this success in terms of Western medicine. There are three possible explanations at this time:

- Scalp acupuncture may enhance brain plasticity in promoting brain repair by stimulating the sprouting and formation of new functional connections in surrounding normal brain tissue.[53]

- Neuronal circuits in the central nervous system might be able to reshape themselves in response to external stimuli and experience.[54]
- Scalp acupuncture may stimulate the brain to create a new neuronal pathway or rewire a part of the damaged cortex. The damaged brain can often reorganize itself so that when one part fails, other parts can compensate for it.[55]

In this book, we have given details of many original cases treated by us. Through our years of clinical work as well as extensive teaching, we have greatly expanded the techniques and applications of scalp acupuncture. We have also attempted in this presentation to model the successful integration of Chinese medicine with Western medicine for the betterment of our patients' lives. We believe that the work described in this book gives a solid foundation for clinical application of scalp acupuncture by established acupuncture practitioners, for those new to the field, and for teachers and researchers as well. Furthermore, we hope the material presented here provides non-acupuncture health practitioners with a better understanding of how they might integrate this method into their practice.

The main contributions that we have presented in this book for scalp acupuncture are:

- The setup of treatment protocols for many central nervous system disorders such as multiple sclerosis, Parkinson's disease, phantom pain, residual limb pain, and complex regional pain
- Shortening the length of areas to be stimulated for tremor and chorea, as well as for blood vessel dilation and contraction, according to anatomy and neurophysiology
- Adding the location, function, and indication for stimulating the Head Area, based on our experience
- Increasing the functions and indications for many stimulating areas, such as Foot Motor and Sensory Area, Sensory Area, and Motor Area
- Summarizing special needling methods used in scalp acupuncture treatment
- Creating new, easy-to-understand color figures for stimulation areas, the cerebral hemisphere, insertion, and manipulation.

This book also heralds an exciting time of great interest in scalp acupuncture in both Asia and the West. Physicians need new tools to deal with many disorders that do not respond to currently known techniques, and patients look for new solutions to improve their lives. Scalp acupuncture has been recognized as a very effective process to handle many of these problems. This book provides practitioners with a clear and skillful way to master scalp acupuncture and its applications. We hope that readers will share this knowledge and achieve excellent results in their own practice.

Although this book represents the fruits of our collaboration and our practice to this point, we see it as a work in progress. The clinical applications for using scalp acupuncture are still expanding. For example, we recently discovered that patients can recover from brain damage even decades after the trauma, in contrast to the common assumption that only immediate treatment would be effective.

The authors trust that this book will further enhance the practice, development, and research of scalp acupuncture. If its scope were expanded, we believe scalp acupuncture could have a significant impact on recovery from central nervous system disorders for thousands of patients. There is, therefore, a pressing need for Chinese scalp acupuncture to be studied and perfected using modern research methods, so that its potential can be fully explored and applied.

Appendix:
International Standard Scalp Acupuncture Nomenclature and Locations

As we discussed in the introduction, there have been several different scalp acupuncture schools before and after Jiao Shun-fa's nomenclature and locations. International Standard Scalp Acupuncture Nomenclature and Location was proposed at the conference held by the Western Pacific Regional Office of the World Health Organization (WHO) in 1984 and was adopted at the International Standard Scalp Acupuncture Nomenclature Symposium of WHO in Geneva in 1989.[56] In accordance with the standard regular acupuncture nomenclature of the 14 channels, international standard scalp acupuncture nomenclature includes three parts: the English name, Chinese Pinyin name, and alphanumeric code. Alphanumeric code is written as MS 1–14. In this system, 'M' represents micro-acupuncture and 'S' represents scalp acupuncture. There are 14 treating lines in International Standard Scalp Acupuncture. Most of those 14 lines are based on Jiao Shun-fa's locations, functions, and indications. As WHO states,

These scalp acupuncture lines were formerly named in functional terms. The proposed standard international nomenclature is based on surface anatomy so as to facilitate localization of the lines but their relationship to the underlying functional structures has not changed.[57]

Some scholars argued that the new standard names are relatively difficult for acupuncture practitioners to remember and use in their practice and research.[58]

A brief introduction of the 14 lines[59]

The Four Standard Lines in the Forehead

Middle Line of Forehead, Ezhongxian (MS 1): 1 *cun* down from Shen Ting (DU 24) straight downward along the channel. The location and indication of this line is the same as the Head Area in our book.

Lateral Line 1 of Forehead, Epangxian I (MS 2): 1 *cun* from Mei Chong (Bl 3) straight downward along the channel. The location and indication of this line is the same as the Thoracic Cavity Area in our book.

Lateral Line 2 of Forehead, Epangxian II (MS 3): 1 *cun* from Tou Lin Qi (GB 15) straight downward along the channel. The location and indication of this line is the same as the Liver and Gallbladder Area and Stomach Area in our book.

Lateral Line 3 of Forehead Epangxian III (MS 4): 1 *cun* from a point 0.75 *cun* medial to Tou Wei (St 8) straight downward. The location and indication of this line is the same as the Reproductive Area and Intestine Area in our boo.

The Five Standard Lines in the Vertex

Middle Line of Vertex, Dingzhongxian (MS 5): from Bai Hui (DU 20) to Qian Ding (DU 21) along the midline of the head. The indication of this line is similar to the Foot Motor and Ssensory Area in our book.

Anterior Oblique Line of Vertex-Temporal, Dignie Qianxienxian (MS 6): from Qian Ding (1.5 *cun* anterior to Bai Hui) obliquely to Xuan Li (GB 6). The location and indication of this line is similar to the Motor Area in our book.

Posterior Oblique Line of Vertex-Temporal, Dignie Houxiexian (MS 7): from Bai Hui (DU 20) obliquely to Qu Bin (GB 7). The location and indication of this line is similar to the Sensory Area in our book.

Lateral Line 1 of Vertex, Dingpangxian I (MS 8): 1 *cun* lateral to Middle Line of Vertex, 2 *cun* from Cheng Guang (Bl 6) backward along the channel. The indication of this line is close to the Foot Motor and Sensory Area in our book.

Lateral Line 2 of Vertex, Dingpangxian II (MS 9): 2.25 *cun* lateral to Middle Line of Vertex, 1.5 *cun* from Zheng Ying (GB 17) backward along the channel. The location and indication of this line is close to the middle 2/5 Motor Area and middle 2/5 Sensory Area in our book.

The Two Standard Lines in Temporal Area

Anterior Temporal Line, Nieqianxian (MS 10): from Han Yan (GB 4) to Xuan Li (GB 6). The indication of this line is close to the Speech I Area in our book.

Posterior Temporal Line, Niehouxian (MS 11): from Shuai Gu (GB 8) to Qu Bin (GB 7). The location and indication of this line is close to the Vertigo and Hearing Area in our book.

The Three Standard Lines in Occipital Area (altogether five lines)

Upper Middle Line of Occipital, Zhengzhongxian (MS 12): from Qiang Jian (DU 18) to Nao Hu (DU 17). The indication of this line is similar to the Vision Area in our book.

Upper Lateral Line of Occipital Zhenshangpangxian (MS 13): 0.5 *cun* lateral and parallel to Upper Middle Line of Occipital. The location and indication of this line is similar to the Vision Area in our book.

Lower Lateral Line of Occipital, Zhenxiapangxian (MS 14): 2 *cun* long from Yu Zhen (Bl 9) straight downward. The location and indication of this line is similar to the Balance Area in our book.

References

1. Feng Cun-xiang et al., *Practical Handbook of Scalp Acupuncture*, Chinese Medicine and Science Publishing House, 1999, p. 30–36
2. Wang Fu-chun, Yu Xian-mei, Deng Yu, *Scalp Acupuncture Therapy*, People's Medical Publishing House, Beijing, 2003, p. 61–68
3. Wu Bo-li et al., "Yu Zhi-shun's Experience on Head Points for Paralysis," *Chinese Acupuncture & Moxibustion*, 1997, Vol.17 No. 3, p. 153–154
4. Zhu Ming-qing et al., *Scalp Acupuncture*, Guangdong Technology and Science Press, 1992, p. 8–11
5. Jiao Shun-fa, *Head Acupuncture*, Foreign Languages Press, Beijing, 1993, p.17–22
6. E.C.B. Hall-Craggs, *Anatomy As a Basis for Clinical Medicine*, Urban & Schwarzenberg, Inc., West Germany, 1985, p. 493
7. Van Heertum, Ranalk L., and Tikofsky, Ronald S., *Functional Cerebral SPECT and PET Imaging*, Third edition, Lippincott Williams & Wilkins, Philadelphia, PA, 2000, p. 56–57
8. Tortora, Gerald J., and Anagnostakos, Nicholas P., *Principles of Anatomy and Physiology*, Fifth edition, Harper & Row, Publishers, New York, 1987, p. 349
9. Blumenfeld, Hal, *Neuroanatomy Through Clinical Cases*, Sinauer Associates, Inc., Sunderland, MA, 2002, p. 743–750
10. Arslan, Orhan, *Neuroanatomical Basis of Clinical Neurology*, The Parthenon Publishing Group Inc., New York, 2001, p. 326–329
11. Wang Xue-tai et al., *Complete Works of Chinese Acupuncture and Moxibustion*, Henan Scientific and Technical Publishing House, Henan, 1993, p. 49
12. Cheng Xin-nong, *Chinese Acupuncture and Moxibustion*, Revised edition, Foreign Languages Press, Beijing, 1990, p. 41

13. Beijing University of Traditional Chinese Medicine et al., *The Foundation of Traditional Chinese Medicine*, Shanghai Scientific and Technical Publishing House, Shanghai, 1977, p. 18

14. Jia, Huai-yu et al., *Scalp Acupuncture Therapy*, People's Medical Publishing House, Beijing, 1994, p. 29

15. Wang et al., *op.cit.*, p. 106

16. Jia et al., *op.cit.*, p. 28

17. O'Connor, John and Dan Bensky, *Acupuncture A Comprehensive Text*, Eastland Press, Seattle, 1981, p. 59–60

18. Jiao, *op.cit.*, p. 88–89

19. O'Connor and Bensky, *op.cit.*, p. 498–501

20. Zhu et al., *op.cit.*, p. 77–81

21. Jiao Shun-fa, *Scalp Acupuncture and Clinical Cases*, Foreign Languages Press, Beijing, 1997, p. 23–25

22. Wang et al., *op.cit.*, p. 95–97

23. Helms, Joseph M., *Acupuncture Energetics*, Medical Acupuncture Publishers, Berkeley, CA, 1995, p. 649–652

24. Blumenfeld, *op.cit.*, p. 64

25. Olmstead, Donna, "Acupuncture: The Medicine Is Powerful," *Albuquerque Journal*, February 19, 1996, p. A1

26. Chang, Richard, "Fertile Ground for Alternative Medicine," *The New Mexican*, June 1, 1997, p. E2–4

27. Chang, Richard, "Acupuncture Rehab," *The New Mexican*, April 3, 1998, p. C-3

28. McMillan, Brett B., "Easing the Pain, Acupuncture Program Looks to Help Relieve Discomfort of Troops," *Stripe*, February 17, 2006, p. 1

29. Zhou Ying, "He Teaches and Popularizes Chinese Medicine in USA," *China News On Traditional Chinese Medicine*, April 5, 2006, p. 8

30. Lampe, Frank, and Suzanne Snyder, "Jason Hao, DOM: Pioneering the Use of Scalp Acupuncture to Transform Healing," *Alternative Therapies*, March/April 2009, Vol.15 No. 2, p. 62–71

31. Kong Yao-qi et al., *The Acupuncture Treatment for Paralysis*, Science Press, Beijing, 2000, p. 23

32. Jiao, *op.cit.*, p. 47

33. Jia, *op.cit.*, p. 74

34. Liu Jian-hao et al., "Observation on Specificity of Acupuncture Location in Treatment of Acute Apoplexy by Scalp Penetration Needling," *Chinese Acupuncture & Moxibustion*, April 2010, Vol. 30 No. 4, p. 275–278

35. Li Min et al., "Observation on Therapeutic Effect of Five-Needle-in-Nape Acupuncture for Treatment of Post-stroke Pseudobulbar Paralysis Dysphagia," *Chinese Acupuncture & Moxibustion*, November 2009, Vol. 29 No. 11, p. 873–875

36. Hao, Jason and Linda Hao, "Treatment of Multiple Sclerosis by Scalp Acupuncture," *Acupuncture Today*, April 2008, Vol. 9 No. 4, p. 12–13

37. Gao Wei-bin and Gao Jing-li, *Acupuncture and Moxibustion Six Unique Skills*, Chinese Medical Science Publishing House, 1998, p. 243–244

38. Wu Jian-min, "Clinical Observation of 80 Cases of Facial Paralysis by Scalp Acupuncture," *Shanxi Journal of Traditional Chinese Medicine*, 1989, Vol. 10 No. 2, p. 81

39. Liu Fang-shi et al., "Clinical Observation of 48 Cases of Facial Paralysis by Scalp Acupuncture," *Shanghai Journal of Acupuncture and Moxibustion*, 1994, Vol. 13 No. 4, p. 166

40. Hao, Jason and Linda Hao, "Treatment of Phantom Pain by Scalp Acupuncture," *Acupuncture Today*, September, 2006, Vol. 7 No. 9, p. 10–11

41. Shi Ling-zhi and Hao Ji-shun, "Treatment of Fibromyalgia by Eight-needle Penetrating Technique", *Chinese Journal of Information on Traditional Chinese Medicine*, February 2005, Vol. 12 No. 2, p. 64

42. Hoy Ping Yee Chan et al., *Acupuncture for Stroke Rehabilitation*, Blue Poppy Press, Boulder, CO, 2006, p. 84–85

43. Chen Dao-yi, "Clinical Observation on the Scalp Acupuncture for 444 Cases of Cerebral Paralysis and Aphasia," *Chinese Acupuncture & Moxibustion*, 1987, Vol. 7 No. 2, p. 9–14

44. Damone, Bob, *Principles of Chinese Medical Andrology: An Integrated Approach to Male Reproductive and Urological Health*, Blue Poppy Press, Boulder, CO, 2008, p. 219–250

45. Flaws, Bob, and James Lake, MD, *Chinese Medical Psychiatry*, Blue Poppy Press, Boulder, CO, 2001, p. 277–288

46. Shen Xiu-lan et al., "Clinical Observation on the Scalp Electro-acupuncture for 240 Cases of Seizure," *Journal of Guiyang College of Traditional Chinese Medicine*, 1989, (3), p. 48–49

47. Wang Tai-dong et al., "Clinical Analysis on the Scalp Acupuncture for 163 Cases of Nocturnal Enuresis," *Journal of Combining Western and Chinese Medicine*, 1987, Vol. 7 No. 8, p. 50

48. Zhang Yu-lian et al., "A Clinical Study on the Treatment of Apoplectic Ataxia with Scalp and Body Acupuncture," *Shanghai Journal of Acupuncture & Moxibustion*, No. 8, 2003, p. 7–8

49. Flaws, Bob, and Philippe Sionneau, *The Treatment of Modern Western Medical Diseases with Chinese Medicine*, 2nd Edition, Blue Poppy Press, 2001, p. 53–58

50. Sui Kang-min et al., "Clinical Observation on Acupuncture Combined with Medication for Treatment of Essential Tremor," *Chinese Acupuncture and Moxibustion*, February 2010, Vol. 30 No. 2, p. 107–109

51. Flaws and Sionneau, *op.cit.*, p. 141–145

52. Jia, *op.cit.*, p. 92–97

53. Larsen, Stephen, *The Healing Power of Neurofeedback*, Healing Arts Press, Rochester, VT, 2006, p. xiii-xv

54. Brown, David, "Brain Rebuilding," *Albuquerque Journal*, January 31, 2011, p. C-1

55. Doidge, Norman, *The Brain That Changes Itself*, Penguin Group, Inc., New York, 2007, p. xix

56. Wang Fu-chun, *Scalp Acupuncture Therapy*, People's Medical Publishing House, Beijing, 2007, p. 53–60.

57. World Health Organization, "The International Standard of scalp Acupuncture Nomenclature", http://apps.who.int/medicinedocs/en/q/Traditional Medicine, 2011, p.4

58. An Bao-zhen, "Discussion About the Divided Methods and Unification on the Location of Scalp Acupuncture," *Chinese Acupuncture & Moxibustion*, June 2009 Vol. 29, No .6, p. 498–500

59. World Health Organization, *op.cit.*, p. 1–4

Index

Biographies

Jason Jishun Hao received his bachelor and master degrees of Traditional Chinese Medicine from Heilongjiang University of Traditional Chinese medicine in Harbin, China, in 1982 and 1987, respectively. He received his MBA from the University of Phoenix in 2004.

He was among an early group of doctors who studied scalp acupuncture. He had the opportunity to learn it directly from famous experts including Jiao Shun-fa, the founder of Chinese scalp acupuncture, Yu Zhi-shun, professor of scalp acupuncture development, and Sun Shen-tian, professor of scalp acupuncture research.

Dr. Jason Hao has been practicing and researching scalp acupuncture for 29 years and has been teaching classes and seminars in the West since 1989. He has trained hundreds of acupuncture practitioners and treated thousands of patients with disorders of the central nervous system in the United States and Europe. He has taught scalp acupuncture seminars sponsored by UCLA and Stanford for nine years. In 2006 Dr. Hao gave a scalp acupuncture seminar at Walter Reed Army Medical Center in Washington, DC, where he successfully demonstrated scalp acupuncture treatment of phantom limb pain for veterans. His case histories have been printed in the US Army publication *Stripes*, in *China Daily*, and in *Alternative Therapies*.

Jason Hao currently serves as chairman of the acupuncture committee in the National Certification Commission of Acupuncture and Oriental Medicine, as president of the board of directors at Southwest Acupuncture College, and as president of the International Academy of Scalp Acupuncture.

Linda Lingzhi Hao, PhD, was born in Harbin, Heilongjiang, China. She is a licensed and certified Doctor of Oriental Medicine. Beyond that training, she holds a doctorate degree of acupuncture from Heilongjiang University of Traditional Chinese Medicine in China, with a concentration in scalp acupuncture. She is also an appointed professor at Southwest Acupuncture College in Santa Fe, NM, where she received her master's degree of Traditional Chinese Medicine.

Dr. Linda Hao studied for four years under Dr. Sun Shen-tian, a highly acclaimed professor of scalp acupuncture development and research. She also learned it from Dr. Jiao Shun-fa, the founder of scalp acupuncture. She is a successful practitioner of scalp acupuncture with a well-established practice. Her expertise with this specialized method of treatment has been the subject of her lectures. She has collaborated with her husband, Dr. Jason Hao, in presenting seminars in various US cities, including Santa Fe, Denver, Dallas, New York, and Washington DC, and most recently, in Europe.

Throughout her professional career, Dr. Linda Hao has published several articles in *Acupuncture Today* in the US, and the *Chinese Journal of Information of Traditional Chinese Medicine* and *The World Federation of Acupuncture* in Beijing. Her article about clinical research on fibromyalgia, published in *Traditional Medicine and People's Health* by the Third International Congress on Traditional Medicine, was awarded the highest honor in Beijing, in 2003. Linda Hao was the associate editor-in-chief for a university textbook on Chinese herbal medicine published in China. She has also been featured in the *Albuquerque Journal* and *New Mexico Women* Magazine.

Dr. Linda Hao is president of the National Healthcare Center in Albuquerque, New Mexico, and is also the founder and vice president of the International Academy of Scalp Acupuncture.

OTHER BOOKS ON CHINESE MEDICINE AVAILABLE FROM:
BLUE POPPY ENTERPRISES, INC.

Oregon: 4804 SE 69th Avenue, Portland, OR 97206
For ordering 1-800-487-9296 PH. 503-650-6077 FAX 503-650-6076
Email: info@bluepoppy.com Website: www.bluepoppy.com

ACUPOINT POCKET REFERENCE by Bob Flaws
ISBN 0-936185-93-7
ISBN 978-0-936185-93-4

ACUPUNCTURE, CHINESE MEDICINE &
 HEALTHY WEIGHT LOSS   Revised Edition
by Juliette Aiyana, L. Ac.
ISBN 1-891845-61-6
ISBN 978-1-891845-61-1

ACUPUNCTURE & IVF by Lifang Liang
ISBN 0-891845-24-1
ISBN 978-0-891845-24-6

ACUPUNCTURE FOR STROKE REHABILITATION
Three Decades of Information from China
by Hoy Ping Yee Chan, et al.
ISBN 1-891845-35-7
ISBN 978-1-891845-35-2

ACUPUNCTURE PHYSICAL MEDICINE: An Acupuncture
Touchpoint Approach to the Treatment
of Chronic Pain, Fatigue, and Stress Disorders
by Mark Seem
ISBN 1-891845-13-6
ISBN 978-1-891845-13-0

ACUPUNCTURE MEDICINE: Bodymind Integration for Bodily
Distress and Mental Pain by Mark Seem
ISBN 1-891845-70-5
ISBN 978-1-891845-70-3

AGING & BLOOD STASIS: A New Approach
to TCM Geriatrics by Yan De-xin
ISBN 0-936185-63-6
ISBN 978-0-936185-63-7

AN ACUPUNCTURISTS GUIDE TO MEDICAL RED FLAGS &
REFERRALS by Dr. David Anzaldua, MD
ISBN 1-891845-54-3
ISBN 978-1-891845-54-3

BETTER BREAST HEALTH NATURALLY with
CHINESE MEDICINE
by Honora Lee Wolfe & Bob Flaws
ISBN 0-936185-90-2
ISBN 978-0-936185-90-3

BIOMEDICINE: A TEXTBOOK FOR PRACTITIONERS OF
ACUPUNCTURE AND ORIENTAL MEDICINE by Bruce H.
Robinson, MD Second Edition
ISBN 1-891845-62-4
ISBN 978-1-891845-62-8

THE BOOK OF JOOK: Chinese Medicinal Porridges
by Bob Flaws
ISBN 0-936185-60-6
ISBN 978-0-936185-60-0

CHANNEL DIVERGENCES Deeper Pathways of the Web by
Miki Shima and Charles Chase
ISBN 1-891845-15-2
ISBN 978-1-891845-15-4

CHINESE MEDICAL OBSTETRICS by Bob Flaws
ISBN 1-891845-30-6
ISBN 978-1-891845-30-7

CHINESE MEDICAL PALMISTRY: Your Health in Your Hand by
Zong Xiao-fan & Gary Liscum
ISBN 0-936185-64-3
ISBN 978-0-936185-64-4

CHINESE MEDICAL PSYCHIATRY: A Textbook and Clinical
Manual by Bob Flaws and James Lake, MD
ISBN 1-845891-17-9
ISBN 978-1-845891-17-8

CHINESE MEDICINAL TEAS: Simple, Proven, Folk Formulas for
Common Diseases & Promoting Health
by Zong Xiao-fan & Gary Liscum
ISBN 0-936185-76-7
ISBN 978-0-936185-76-7

CHINESE MEDICINAL WINES & ELIXIRS
by Bob Flaws Revised Edition
ISBN 0-936185-58-9
ISBN 978-0-936185-58-3

CHINESE PEDIATRIC MASSAGE THERAPY: A Parent's & Practi-
tioner's Guide to the Prevention
& Treatment of Childhood Illness by Fan Ya-li
ISBN 0-936185-54-6
ISBN 978-0-936185-54-5

CHINESE SCALP ACUPUNCTURE
by Jason Jishun Hao & Linda Lingzhi Hao
ISBN 1-891845-60-8
ISBN 978-1-891845-60-4

CHINESE SELF-MASSAGE THERAPY:
The Easy Way to Health by Fan Ya-li
ISBN 0-936185-74-0
ISBN 978-0-936185-74-3

THE CLASSIC OF DIFFICULTIES: A Translation
of the Nan Jing translation by Bob Flaws
ISBN 1-891845-07-1
ISBN 978-1-891845-07-9

A CLINICIAN'S GUIDE TO USING GRANULE
EXTRACTS by Eric Brand
ISBN 1-891845-51-9
ISBN 978-1-891845-51-2

A COMPENDIUM OF CHINESE MEDICAL
MENSTRUAL DISEASES by Bob Flaws
ISBN 1-891845-31-4
ISBN 978-1-891845-31-4

CONCISE CHINESE MATERIA MEDICA
by Eric Brand and Nigel Wiseman
ISBN 0-912111-82-8
ISBN 978-0-912111-82-7

CONTEMPORARY GYNECOLOGY: An Integrated Chinese-West-
ern Approach by Lifang Liang
ISBN 1-891845-50-0
ISBN 978-1-891845-50-5

CONTROLLING DIABETES NATURALLY WITH
CHINESE MEDICINE by Lynn Kuchinski
ISBN 0-936185-06-3
ISBN 978-0-936185-06-2

INTRODUCTION TO THE USE OF PROCESSED CHINESE
MEDICINALS by Philippe Sionneau
ISBN 0-936185-62-7
ISBN 978-0-936185-62-0

KEEPING YOUR CHILD HEALTHY WITH
CHINESE MEDICINE by Bob Flaws
ISBN 0-936185-71-6
ISBN 978-0-936185-71-2

THE LAKESIDE MASTER'S STUDY OF THE PULSE
by Li Shi-zhen, trans. by Bob Flaws
ISBN 1-891845-01-2
ISBN 978-1-891845-01-7

MANAGING MENOPAUSE NATURALLY WITH
CHINESE MEDICINE by Honora Lee Wolfe
ISBN 0-936185-98-8
ISBN 978-0-936185-98-9

MASTER HUA'S CLASSIC OF THE CENTRAL
VISCERA by Hua Tuo, trans. by Yang Shou-zhong
ISBN 0-936185-43-0
ISBN 978-0-936185-43-9

THE MEDICAL I CHING: Oracle of the Healer Within by Miki
Shima
ISBN 0-936185-38-4
ISBN 978-0-936185-38-5

MENOPAUSE & CHINESE MEDICINE
by Bob Flaws
ISBN 1-891845-40-3
ISBN 978-1-891845-40-6

MOXIBUSTION: A MODERN CLINICAL HANDBOOK by Lorraine
Wilcox
ISBN 1-891845-49-7
ISBN 978-1-891845-49-9

MOXIBUSTION: THE POWER OF MUGWORT FIRE by Lorraine
Wilcox
ISBN 1-891845-46-2
ISBN 978-1-891845-46-8

A NEW AMERICAN ACUPUNTURE By Mark Seem
ISBN 0-936185-44-9
ISBN 978-0-936185-44-6

PLAYING THE GAME: A Step-by-Step Approach to Accepting Insurance as an Acupuncturist
by Greg Sperber & Tiffany Anderson-Hefner
ISBN 3-131416-11-7
ISBN 978-3-131416-11-7

POCKET ATLAS OF CHINESE MEDICINE
Edited by Marne and Kevin Ergil
ISBN 1-891-845-59-4
ISBN 978-1-891845-59-8

POINTS FOR PROFIT: The Essential Guide to Practice Success
for Acupuncturists   5th Fully Edited Edition
by Honora Wolfe with Marilyn Allen
ISBN 1-891845-64-0
ISBN 978-1-891845-64-2

PRINCIPLES OF CHINESE MEDICAL ANDROLOGY: An Inte-
grated Approach to Male Reproductive and Urological Health by
Bob Damone
ISBN 1-891845-45-4
ISBN 978-1-891845-45-1

PRINCE WEN HUI's COOK: Chinese Dietary Therapy by Bob
Flaws & Honora Wolfe
ISBN 0-912111-05-4
ISBN 978-0-912111-05-6

THE PULSE CLASSIC: A Translation of the Mai Jing
by Wang Shu-he, trans. by Yang Shou-zhong
ISBN 0-936185-75-9
ISBN 978-0-936185-75-0

THE SECRET OF CHINESE PULSE DIAGNOSIS
by Bob Flaws
ISBN 0-936185-67-8
ISBN 978-0-936185-67-5

SECRET SHAOLIN FORMULAS FOR THE
TREATMENT OF EXTERNAL INJURY
by De Chan, trans. by Zhang Ting-liang & Bob Flaws
ISBN 0-936185-08-2
ISBN 978-0-936185-08-8

STATEMENTS OF FACT IN TRADITIONAL CHINESE MEDICINE
by Bob Flaws   Revised & Expanded
ISBN 0-936185-52-X
ISBN 978-0-936185-52-1

STICKING TO THE POINT: A Step-by-Step Approach to TCM
Acupuncture Therapy
by Bob Flaws & Honora Wolfe (2 Condensed Books)
ISBN 1-891845-47-0
ISBN 978-1-891845-47-5

A STUDY OF DAOIST ACUPUNCTURE
by Liu Zheng-cai
ISBN 1-891845-08-X
ISBN 978-1-891845-08-6

THE SUCCESSFUL CHINESE HERBALIST
by Bob Flaws and Honora Lee Wolfe
ISBN 1-891845-29-2
ISBN 978-1-891845-29-1

THE SYSTEMATIC CLASSIC OF ACUPUNCTURE
& MOXIBUSTION: A translation of the Jia Yi Jing
by Huang-fu Mi, trans. by Yang Shou-zhong & Charles Chace
ISBN 0-936185-29-5
ISBN 978-0-936185-29-3

THE TAO OF HEALTHY EATING: DIETARY
WISDOM ACCORDING TO CHINESE MEDICINE
by Bob Flaws Second Edition
ISBN 0-936185-92-9
ISBN 978-0-936185-92-7

TEACH YOURSELF TO READ MODERN MEDICAL CHINESE
by Bob Flaws
ISBN 0-936185-99-6
ISBN 978-0-936185-99-6

TEST PREP WORKBOOK FOR BASIC TCM THEORY
by Zhong Bai-song
ISBN 1-891845-43-8
ISBN 978-1-891845-43-7

TEST PREP WORKBOOK FOR THE NCCAOM
BIOMEDICINE MODULE: Exam Preparation & Study Guide by
Zhong Bai-song
ISBN 1-891845-34-9
ISBN 978-1-891845-34-5

TREATING PEDIATRIC BED-WETTING WITH ACUPUNCTURE
& CHINESE MEDICINE
by Robert Helmer
ISBN 1-891845-33-0
ISBN 978-1-891845-33-8

TREATISE on the SPLEEN & STOMACH: A Translation and an-
notation of Li Dong-yuan's Pi Wei Lun by Bob Flaws
ISBN 0-936185-41-4
ISBN 978-0-936185-41-5